Myths, Politicians and Money

Myths, Politicians and Money

The Truth behind the Free Market

by

Bryan Gould

First published 2013 by
PALGRAVE MACMILLAN

Palgrave Macmillan in the UK is an imprint of Macmillan Publishers Limited,
registered in England, company number 785998, of Houndmills, Basingstoke,
Hampshire RG21 6XS.

Palgrave Macmillan in the US is a division of St Martin's Press LLC,
175 Fifth Avenue, New York, NY 10010.

Palgrave Macmillan is the global academic imprint of the above companies
and has companies and representatives throughout the world.

Palgrave® and Macmillan® are registered trademarks in the United States,
the United Kingdom, Europe and other countries.

ISBN 978–1–137–35862–2

This book is printed on paper suitable for recycling and made from fully
managed and sustained forest sources. Logging, pulping and manufacturing
processes are expected to conform to the environmental regulations of the
country of origin.

A catalogue record for this book is available from the British Library.

A catalog record for this book is available from the Library of Congress.

Typeset by MPS Limited, Chennai, India.

Contents

Preface

I was born in New Zealand just before the outbreak of the Second World War. New Zealand's contribution to the winning of that war meant that it played a role that was significantly greater than its then relative isolation might have suggested. Partly as a result, no doubt, I took a lively interest as I grew up in international affairs. The war, some of which – and especially whose end – I clearly recall, had left me in no doubt as to what was worth defending; and a sense that I was a privileged heir to a great and beneficent civilisation continued to inform my attitudes as the Cold War gathered force and eventually ran its course.

By the time I had won a Rhodes Scholarship to study law at Oxford in 1962 it seemed to me that the values that distinguished western liberal civilisation were likely to be adopted by an increasing proportion of the world's population – a belief that was underpinned by the rapid demise of colonialism and by the prospect of a hoped-for spread of democracy and self-government across the globe. I looked forward to playing my own small part in that development. I was proud of my New Zealand heritage; and the fact that my passport at that time described me not only as a New Zealand citizen but also as a British subject seemed to confirm my identity as a scion of a long-established civilisation of which Oxford was a leading ornament. As a self-appointed representative of western civilisation (of which English-speaking countries seemed to be the leading practitioners), and as a former schoolboy student of Latin, I was inclined to say to myself *civis britannicus sum*!

After a spell in the British Diplomatic Service (which gave me a bird's-eye view from Brussels of the early days of what has become the European Union) and some years as an Oxford law don, I was eventually elected to the House of Commons in 1974 as a Labour MP. I had first joined the Labour Party in 1964 when, after Harold Wilson's election victory, the foreign exchange markets had engineered an immediate run on sterling; I was outraged by what I saw as an attempt by the City of London to undo the outcome of a democratic election.

As a new MP, I rapidly reached the conclusion that, while there were many other matters of interest and importance right across the board, the central issue of politics was the question of who controlled the economic process and in whose interests that was done. I became interested – and, I like to think, to some extent expert – in issues of macroeconomic policy. I developed positions on a number of the issues which I saw as both distorting economic policy against the interests of ordinary people and as inhibiting the ability of those same people to use the power of democracy to defend themselves against the unfair hand they were being dealt.

So, I was concerned at what I saw as the disproportionate influence wielded by the City of London over economic policy and at the priority given to financial interests. The corollary of this bias was the decline of manufacturing industry, on which so many British workers depended. The refusal to accept the importance of the exchange rate in determining the competitiveness of British industry and the adoption of monetarist doctrines in the late 1970s prompted me in 1981 to write, with two colleagues, *Monetarism Or Prosperity*, a critique of then current and developing policy, a critique which I believe stands up very well today.

I was also concerned at the risks inherent in what seemed to me to be anti-democratic efforts to create a European super-state – a vision nurtured by a small elite but not shared by most ordinary people – and at the growing power of international capital following the removal of exchange controls by the Thatcher government. I was dismayed, too, when in 1986, leading for the Opposition in the Committee stage of the Financial Services Bill, I saw at close quarters the emerging blueprint for hugely more powerful financial markets and institutions that would be subject to no effective regulation.

I had the misfortune, as I saw it, of spending much of my political career in opposition at a time when the Thatcherite assertion that 'there is no alternative' to what we would now call neo-liberalism was widely accepted. I, along with others, was compelled to observe and criticise from the sidelines, as the interests of working people were sacrificed to those of powerful national, European and international financial interests and institutions.

One of my principal concerns was the failure of the Labour Party in Britain, and of progressive and pragmatic politicians across the globe, to mount any proper defence of democracy or to argue for an economic policy that took account of the interests of everyone and not just of a privileged few. By the time I had unsuccessfully contested the leadership of the British Labour Party in 1992, it was clear to me that my chances of persuading my colleagues that we needed to do better had become very slight.

As New Labour began to take shape, I accepted an offer to return to my native New Zealand in 1994 to take up the vice-chancellorship of Waikato University. During my ten-year term of office at the university, I largely eschewed any direct political involvement, although I did not abandon my interest in political and economic issues. But since stepping down from the university in 2004, I have been free to express – in a series of books and articles in both New Zealand and the United Kingdom – my distress at the overwhelming power of international capital in the global economy and at the diminution of any hope that this could be restrained by governments claiming the legitimacy of having been democratically elected.

The global financial crisis in 2008 and the recession that followed represented what should have been, in my view, a conclusive and adverse judgement on the regime created by the new masters of the global economy. The failure, or perhaps refusal, on the part of those powerful people to learn the obvious lessons seems to illustrate and emphasise just how fundamental has been the transfer of power from democratic governments to a relatively small cabal of extremely rich and powerful people and institutions, a development that I believe now calls into question the fundamentals of what we used to regard as western civilisation. True to the values I have tried to uphold over a long period in public life, I have felt compelled to raise my small voice to warn about what we are in the course of losing before it is too late.

In making this attempt, I have often drawn on the lessons I have learnt by virtue of the time I have spent in both my native New Zealand and in the United Kingdom. I have also prayed in aid examples drawn from the experience of the United States, and to a lesser extent, Australia and Canada. It will not escape notice that these are English-speaking countries, exhibiting a particularly Anglo-American approach to the issues that the West as a whole now faces. I make no apology for this; while other western countries may have avoided the worst of the errors and excesses that have assumed their most virulent form in English-speaking countries, it is western civilisation as a whole that is paying the price.

Introduction

It was just over twenty years ago, in 1989, that Francis Fukuyama proclaimed 'the end of history' in his famous essay of that name.[1] In that essay, and in *The End of History and the Last Man*,[2] the 1992 book in which he subsequently developed and elaborated his ideas, he took a hugely optimistic view of what he saw as the more or less permanent triumph of the West – of what he called 'liberal democracy'.

Fukuyama took as his starting point the defeat of fascism four decades earlier and what was by 1989 emerging as the decisive rejection of communism, but his thesis involved much more than a celebration of the demise of what he described as 'the strong state' – authoritarian alternatives to democracy. He maintained that what had been achieved was no less than the end state of human political, economic and social development, a state so agreeable and acceptable to all, so clearly the best of all possible worlds, that it was doubtful that anyone could be found to resist or criticise it in any serious way; nor, he thought, could those who currently did not enjoy its benefits fail to flock to its banner.

Liberal democracy, he accepted rather than argued since it seemed so self-evident, combined a political organisation in which everyone had at least the right and opportunity to make their voices heard, an economic organisation which, through the magic worked by the free market, guaranteed to everyone at least a reasonable share of the riches produced by an efficient and responsive economy (and, to those of particular talents and worth, much more than that), and a social organisation in which a natural balance was struck between mobility and stability, between self-interest and community awareness.

So confident was Fukuyama in 1992 of the fundamental and permanent nature of these virtues, and of the fact that most of the major problems of earlier societies had accordingly been resolved, that he spent a good deal of time in speculating about the nature of any further challenges that would help to keep people interested and occupied. He argued that those challenges were more likely to come from within, from human nature itself, rather than from the wider social and political movements that had characterised our history in the past; he predicted that, without such impulses (whose nature he was keen to explore), the absence of the more familiar political, social and economic problems might mean a kind of stultification and stasis. He speculated at length about how those challenges might be met.

No one, in today's rapidly changing world, can reasonably expect an account of the immediate future that is as comprehensive, wide-ranging and learned as Fukuyama's to be accurate in all respects when it is read twenty-odd years later. It is, though, remarkable that as recently as twenty years ago there was hardly any reference to developments such as the greatly increased importance of Islam as a world force or the immense power of the global economy. We can also see that his belief that democracy, once it had a foothold, would grow strong roots in countries such as Russia or in regions such as the Middle East or Africa was destined to be substantially disappointed.

One of Fukuyama's more obvious failings (admittedly, evident only with the great benefit of hindsight), was his failure or perhaps unwillingness to recognise that what he described as economic liberalism was not the only form of economic organisation that could coexist with and partner democratic political organisation. He spent no time in considering other forms of economic organisation, such as a market economy in which the market is regulated in the public interest. He thereby excludes from any real consideration a whole range of political approaches that could appropriately support democratic social and political organisation; and he compounds this oversight by adopting the familiar American terminology of treating 'socialist' as synonymous with 'communist' or 'Marxist' – a practice that does little justice to a number of democratic European political movements.

Fukuyama assumed instead that the equation of economic liberalism, or what we might today more probably call neo-liberalism or faith in the supposed 'free market', with political democracy was an unchallenged and unchallengeable feature of the western society whose triumph he celebrated. He saw the 'free market' and democracy as not only compatible but mutually supportive, and this perception was to him so natural and self-evident that he saw no need to argue it. To Fukuyama, the market – more or less unfettered – was the natural equivalent in economic terms of political democracy, achieving the same dispersal of economic power throughout society as democracy achieved in political terms. He saw no need for democracy to act as a restraint on the economic outcomes determined by the market, and he saw no danger that the 'free market' might in some, perhaps many, ways prove inimical to effective democracy.

We can now see that, for all these and many other reasons, Fukuyama's optimism in believing that the western world and its values had prevailed and would rapidly become the norm for everyone was sadly misplaced. But, looking at the world as he did twenty years before the end of the twentieth century, it is understandable that he saw it as he did. The post-war world he described seemed to have reached a landing point. The Cold War, which had dominated international relations, was drawing to a close. The fall of the Berlin Wall in 1989 had been the culmination of what had increasingly seemed to be the inevitable disintegration of the Soviet Union. Within Russia itself, Mikhail Gorbachev had put his weight behind an irreversible reform process that seemed destined to replace communism and economic centralism with some form of market economy; other countries that had formed part of the Soviet Union were pressing for and achieving independence, and the opportunity to pursue their own routes to reform.

In Eastern Europe, the process of throwing off Moscow's shackles of domination was gathering pace. Countries whose ancient history had been submerged by that domination began to emerge as independent countries once more, and were clearly preparing to re-engage with western liberalism – a civilisation, culture and economy from which they had never wished to be parted.

As these trends became clearer, it became apparent that communism, which had seemed for much of the twentieth century to present a major challenge to the western liberal approach to politics and economics, was a busted flush. Supposedly communist regimes remained in power in countries as diverse as China, Cuba, Vietnam and North Korea, but in each case such instances seemed mere disjointed remnants of a discredited approach to social and economic organisation that was destined, dinosaur-like, for extinction.

There were, of course, many regimes around the globe that, while in no sense communist, fell far short of western standards of governance – regimes that denied democracy and the rule of law to their citizens, and whose failure to implement market-based reforms meant that living standards were much lower than those achieved in the West. But most of these regimes seemed to rest on the excesses of individual tyrants and dictators; it was not unreasonable to expect that their day, too, would soon be done, as the peoples they had tyrannised demanded access to the freedom and prosperity that were made possible by political democracy and the market economy.

In the last two decades of the twentieth century, democracy seemed to have established itself as, without question, not only the most desirable, socially congenial and ethically supportable form of government but also the most efficient. Winston Churchill's famous aphorism that 'democracy is the worst form of government – except for all those others that have been tried' seemed to have been conclusively validated. Little wonder, perhaps, that Fukuyama overstated democracy's appeal to those who had not yet enjoyed its advantages.

Not only was democracy in its various forms seen as the highest model of government and the end state of human progress, but the market economy which it supported and made possible was acknowledged to have produced a level of economic freedom and of material living standards for ordinary people that had no parallel in the whole of human history. The difficult issues that had confounded generations of leaders and economists in terms of managing the economy and keeping it on an even keel, free from cyclical variations and excesses, seemed to have been resolved.

The confidence felt by western opinion that progress was not only inevitable but was to be defined exclusively in terms of the adoption of western models was helped greatly in the last two decades of the twentieth century by what appeared to be a conclusive resolution of a contentious debate within western countries and economies themselves about the form that a market economy should properly take.

In the immediate aftermath of the Second World War, that debate had been strenuously engaged and had increasingly been seen as dominated by the apparent validation – by virtue of the unifying influence of the collective effort needed to win the war – of Keynesian economics, collective and community provision, and a deliberate effort to create a more egalitarian society. The attempt to create a more balanced economy in whose success everyone shared, and a more participatory democracy in which the legitimacy of political power was consciously used to offset and restrain economic inequality, had been made with the legacy of the Great Depression of the 1930s still present in many minds.

So, in many western countries, especially in Europe and Australasia, a substantially modified market economy had, in the decades following the end of the Second World War, become the norm; a writer and politician such as Anthony Crosland in the UK could, in publishing *The Future of Socialism* in 1956,[3] take it for granted that the broad outlines of full employment as the prime goal of economic policy, collective public provision as the means of guaranteeing basic standards of essential services, and the need to restrain market excesses through careful regulation, were unlikely to be challenged – and were in fact accepted by opinion right across the political spectrum.

By the 1970s, however, a real debate had opened up, so that the received wisdom of the immediate post-war years was subject to new challenges. New ideas began to surface; the individual, rather than society, was seen as the pivotal point of human endeavour and progress; writers such as Friedrich Hayek and Robert Nozick questioned the need for or appropriateness of an extended role for government or the acceptability of meddling in 'free-market' solutions; redistributive taxation, the provision of taxpayer-funded benefits to the disadvantaged and the power of organised labour came to be seen as obstacles to economic growth rather than as guarantees of an equitable distribution of wealth; economists such as Milton Friedman questioned the efficacy in peacetime of Keynesian intervention, and promoted the idea that macroeconomic policy was really just a simple matter of controlling the money supply in order to restrain inflation; while global developments such as the oil-price shock of the early 1970s meant that inflation rather than full employment was seen as the primary issue for economic policy.

What had been regarded as the 'post-war consensus' had begun, in other words, to unravel. That process was helped along, especially in the UK, by the awareness of what seemed to be an increasingly difficult economic conundrum: how was the welfare state to be maintained in the face of the pressing need to improve competitiveness and productivity so as to meet the challenges of newly efficient rivals? In the late 1970s, 'stagflation', the failure to secure an acceptable rate of growth, combined with the threat that even if a faster rate of growth could be achieved it could be only at the cost of higher inflation, was seen to present (in the absence of any disposition to use the exchange rate to improve competitiveness) an impassable brick wall and dead end.

By the 1980s, many of these issues had been resolved in favour of the 'free-market' reformers. Many of their ideas had been carried into government by Ronald Reagan in the USA and Margaret Thatcher in the UK. In both cases, the new leaders had – without necessarily developing these ideas themselves – gratefully accepted agendas prepared for them by right-wing thinkers; they were then gratified to discover that their opponents on the left had either lost confidence in their own prescriptions or had taken refuge in political positions which were easily portrayed as extreme, at least when judged in relation to the new orthodoxy.

The two leaders made common cause at the beginning of the penultimate decade of the century in taking a step whose significance perhaps even they did not fully grasp at the time. The global economy had, in the post-war era, rested on the 1944 Bretton Woods agreement, which had established a regime of more or less fixed exchange rates and restricted international capital movements; but the pressure to introduce greater flexibility in both exchange rates and capital movements began to grow as the world entered the 1980s.

This pressure reflected the interests of a growing group of powerful international investors, mainly based in the USA and, to a lesser extent, in the UK, who were beginning to accumulate large volumes of capital and who were anxious to move it to those parts of an increasingly global economy that offered the lowest costs and therefore the biggest returns. The portentous decision was accordingly taken in the USA and in the UK to float their currencies and to remove exchange controls. The way was now clear not only for an explosion in international trade and foreign investment but for a determined assault by international capital on the political power of democratically elected governments across the globe.

The ability to move capital at will across national boundaries not only meant that international investors could bypass national governments but also enabled them to threaten such governments that they would lose essential investment if they did not comply with the investors' demands. This shifted the balance of power dramatically back in the direction of capital, and set the seal on the triumph of those 'free-market' principles of economic policy that became known as the 'Washington consensus'.

That triumph was widely seen as decisive and probably irreversible. Fukuyama's thesis rested on this assumption. As the horizon was scanned for future problems, the broad principles of politics and economics at least – not just the traditional virtues and values of a western liberalism dating back to the Renaissance, and before that to classical times, but the more modern elements of neo-liberalism as well – seemed to be well established and immune from challenge. As recently as 2007, Gordon Brown, in his annual Mansion House speech, his swansong after a decade at the Treasury, heaped praise on the financial services industry developed by the City of London, and predicted that 'it will be said of this age, the first decades of the twenty-first century, that out of the greatest restructuring of the global economy, perhaps even greater than the industrial revolution, a new world order was created'.[4]

As this encomium demonstrates, the political left played an important part in securing this apparently permanent victory for neo-liberalism. Far from developing an effective critique of what was happening, mounting a fierce opposition to it and offering a persuasive alternative, progressive parties in most western countries, and particularly in the UK, abandoned pragmatism and conceded the correctness of the newly established orthodoxy. They opted to concentrate, through rationalisations such as the Third Way and New Labour, on developing hoped-for palliatives which would tack on to the absolutism of 'free-market' prescriptions at least a token attempt to provide the softening effect of measures designed to achieve a modicum of social justice.

This gloss on neo-liberal orthodoxy was, as statistics on growing inequality demonstrate, largely ineffective. But its wide acceptance meant that no substantial challenge to that orthodoxy was likely to be mounted, a reinforcement of the mantra made famous by Mrs Thatcher that 'there is no alternative'.

Margaret Thatcher and Ronald Reagan had come to power on a tide of opinion which held that the benefits of democracy and the market economy – particularly in what might be termed its 'Anglo-American' form – could be multiplied in scale and extended in time and global reach to an unprecedented degree, if only those in charge had the courage to push back the boundaries. The way seemed clear to extend this domestic and national triumph on to the global scale, and Fukuyama was by no means alone in celebrating that increasingly real prospect.

Western thinking and achievements seemed to dominate not only in economic terms but in most other respects as well. Western technology was paramount and led the world. The USA, as leader of the West, was by some distance the dominant military power, and led a NATO alliance that could enforce its will – as in the Gulf War of 1990–1 – as though it were a global police force.

English was well on the way to becoming the world language, the lingua franca not only of trade and commerce but of culture as well. Western philosophy shaped the world's thinking. Western values defined concepts of progress and civilisation. Human rights and the rule of law were accepted as the cardinal attributes of the modern state.

So it was, it seemed, game over. There was, on the part of the ideologues of the widely accepted orthodoxy, a sense of self-satisfaction, confidence and invulnerability that could almost be described as triumphalist. And, as the political leaders of the major western economies – especially the English-speaking ones – surveyed the scene, they could be forgiven for thinking that this was just the beginning.

So, what happened? Why is it that, a mere twenty or so years later, the world seems very different from that observed, celebrated and foreseen by Francis Fukuyama? Why is it that the West, and its values, ideology and track record, are today under serious threat from a variety of challengers – political, economic, ideological, cultural and religious – and suffering a seemingly debilitating crisis of confidence?

In economic terms, the West's pre-eminence is now under serious threat. The USA, for so long accepted without question as the world's most economically powerful country, is now being challenged by China and by other newly developing countries, whose economic success in dominating export markets for high-technology manufactured goods, and their ability to amass through trade surpluses large volumes of capital that enable them to buy up assets across the globe, mean that the twenty-first century seems likely to see economic leadership pass from the West into new hands.

In addition, Europe's difficulties in escaping from economic problems of its own making seem likely to condemn the sub-continent to a reduced role. And, as with the USA, this comparative decline seems likely to be both consequence and cause of conceding leadership in technological terms, as well as of obvious but persistent mistakes in managing economies, political structures and societies.

These frailties have led in turn to a reappraisal of and loss of confidence in western education systems and cultural achievements, and the wider political and economic bases on which western societies and economies operate. If other modes of operation appear to produce better economic outcomes, who can be surprised that interest and attention switch to those apparently superior models?

And if western countries are no longer seen to epitomise the success that others wish to emulate, why should other western values – values of individual freedom, social responsibility, political democracy, the rule of law, mutual respect and support – be given any respect, especially when they seem to be celebrated, in the practice of western countries, more in the breach than in the observance?

The moral leadership claimed by the West is now, in other words, challenged and disputed by those who prefer to set their own standards; and western leaders have made their own significant contribution to this by contradicting, in their interactions with other countries and interests, the principles they purport to represent. The ignorance demonstrated by western leaders of other civilisations and the arrogant disregard for other values have reduced the standing of the West in many eyes.

The picture that Fukuyama described in 1992 looks, in other words, very different now. 'History' has made a comeback with a vengeance. But how did this come about – and so quickly? Was Fukuyama simply wrong? Did he, and many others, misread the runes? Was the decline of the West inevitable? Was it a return, after an aberration of a few centuries, to a more normal world order in which western countries have to make do with a peripheral role in world affairs? Or did something go wrong? Have western leaders thrown away the great virtues and benefits of western civilisation and – through distorting the inheritance that fell into their laps – brought this situation about through their own arrogance and stupidity?

The challenges that are now apparent had their origins in developments that were well under way by 1992, of course. The fact that their true significance and potential was overlooked for so long was a measure of the arrogance and self-satisfaction that characterised western attitudes at that time, and that still obscure for us the reality of what has happened.

As is so often the case, just as victory seemed complete the seeds of decline were being sown. It is the thesis of this book that the triumphal progress towards the unchallenged dominance of the 'free market' has had unexpected and unwelcome consequences, which have meant that the western civilisation of which it claimed to be the supreme expression has actually been brought low by the excesses which it has permitted, required and endorsed.

The 'free market' has not only determined how we run our economic activity (and even there it has been revealed to have major drawbacks) but it has been allowed to extend itself into every facet of our society, culture and civilisation – and it has done so by replacing the values which were believed to underpin western civilisation as a whole with that much narrower range of values that commend themselves only to a small and self-centred minority.

Very few people seem to realise how thoroughly our civilisation has been transformed by the triumph of the 'free-market' ideology. They do not see that western liberalism, which has informed, supported and extended human progress for perhaps 700 years, has now been supplanted by an aggressive self-interested doctrine of the individual which leaves no room for community and cooperation. Even the victims of this comprehensive and fundamental change seem hardly aware of what has happened.

These are the issues that this book addresses. I hope to show that the West has lost its way because we have not cherished and made a reality of our democracy. We have instead allowed the substance of that democracy to be sucked out, so that only the shell, the forms, of democracy remain.

Fukuyama failed, in other words, to recognise that the threat to western democracy came not only from important external forces whose significance had eluded him, such as the rise of Islam or the development of other economic models in countries such as China, but, even more importantly, from within those democracies themselves. The threats came from the greed and self-interest of the rich and powerful, and also from the quiescence and apathy of that much greater number who forgot what democracy meant and the value that it delivered to them, and who are left confused and puzzled about what has gone wrong.

It is my aim to explain what lies behind that confusion and puzzlement, and to show that on all of these issues we had choices; and that we have suffered greatly from making the wrong ones.

Chapter 1

The Triumph of the 'Free Market'

The individual versus the state

The global history of the past three decades, during which the western world's comparative standing and fortunes have plummeted, has seen the widespread propagation and acceptance in the western world of a number of significant and game-changing ideas – about how economies should be run, how societies should function, and how the relationship between the individual and the state should be managed. It has been a period that has seen a conclusive victory for doctrines that, until quite recently, were dismissed as the preserve of a small and extreme minority on the fringes of politics, economics and philosophy.

In many ways, it was the unexpected coming together of initially somewhat disparate and unrelated ideas – in philosophy, economics and politics – that eventually created and underpinned a victory that proved to be so comprehensive and decisive. The ideas that came to prevail over this period across the whole spectrum were consistent with and reinforced each other; and that interlinking consistency established such a comprehensive orthodoxy across the board, supported not only by intellectual argument but also by the realities of economic power, that any dissent was virtually stifled at birth. In any assessment of what has happened over this period, it is that recently established orthodoxy that must take centre stage.

Perhaps the starting point for that assessment is to consider the revival of a philosophical doctrine that, emerging in a new and more extreme form, has underpinned much that has happened in wider economic and social policy over the last thirty years. For much of the twentieth century, and long before that, it had been recognised that societies were more than collections of atomised individuals, that their strength and cohesion were the result of a collective effort, and that it was that effort which allowed individuals – enjoying the support provided by many others – to flourish.

This belief came increasingly under attack, however, from a group of writers that included Friedrich Hayek and Robert Nozick, to say nothing of Ayn Rand, who were thought to argue that the individual was the only entity that mattered, and that any attempt to constrain individual freedom of action was anathema to any proper concept of liberty and free expression.

Hayek's *The Road to Serfdom* was primarily intended as a wartime critique of central planning, and is not quite the rallying cry for *laissez-faire* that it is often claimed to be;[1] indeed, Hayek explicitly rejects that doctrine. But, in an increasingly familiar process, his message has been simplified and sharpened so that he has been recruited to a cause that he almost certainly would not have fully endorsed.

There can be less ambivalence about Nozick's argument for a severely limited role for government:[2] he argued that government should limit itself to the defence of the realm, the maintenance of internal law and order, and defending the value of the currency; and even less about Rand's glorification of the individual,[3] her condemnation of any attempt to shackle individual advancement and her dismissal of any need to consider the wider common interest. These writers and thinkers, and others, popularised the idea that the claims of society, and even more, therefore, of government, to constrain the pursuit of individual claims in the wider interest must be resisted if the individual was to enjoy the freedom which alone would allow the highest peaks of human achievement to be scaled; and society itself, if it existed at all, would be best served by allowing individuals to pursue their individual destinies without let or hindrance.

As politicians such as Ronald Reagan and Margaret Thatcher came to power in the early 1980s, these theories about the relationship of the individual citizen with the state and the belief that it was the individual, not society, who held the key to human progress became widely discussed and increasingly accepted.

Margaret Thatcher was an enthusiastic devotee of Hayek. Her famous dictum that 'there is no such thing as society' and Ronald Reagan's equally memorable assertion that 'government is not the solution – government is the problem' were quickly adopted as mantras by many, and particularly by those who considered themselves as the new wave of enlightened intelligentsia.

These new doctrines at times reached extreme proportions. For some, government (and by extension any organised form of society) was, by definition, an affront to a proper social order and to individual freedom. Consistent with this view, taxation could only be regarded as theft, and should be resisted; the purposes to which taxation was put were, accordingly, illegitimate.

The role of the state, such people believed, was – at most – simply to hold the ring so as to allow an unfettered competition in which the strongest, cleverest, richest, most privileged or luckiest individuals could make their advantages count and would accordingly prevail. The winners in that competition would rightly claim the rewards, which no one else should resent, since their achievements were a proper recognition of their worth and would benefit society as a whole. And, because society would be stronger, even the losers – the vast majority – would be carried forward to benefits they could never hope to gain by their own efforts.

Human progress was seen to depend on the achievements of a few outstanding individuals. It was essential, therefore, that those individuals should be allowed the freedom to pursue their destinies. If weaker individuals could not stay the course, they could have no complaint. And since it could not be predicted which individuals were potentially capable of joining that elite group, it followed that every single person was entitled to the same freedom from restraint.

The significance and value, even existence, of social organisation and collective or community action were ignored or denigrated as factors in advancing human progress. The contributions, large and small, made by literally billions of people over the whole of history and from every corner of the globe to the infrastructure on which modern society was based, and from which each individual member of society benefited, were given no value. There was increasingly little understanding of the importance of a healthy, integrated, united society, a mutually supportive society in which all individuals could flourish and share in the benefits of living in society, not just economically, but creatively, culturally and in every other way.

There was no recognition of the fact that in today's world no single individual – however clever, strong, rich, privileged or lucky – could hope, unaided, even to make the shirt on his back. That even an apparently small-scale achievement like that is unavoidably a social enterprise, relying on the contributions, technical, physical, intellectual, economic, entrepreneurial, of literally the whole of society over the whole of human history – and that what is true of that simple feat is also true of the whole of human progress – was ignored or denied.

It became the accepted wisdom instead that, if economic success rested almost entirely on the achievements of a few successful individuals, no reward was too great if they were to be properly recognised and encouraged to achieve even more. In the era of the huge salaries, bonuses and share issues for business leaders that preceded the global financial crisis in 2008, influential journals (such as *The Economist*) argued that, provided they were sanctioned by the market, there was literally no limit to the riches that could and should be paid to the most highly rewarded individuals.

The perception that huge rewards were appropriate for people of exceptional talents was, of course, encouraged by the adulation heaped by the popular media (about which more later) upon pop stars, film actors and sports champions – all occupations requiring particular abilities that attracted enormous popular attention (if only for a time) and therefore warranted exceptional rewards. Persuading an adoring public that disproportionate wealth for such people is appropriate was much easier than persuading the same (but on this issue sometimes more cynical) public that similar rewards for business leaders were justified.

While these doctrines were advanced in the name of individual freedom, there was no acknowledgement of the fact that excessive wealth and power (and therefore freedom) for a few inevitably meant that the majority had less freedom or ability to choose, and that – on the basis that the true measure of the degree of freedom in any society is arguably the degree of freedom enjoyed on average by all citizens or even by the least free – the net result was that society as a whole became less free, even while a few individuals celebrated their liberation from normal constraints.

Whereas historically, in most western countries, social organisation in general and democratic politics in particular had had the intended effect of dispersing power and restricting privilege, the newly reinvigorated doctrine of the sanctity of the individual, combined with an assertion of the market's infallibility, provided a blueprint for a quite different kind of society – one in which the concentration of that power in a few hands was legitimised by the market, and accordingly represented as a matter for celebration rather than concern. So it was, as we shall see, that the fundamental values of a western democracy were undermined.

The 'infallible' market

The economic and social context in which the individual was best able to flourish, it was argued, was the 'free' or unfettered market – that is, the market allowed to operate without any intervention from government or anyone else. This, it was thought, provided the only guarantee of the best outcomes. The market was not only essential as an allocator of scarce resources but possessed an almost moral force and authority in deciding the appropriate distribution of rewards to those who succeeded in manipulating it to their advantage. This supposedly dispassionate, objective and value-free mechanism for rewarding the successful was the key to encouraging the innovation on which economic success, it was said, depended.

The market's infallibility was akin to a force of nature, and – like nature – the market was often 'red in tooth and claw'. There was no point in bemoaning the fact that the market produced losers as well as winners; in that respect the market was an evolutionary force, jettisoning the weak while rewarding and preserving the strong.

There was little point in governments or anyone else attempting to second-guess the market, since any divergence from the outcomes it would normally produce would be literally counterproductive. Economic models showed that the market operated with perfect fairness and efficacy, and ensured that each actor in the marketplace was perfectly informed; if decisions were made on the basis of imperfect information, this deficiency on the part of the individual market operator would be appropriately punished, so that the best informed operators would, as was desirable, prosper and guide the market to new heights.

The market was a mechanism that was constantly seeking equilibrium in any case without any need for intervention – and when it moved away temporarily from that equilibrium, it was naturally self-correcting. It therefore provided its own antidote to any threat of monopoly or imperfect competition.

The risk that a dominant position in the marketplace could be used to entrench and intensify that advantage was dismissed. The market would automatically restrain such long-term imbalances because it would constantly allow and encourage new entrants, new ideas and new products, to restore equilibrium.

For all of these reasons, it could remain largely unregulated – and if by any chance regulation was seen as required, it could either be self-regulation or, at worst, 'light-handed' regulation, neither of which would unduly trouble the delivery of normal market outcomes.

If the outcomes produced by the market were the best that could be obtained, it also became accepted, or at least plausibly argued, that to counteract the market by altering the outcomes it produced ex post facto would be to jeopardise the very benefits that the market economy was best able to produce. The dice must be allowed to lie where they fell. Otherwise, the full and beneficial effects of market incentives – as spurs to even greater innovation, profitability and growth – would be lost.

So, for example, redistributive taxation (and, by necessary implication, the public spending that depended for funding on tax revenue) could not be supported. Tears need not be shed over this, however, since those who might feel that they would benefit from any such redistribution were in fact wrong. Their best bet was not to look for 'hand-outs' but to allow market forces to run their course without interference; in that way, economic benefits would be maximised not only for those who succeeded in the marketplace but for everyone else as well. Everyone would prosper, in other words, if the successful were able to keep their gains, since these would eventually be spent in the economy; and that spending would generate more and better-paid jobs for everyone. The good fortune of the successful would 'trickle down' to everyone else; there would be no losers, only winners, though winners to widely varying degrees. And if, however fast the trickle flowed, the gap between the rich and poor widened, that was the price that had to be paid if the successful were to be properly rewarded.

The market was such a perfect and self-correcting mechanism that, far from introducing countervailing measures to correct or modify its outcomes, policy should be directed at removing any factors that might inhibit its unfettered operation. So, for example, 'labour market rigidities', by which was meant the power that a unionised workforce might use to protect jobs, and conditions such as health and safety at work, were attacked, and labour laws generally were significantly redrafted in favour of employers.

In most countries, as a result, union membership was discouraged, the right to strike was weakened, and employers were given new rights to hire and fire as they chose. The goal was to treat the labour market as being no different from the market in any other commodity; an efficient market had no place for the kind of sentimentality that might tempt employers to treat workers as people rather than as factors of production.

Similar arguments could be used to address other issues. The shortage of affordable housing – an increasingly pressing problem in a number of countries? The fault was not that of the 'free market', but of 'rigidities' such as the restraints on development imposed by planning law and the processes insisted upon by local government.

The remedy was to encourage developers (whose profits were not seen as a problem but rather as a proper recognition of their efforts), by removing the rigidities and protecting and even extending the tax advantages they enjoyed.

Environmental issues – such as the pollution of air or water, or the exhaustion of finite resources, or global warming? Rather than outlaw undesirable activities, the correct market approach would be to regulate or restrain them by selling the right to undertake them to the highest bidder; this use of the market or price mechanism would be more elegant and effective, and in the end fairer, than any solution imposed by regulation or restriction. The consequence that the richest and most powerful people might be able to use their wealth to buy exemption from constraints that were seen as essential in the general interest was ignored.

The allocation of scarce resources? The market was again the best way of deciding, painlessly and automatically, who should get what, by allowing the price mechanism to identify the most deserving bidder – the one willing to pay the highest price for the use of the resource. Those who lost out in the bidding, which meant the great majority, would derive a benefit from the fact that the scarce resources were efficiently exploited, as witness the profits made by the exploiters, profits which again, it was asserted, would 'trickle down' to the rest of the community.

A further feature of orthodox 'free-market' doctrine was the supposed need to 'externalise' costs, and the propriety of doing so. Accounting practice ensured that the only costs that appeared in the accounts of an individual company were those which had a quantifiable market value that could be directly and uniquely attributed to the operations of that company – in other words, costs incurred through payments made to other market operators. Anything else – adverse impacts on air or water quality, for example, or on the remaining store of scarce resources – were not the concern of individual companies but were to be 'externalised', that is, excluded from the cost of market transactions and passed on to some other unidentified person, which usually meant to the community as a whole. The bottom line would, in other words, always trump the concerns of wider society. To do otherwise, it was held, would distort the market and reduce economic, that is profit-seeking, efficiency and activity.

These convictions about the infallibility of the market and its sacrosanct nature were treated with almost religious zeal as articles of faith by true believers. There was a sense that scales had dropped from people's eyes, and that what had always been true had at last been revealed. What was surprising was that there was no understanding that these doctrines had a long and chequered history, and that they represented just one (almost always minority) side of a debate that had waxed and waned for 200 years.

A new and extended version of an old doctrine

Adam Smith's great work, *The Wealth of Nations*,[4] perhaps the first real study of what we would today describe as 'economics', was adopted as the bible of many free marketeers, many of whom gave no evidence of ever having read it. According to such people, Adam Smith's description of the market's 'hidden hand' was all that was needed to justify the assertion that the market was infallible and could be relied upon always to arrive at the optimal answer.

There was little recognition of the fact that the market was a social construction, resting on a range of policy interventions and innovations (such as the legal protection of the rights of private property, the law of contract by which agreements could be enforced, the special privileges by which private banks were allowed a monopoly over the creation of credit, the availability of insurance cover and particularly the special privileges accorded to limited liability companies) without which the market economy could not have functioned.

The intervention of both statute and common law in the development of the limited liability company was, of course, a fundamental, hugely valuable but largely and conveniently unrecognised concession made to corporate activities. It is safe to say that today's market economy could not have developed without it. Yet no matter how often employees, customers, investors and ordinary citizens suffer losses from failed companies, and no matter how often company owners walk away from the wreckage, having protected their own wealth and leaving others to take the losses, limited liability is such a commonplace feature of our commercial life that we are conditioned to see it as part of natural law and not as an extraordinary intervention by the lawmakers. So much has this come to be regarded as an unremarkable part of the natural landscape in which business is conducted that those who are the greatest beneficiaries from this remarkable intervention are often those who complain most loudly about government 'interference' in their affairs, and in market operations more generally.

This is not to say that developments such as these have not been valuable and beneficial; but the fact that they all depend on the intervention of lawmakers shows that it cannot be argued that the market operates as part of the natural order of things with which it would be sacrilege to interfere.

Even the most fervent adherents of Adam Smith had not in any case, until very recently, read him as arguing that the market should never be challenged. One need only recall his famous dictum that 'people of the same trade seldom meet together, even for merriment and diversion, but the conversation ends in a conspiracy against the public, or in some contrivance to raise prices' to understand that he well recognised the market's deficiencies; and he made many other comments that make similar points.

Take, for example, 'Our merchants and master-manufacturers complain much of the bad effects of high wages in raising the price, and thereby lessening the sale of their goods both at home and abroad. They say nothing concerning the bad effects of high profits. They are silent with regard to the pernicious effects of their own gains. They complain only of those of other people.'

Or, 'Labour was the first price, the original purchase-money that was paid for all things. It was not by gold or by silver, but by labour, that all the wealth of the world was originally purchased.' And consider his remark that there are 'two distinct objects' of an economy: 'first, to provide a plentiful revenue or subsistence for the people, or, more properly, to enable them to provide such a revenue or subsistence for themselves; and secondly, to supply the state or commonwealth with a revenue sufficient for the public services'.

Adam Smith, it may be safely concluded, had a much more nuanced view of the market's operations than many of his modern-day adherents would choose to accept. Nor is it true, as is often suggested, that there was at some point in the past a golden age of the market or capitalist economy, when the free market was unfettered by any intervention by the state. Economic history shows conclusively that the state was active in providing the conditions that were necessary for the development of the market economy, and that such intervention was constantly sought by those who were most anxious to advance the basis on which a market economy could successfully operate.

In the case of the first major industrial economy, Great Britain, the state intervened through legislative innovation and by using its power – both domestically and internationally – to support the new class of merchants and entrepreneurs. Other European countries, such as Germany and France, found it necessary – if they were to close the gap with the British who had got off to such a fast start – to use the power of the state to encourage and support their industrialists. The links between government and industry in these countries remain very close even today, especially in Germany, where the partnership with government commonly undertaken by business is at the regional or state level; and even in the USA, right up to the present, despite the ideological objections to government involvement in industry, the military/industrial nexus provides a powerful link between government and industry, and remains of huge importance to the continued power of the American economy.

In more modern times, and even more strikingly, the new generation of economies in Asia, South America and Eastern Europe that have seen rapid development have all, without exception, achieved their success through a close partnership between government and business, albeit that this partnership has taken widely differing forms. It is safe to say that the support from government for rapid industrialisation has been the cardinal feature of economic development in those countries, and has produced an economic context which is very different from that currently favoured in the West. We shall look later at the Chinese model, whereby the state decides all the most important strategic issues of economic development and then ensures that the private sector complies with the framework thereby established. It is only in the developed economies of the West (especially the English-speaking countries), and only in the last thirty years or so, that the conviction has grown in some quarters that the market economy operates best if business is left entirely to its own devices, and that the only role of government is to hold the ring so that the 'natural laws' of the unfettered market can produce its winners and losers.

That is not to say that the proper role of government in relation to business and the economy has not been the subject of lively debate over a long period. That debate over probably the central issue of modern politics is the one that has most divided protagonists from different parts of the political spectrum. It has raged for as long as we have had what would be recognised in modern terms as an economy.

An early statement of the positions of the protagonists in that debate is to be found as long ago as 1810 in the majority and minority reports respectively of the British Parliament's Select Committee on the High Price of Gold Bullion. The select committee focused on a relatively narrow point – whose responsibility it was to determine the volume and value of the money stock – but the debate reflected much wider issues concerning the responsibilities of government and the extent of its role in the management of a market economy. While the language may be outdated, the ideas are contemporary in a debate that continues to this day.

On one side of the debate has been the view – generally supported by the majority in 1810, who concluded that government should have no discretionary power to adjust the money stock – that governments have very limited capacity to manage the economy. Any pretension to extend that power will not only be self-defeating but also, because of the distorting effect on the proper and unfettered operation of the free market, positively damaging. Governments, according to this view, are not, or at least should not be, actors in the economy in their own right. Their motivation will usually be a non-market one, and to use the power of government to intervene for non-market purposes in the marketplace will inevitably distort the market's proper operation. More importantly, they should not even claim a role as policymaker in shaping the course of the economy, since it is very unlikely that policymakers will reach judgements as good as those made by the unfettered market.

Governments should instead limit themselves to those purposes that are their proper concern. As Robert Nozick has argued more recently, the defence of the realm, the maintenance of law and order, the underpinning of a system of law and practice that allows commerce and business to operate efficiently – this is the proper role of government. In the field of economics, the role of government is similarly restricted. It is limited to the maintenance of the value of the currency, as an essential part of the context in which business can operate efficiently. It matters little what the numerical value of the currency might be, as long as it is stable enough over a sufficient length of time to enable business decisions to be taken with confidence. Government is entitled to use those instruments of monetary policy as are necessary, such as interest rates, to secure the desired stability.

Beyond that, however, governments should withdraw. Once monetary stability has been established (and this is essentially a technical operation that can safely be left to officials and is thereby insulated against the vagaries of democratic pressures), the economy can be left to operate by itself. This is not a failure of responsibility but a proper recognition of the respective roles of government and business.

The clarity and certainty of this approach has been, it is fair to say, more strongly maintained – at least until recently – in theory rather than practice. Most often, however strongly the doctrine may have been supported in argument, the exigencies of practical operations in the marketplace have usually ensured that government help and support has been sought and accorded when needed. While the pendulum has swung regularly in favour of one view rather than another over the past two centuries, it is fair to say that the default position has denied the purity of the 'free-market' doctrine, and on those relatively infrequent occasions when it has been given an extended trial it has rapidly been abandoned. It is only in the last few decades that 'free-market' ideologues have succeeded in imposing their views in practice as well as theory.

The alternative view postulates a much greater role for government. According to this view, supported in the Select Committee's powerful minority report, government is a major player in the economy, whether it likes it or not, both as a direct and significant actor in its own right, as a coordinator of other actors and as a maker of policy. This inescapable role means that government should accept and, according to some views, seek and welcome a responsibility for the performance of the economy as a whole.

That performance is to be measured not according to purely monetary criteria but according to real phenomena such as output, employment and investment. Government should therefore set its sights on achieving targets such as full employment, a reasonable and (today) sustainable rate of growth in output, and an effective level of public services which are needed to supplement market provision for those with limited purchasing power. Stability should be sought not only in terms of monetary conditions but also in matters such as the level of demand. Particularly in the matter of demand management, governments will often aid economic performance by taking a deliberately countercyclical stance. The economy will also perform better if the power of government is harnessed to the needs and interests of industry, and if government undertakes those functions – such as the provision of major infrastructure – that cannot easily be carried out by private industry.

Historically, the right in politics has on the whole identified with the first view, while the left has endorsed the second. It is hard to exaggerate the significance of the left's abandonment over the last three decades of its historic commitment to the idea that the power of government should be used to promote the general good, in favour of an acceptance that the task can safely be entrusted to the 'free market' instead. We shall now explore what has brought this about.

Chapter 2

Globalisation

How was it that the battle of ideas was resolved so conclusively in favour of what had hitherto been the preserve of an unrepresentative minority? How did extreme and unprecedented 'free-market' doctrines become so dominant? Why did governments, particularly those with progressive views, not ensure that market forces were tempered by a concern for the interests of the majority? However dominant the 'free-market' orthodoxy had become towards the end of the last century, why did the pendulum of political fashion not swing in due course in its normal fashion? Why did its opponents abandon the debate, declare themselves to be true believers, and focus instead on largely ineffectual efforts to mitigate the consequences of the orthodoxy they had now adopted?

A large part of the answer to these questions lies in a single word – globalisation. It was not that the neo-liberal triumph was the outcome of a full-scale intellectual argument, in which the pros and cons were fully explored and from which the champions of the 'free market' emerged triumphant because they had the better arguments. It was rather that the sheer force and power, in economic and political terms, that was brought to bear by a small minority eventually reshaped the real world to suit their interests. Foremost among those real developments was the development of the global economy; it was this which incapacitated governments and left the field uncontested to market forces. We need to examine how this happened.

The rise of the global economy

Any consideration of how our lives are affected in the early part of the twenty-first century by both political action and economic development should begin with the global economy. It is, after all, an overwhelming fact of life: it is where we live, it pervades all aspects of our lives and its impact is felt in everything we do.

But what is the global economy? How is it best described and what are its essential elements? It is such a comprehensive, multifaceted and all-pervasive phenomenon that it can mean many different things to different people. Sometimes it means a world economy dominated by a handful of huge multinational corporations, while at other times it denotes the increasingly free movement of goods and services across wide areas of the globe. At yet other times, commentators will highlight the worldwide spread of new technologies and communications networks.

A good working definition of the global economy, which captures its comprehensive nature and avoids value judgements, is that it is a world economic order in which capital, trade, production, information and technology flow to and from the destinations determined by market forces, without having regard to the barriers erected or regulations implemented by national or regional governments, policies and jurisdictions.

Even this, however, fails to capture the essential element of the contemporary global economy – the freedom it confers on international capital to roam the world, seeking the conditions most favourable to its interests and recognising little obligation to pay regard to the requirements of elected governments and the populations whose interests they represent.

In today's global economy, international capital has, by virtue of this freedom, been able to alter the balance of power between itself and other forces, including elected governments. It is the ability of capital to move freely that has transformed the world economy, so that it is now dominated by a single view of what economic policy should be about.

The growth of the global economy has meant that the broad structure of political discussion in most countries now proceeds on the basis of a universally accepted orthodoxy, to the effect that globalisation is both inevitable and desirable, and that it has produced better outcomes than we would have seen otherwise. This orthodoxy is reinforced by the presumed reliance of national economies on international investment, and the requirement that they should toe the line if that investment is to be attracted.

It is the broad and uncontested acceptance of these views, even by those who might have been expected to take a more critical attitude, that has helped to constrain political debate and restricted the options offered to voters in most democratic countries. The consequence of these largely unremarked constraints is that international capital has succeeded in establishing a global political hegemony that would never have become dominant if democratic opinion had been properly consulted and democratic consent obtained in each individual country.

What is different about today's globalisation?

Most supporters of this new world economic order will number among its virtues the claim that it is groundbreaking and innovative, and that it has ushered in a new era of economic opportunity. In fact, economic globalisation is not as novel as it may seem. It has a long and chequered history, reaching back at least to the heyday of the great European mercantile companies, such as the Dutch and British East India companies. It was during this period, the seventeenth and eighteenth centuries, that many of the building blocks of today's global economy were put in place. The joint stock company, foreign currency exchanges, international insurance and the stock market all made their appearance at this time.

More recent history provides further parallels to today's global economy. At the outbreak of the First World War, for example, the world economy was dominated by a handful of developed economies. These were able to exploit new technologies that made it possible to ship raw materials halfway across the globe and manufactured goods all the way back again, and they were also able to impose their view of the policies that were thought to provide the only path to economic progress. The proponents of economic orthodoxy asserted that they had a monopoly of wisdom as to how global prosperity should be built and maintained.

But while today's version of the global economy may not therefore be as original and unique as its proponents claim, it demonstrates a number of characteristics that mark it out from earlier versions. Today's commentators are certainly justified in pointing to the unprecedented size, power and reach of economic forces that now operate on a truly global scale and, significantly, are invested with a truly ideological fervour.

Globalisation today has ceased, in other words, to be just a useful way of describing a number of related but more or less accidental economic developments, and has become, in the minds of many, a deliberate, coordinated and politically motivated crusade. As the American Friends Service Committee Working Party on Global Economics has put it, 'Globalisation can also refer to a deliberate project led by powerful institutions, people and countries (particularly the USA) to apply a single template of economic strategy and policy to all countries and all situations.'[1] It is this ideological element that marks out the current development of the global economy as breaking new ground. The market fundamentalism that fuels it is ideologically driven, and is intolerant of debate or challenge.

A worldwide phenomenon

The most striking feature of today's global economy is its spread and reach. It is truly global, in the sense that very few of the world's economies can be said to escape its dominating influence. The major capitalist, industrialised economies are, of course, the principal architects of and actors in the global economy. The USA, the European Union, Japan, Canada and Australia are all founder members, and are hosts to most of the transnational corporations (TNCs) that dominate the world economy.

But what is remarkable is how rapidly other economies have fallen into line. Many of these economies, which would not ordinarily have been regarded as part of what used to be described as the western world, have made valiant attempts to maintain an independent policy, but most have – to some degree or another – succumbed to the power of global capitalism.

India has been more successful than most in developing a form of home-grown capitalism without complying fully with the prescriptions favoured by international capital, but must now be regarded as playing an important part in the global economy and generating its own quantum of capital looking for an international role. Many of the 'Asian tiger' economies, such as South Korea, Taiwan, Singapore and Thailand, and the leading South American economies, have been compelled at various stages of their recent development to subscribe to the 'Washington consensus' – a process compellingly described (and roundly criticised) by Joseph Stiglitz,[2] the former chief economist at the World Bank. They have done so unwillingly at times, and (particularly in the case of Asian economies) despite achieving success through the pursuit of policies that are in some cases the antithesis of current orthodoxy. So thoroughly have some of these countries now become part of the global economy that those in South, East and South East Asia are now a major source of foreign direct investment (FDI), responsible between them for twice as much FDI as Japan.

Russia and most of the countries that once formed part of the Soviet Union or the Soviet sphere of influence have travelled well down the path towards joining the global economy – or have attempted to do so – under varying degrees of coercion, albeit with pain and difficulty. Even China, while maintaining a political system that might appear inimical to the free rein of market forces, has set itself well on the way to becoming a major (if not dominant) player in the global economy. We shall look at how this has been achieved in Chapter 10.

Perhaps the only countries to have avoided a direct participation in the global economy are those – such as so many African economies – that are too poor, too saddled with debt and too short of capital to do much about it. They have not made a decision to stand aside; they simply lack the capability to play an active participatory role. They are nevertheless passive parts of the global economy, impotently tossed around like corks on the global economic ocean.

A rapid transformation

The global economy may carry all before it, yet it has become – in its contemporary form – dominant in a remarkably short time. As recently as the 1950s and 1960s, the world was still made up of national economies, each pursuing its own political preferences, trading relationships and economic policies. When Anthony Crosland wrote *The Future of Socialism* in 1956, he was able to describe the political system in Britain as though it was a virtually self-contained entity, paying little attention to the multinational or international dimension.

The same was true to a large degree of the rest of the world community. National governments were accountable to their own electorates (at least in the case of democracies), and it was accepted as axiomatic that they should exercise the powers of government in respect of all those operating within their jurisdictions, including corporate as well as private citizens. As a precondition of operating within individual economies, companies – however powerful – were required to meet the requirements of national governments.

International economic relations were exactly that – relations between nations. Trade was in the hands of national operators – companies and individuals who traded across national boundaries. Some major companies were international in nature, in the sense that they had a number of operations located in different national jurisdictions, but in most such cases there was little doubt as to the country where their major activities and investments were located. Where they had markets or operations in other countries, they dealt individually with each relevant national government.

Those governments, reflecting the interests and preferences of their populations, jealously guarded their power to specify their own requirements. The ability to invest in a foreign country was regulated, in particular, because individual governments exercised the power to control the movement of capital across the foreign exchanges. The movement of goods was controlled by trading agreements between countries, and there were significant restrictions on the movement of labour.

Monetary conditions – so far as they were recognised as being significant – were entirely under the control of national governments, who saw as one of their major responsibilities the maintenance of fixed exchange rates, as established in the main by the post-war Bretton Woods agreement. Keynesian policies of demand management were applied, with the major goal of using resources to the full, including labour resources, so that full employment was almost universally accepted as the central and achievable object of government action.

What changed?

From the 1960s onwards, however, this pattern began to change rapidly for a number of reasons. First, there was a rapid growth in international trade, combined with an impulse towards greater political integration of trading partners and the creation of regional trading blocs. Second, multinational corporations rose in importance, operating not so much across national boundaries as irrespective of them. Third, the oil-price shock was delivered to the world economy in the 1970s, along with the recycling of petro-dollars and the development of the euro-dollar market. And finally, there came the adoption of the belief that monetarism offered a new way forward, and the advent of governments – those of Margaret Thatcher and Ronald Reagan, for example – dedicated to putting monetarism at the heart of economic policy. All of these factors combined to produce a powerful momentum towards the creation of a single global economy.

Reflecting many of these developments, but even more importantly, the decision was taken to abandon the Bretton Woods agreement on exchange rates and capital movements in favour of floating exchange rates. It was one of the first decisions of Mrs Thatcher's newly elected government in 1979 that the pound should float and that capital should move freely across the exchanges. As other governments followed suit, this effectively removed from national governments any real ability to determine their own monetary policy and conditions, just at a time when monetary policy was suddenly being touted as the only effective and appropriate lever of economic policy.

Alongside the removal of exchange controls, Mrs Thatcher's government removed credit controls and minimum reserve requirements for the banks, relying purely on interest rates to regulate the growth of credit. How convenient it was for international capital that governments like those of Margaret Thatcher and Ronald Reagan should promote the primacy of monetary policy and then immediately cede control over it to banks and to financial markets that were entirely under the control of international investors!

With these decisions, the single most important step was taken towards the establishment of a global economy in which there is substantially free movement of capital, operating in all its parts in substantially the same way and according to the same 'free-market' principles, and revolutionising the way in which the world economy operates. Differences in the competitiveness of different economies could no longer be accommodated and mitigated by the decisions of national governments to adjust their exchange rates – usually downwards – by means of considered devaluations. With floating exchange rates and the free movement of capital, the markets took over this role. This loss by national governments of the power to fix and regulate their own exchange rates (and therefore their own monetary policy) was the most important of many momentous consequences resulting from the changes.

The impact of these changes was greatly enhanced by the sheer magnitude of the forces unleashed. There is now in effect a single capital market operating continuously, twenty-four hours a day. The principal players in that market control trillions of dollars of resources, sufficient to swamp any attempt by individual companies or governments to gainsay them.

In the early 1970s, before the liberalisation of capital movements, the daily turnover across the world's foreign exchanges totalled around US$18 billion. By 2012, the daily turnover had reached more than US$4 trillion, greater than the annual output of all but a handful of national economies. The magnitude of these flows, which are about a hundred times greater than the value of international trade in goods and services, means that literally no government can now claim the ability to decide the outcomes of these exchanges for the value of its own currency. As UNCTAD reports in its 2012 publication, *Development and Globalization, Facts and Figures*, 'The current ratio of around 100 implies that only about 1 percent of foreign exchange trading is actually related to merchandise trade.'

A large proportion of those flows, in other words, are of what is often called 'hot money'. This term was coined because of the speed and volume of the flows, their often short-term nature, the 'herding' behaviour of those who control them, the tendency of all markets to act in a procyclical fashion and to overshoot, and the consequent and ever-present possibility for recipient countries of large and sudden capital outflows. These features have caused increasing concern, by virtue of their well-attested tendency to inflate asset and currency bubbles, and then leave them deflated as the flow of hot money moves on elsewhere. These concerns have reached the point that even *The Economist* has registered the increasing interest in the possibility of capital controls to restrain flows that are seen as out of control.[3]

Hot money is usually deployed for speculative purposes and short-term gain. Investors of hot money seek a combination of stability (at least over the short term), high interest rates, and the prospect of capital gain as a consequence of the impact of the inflow of hot money on the currency in which they have invested. That capital gain is, of course, usually only a short-term phenomenon – a self-fulfilling consequence of short-term market sentiment – and subsists for only as long as the hot money continues to pour in. It can be realised only if the hot money is moved on at the right moment, before similar decisions by others mean that the outflow causes the currency to fall.

This kind of capital movement does very little for the productive economy, except to distort it. It does this by pushing up the value of a given currency without reference to its real value, to its role in the management of the domestic economy, or to its function as a market-clearing price in the internationally traded goods sector.

The investors of hot money differ from longer-term investors (who would typically take an equity stake in their chosen investment with a view to acquiring a lasting management interest) in that they have an obvious and immediate exit option should they change their view as to where their money could be most profitably deployed. Shareholders cannot exit unless they can find a buyer for their equity stake at an acceptable price. The purveyors of hot money, on the other hand, can exit overnight if they choose, simply making the decision to chase a better return elsewhere.

The deficiencies of hot money as a source of investment, however, should not obscure the fact that international players also dominate the provision of longer-term capital for productive purposes. Inflows of FDI, defined by the World Bank as 'investment that is made to acquire a lasting management interest (usually 10 per cent of voting stock) in an enterprise operating in a country other than that of the investor',[4] grew from US$12.9 billion in 1970 to US$1,524 billion in 2011 (which was actually 25 per cent lower than its peak in 2005–7), and is predicted to grow to US$1,600 billion in 2012. Of that 2011 total, no less than US$1,240 billion came from developed countries, up sharply by 25 per cent over the previous year despite the recession. The global stock of FDI grew thirtyfold in the three decades to 2011, to reach US$20.438 trillion.[5] TNCs are holding record levels of cash, at an estimated total of US$5,000 billion, which so far have not translated into sustained growth in investment, presaging perhaps a future surge in FDI.

This dominance has sharply increased the dependence of individual economies on investment from international sources. Both large economies such as the UK (even though it is itself a major source of international investment) and small economies such as New Zealand now find that the proportion of investment coming from overseas has greatly increased.

One of the consequences of this outflow of FDI is that the world manufacturing economy is rapidly falling into fewer and fewer hands, as huge multinationals take over and buy up smaller producers with narrow national bases, and also merge with each other. UNCTAD defines these multinational companies, or TNCs, according to a 'transnationality index', which takes account of the proportion of the company's total sales generated by foreign subsidiaries, the proportion of total assets owned in foreign countries and the proportion of total employees employed in foreign countries.

This definition, it should be noted, while capturing some of the prime characteristics of multinational operations, excludes many major multinational companies that maintain most of their activities in their home countries but control, on an absolute if not proportionate scale, large volumes of production and trade elsewhere. This has become an important feature of today's global economy, and even more so with the advent of huge IT companies, for example Apple, Google, Facebook, Amazon and Microsoft. The definition also excludes the growing importance of both private equity funds and sovereign wealth funds as investors in cross-border transactions; private equity funds, for example, accounted for nearly 2,000 cross-border mergers and acquisitions in 2011, worth more than US$156 billion or 15 per cent of the total.

The UNCTAD list of the world's top 100 transnational corporations (which excludes financial institutions) shows that by far the greatest number are located in the developed world. Of the foreign affiliates in the developing world, many are located in China, with the result that Chinese wage rates have been widely used as a benchmark to drive down wages elsewhere. In 2011, foreign affiliates of TNCs employed an estimated 69 million workers, who generated US$28 trillion in sales and US$7 trillion in value added, some 9 per cent up from 2010.[6]

The result of these developments is that about one-third of world economic output is now controlled by TNCs, which also control two-thirds of world trade. This latter figure is all the more remarkable given that another consequence of the global economy and the dominance of the multinationals is that there has been a huge increase in the total volume of world trade, both absolutely and in relation to the growth of world GDP, and a similar increase in the number of transactions involving foreign exchange. This rise in the volume of world trade has been much influenced by the movement of raw materials and components, as well as finished goods, within multinational groups and across national boundaries.

In all developed economies, the rate of merger and takeover has also increased rapidly, so that the trend towards greater concentration of ownership has intensified. Mergers and acquisitions worldwide in 2011 totalled well over 40,000, with a total value of over US$3,000 billion, though this was barely half the pre-recession peak of US$6,000 billion.[7]

Major new technologically based industries, such as computers, media and telecommunications, are being reorganised almost daily, so as to create a concentration of control in a few hands. The same is true of major service industries, particularly in the field of financial services, where the reach of the major players is increasingly being extended not only vertically but horizontally, so that all-purpose financial service conglomerates now dominate world markets. Similar developments have occurred in respect of major utilities such as power and transport. An increasingly smaller oligarchy has assumed control of the boards of these new industrial giants. The same names appear in different combinations on the boards of dozens of major corporations.

Interestingly, this concentration of ownership in fewer and fewer hands is now being identified as one of the significant factors in slowing the rate of job creation in the modern economy, at the national as well as the international level. The point has been made well in an article by Barry C. Lynn and Phillip Longman,[8] who register that the net gain in jobs in the USA between 1999 and 2009 was zero, and that this contrasts painfully with the record of the preceding six decades, in each of which job growth had been at least 20 per cent.

Their explanation of this surprising phenomenon is the increasing monopolisation of large sectors of the American economy – and for the American economy, we can equally well read the global economy. As production, distribution and retailing are all increasingly dominated by a handful of major players, the stimulus to innovate and to start new businesses – where the real prospects for job creation lie – is being stifled. A dominant market player will increasingly look to the possibilities, as a means of protecting and increasing profit levels, of exploiting that market power to determine the prices they are able to charge to customers and the costs they are prepared to pay to suppliers, rather than to developing new markets for new products. Such competition as they are compelled to face is to be crushed or sidestepped rather than met head-on. For many such actors in the marketplace, in any case, the most direct means of boosting the bottom line both at home and overseas is to cut costs – that is, jobs.

How has this happened?

As I have already pointed out, the explanation for this shift in the way the world economy came about is not the exponential growth in international trade, or advances in technology, or the increased desire of ordinary people to migrate to the more prosperous parts of the world, important though all of these factors have been. The key that unlocked the door was the dismantling of exchange controls across the world's leading economies, so that capital could move freely across national boundaries.

This has meant that those who control these vast sums of footloose capital are able to scour the world for the best investment opportunities. The investment policies pursued by the providers of capital have, not surprisingly, converged, since they are all essentially looking for the same thing. Their shareholders and their corporate culture demand high profitability (often over a short time frame) and increased market share. In order to achieve these outcomes, they seek the same conditions: political stability (over a reasonably foreseeable time frame); a commitment by governments to free-market policies; competitive – that is, low – costs (particularly of labour); a labour force that is both well educated (at least for industrial purposes) and reasonably quiescent; the absence of what might be considered onerous conditions imposed by national governments in respect of labour conditions and health and safety requirements; the freedom to repatriate profits; an accommodating tax regime; generous investment incentives; cheap raw materials available perhaps at discounted prices; and so on.

The ease with which large corporates are able to bend national governments to their will is shown by a 2010 instance in New Zealand. Warner Brothers threatened the New Zealand government that *The Hobbit* movies would not be made in the country unless they received NZ\$67 million in tax concessions, and changes in New Zealand employment law that would reduce the rights of actors and film crews working there. The New Zealand government complied on both issues.

The conditions required by international investors are, of course, all features of unregulated markets. They have clearly manifested themselves within the national context, but their true theatre of operations has been on a global scale; the triumph of the 'free market' has been, after all, a global victory. The global dimension was an important element in ensuring that, for three decades, it could confidently be claimed that 'there is no alternative'.

The rise of the global economy has been, in other words, as much a political phenomenon as it is an economic one, and as such it has succeeded in turning upside-down many of the assumptions and attitudes politicians and others have acted upon for centuries. The global economy is, by definition, an economy – often described as a single global market – in which there is little or no intervention by governments or other authorities. If there were such intervention in any part of it, so that the intervention made that part operate differently from the rest, it would cease to be a single market and would instead be a series of differentiated markets in which different rules applied. This would run counter to both the theoretical preferences of 'free-market' ideologues and the commercial advantage sought by major global investors. The momentum established by the global economy is necessarily and consistently towards non-intervention.

The global economy therefore operates on the basis of an acceptance by most politicians that intervention is to be eschewed. There is a recognition on the global scale of what at the national level would be described as the monetarist view that governments should limit themselves to establishing conditions of monetary stability and leave the economy to look after itself – a view not, until recently, seen as the blueprint for successful economic development.

International investors have sought not only to establish the primacy of the market as the determinant of policy but to drive home the necessary corollary – that all costs that do not contribute directly to supposed market efficiency, competitiveness and profitability should be externalised and borne by someone else. The effect of this has been to drive down those costs, since no one, other than the hard-pressed taxpayer, can be found to bear them. The impact of international capital in national economies, particularly in the West, has therefore been to limit the propensity to devote resources to non-market social spending

The role of American companies has been particularly significant in this regard. As the most important and in many ways most aggressive international investors, American companies have been able to set the pace. They have, partly for domestic political reasons, been more willing than others to externalise costs or – to use a less value-free term – to pass responsibility for them on to someone else. This ruthlessness has given them a competitive advantage over more responsible investors, who have been forced, if they are to remain competitive, to follow the American example. One of the features of the global economy is that it ensures that everyone has to comply with the lowest common denominator, in terms of social and environmental responsibility, in order to remain competitive.

In many cases, international capital has found willing partners in those national governments that, for their own ideological and political reasons, are opposed to social spending. But even where governments would prefer to undertake significant social spending, they are constrained by the perceived need for international investment in their economies and the consequent imperative to meet the requirements of prospective international investors.

The lesson has been learned that, in the absence of their preferred conditions, multinational investors simply look elsewhere. The result is that there are now many countries, governments and political systems that as a matter of course have aligned themselves with the requirements of the multinational investors. A large proportion of the world economy is now in the hands of governments for whom the main imperative in economic policy is to make themselves attractive to multinational capital.

   This means that not only is the world economy now – as a matter of
its technical operation – one economy, but the imperatives that drive
it are increasingly uniform. The major multinational corporations
behave in an increasingly similar fashion. They watch each other
like hawks, quick to follow when a new management technique is,
or appears to be, successfully adopted by one or other. They are
increasingly agreed on the definition of what constitutes success,
what are the essential contributing factors, what are the required
conditions, and what is the proper relationship between capital and
labour. The precepts that once drove a small minority are now the
orthodoxy that rules the world.

Chapter 3

Stepping Stones to a 'Free-Market' Global Economy

The 'Washington consensus'

The process of developing a global economy, operating largely as a single entity and increasingly directed by a powerful group of international business and political leaders who share a common view of how it should operate, has inevitably spawned a number of institutions, forums and gatherings which reinforce that unity of approach. It is no accident that this approach dominates the thinking of the major institutions that have the power to intervene in national economic policies. Joseph Stiglitz has tellingly revealed the extent to which the assumptions and attitudes that have underpinned the policies enjoined by the World Bank, the International Monetary Fund (IMF) and the World Trade Organization (WTO) reflect the 'Washington consensus'.[1]

It is important to realise that this identity of view between the major world economic agencies on the one hand and the private-sector providers of international capital on the other has not arisen because the agencies and their experts have developed particular views and have then persuaded politicians and business leaders of their merits. The causal connection has operated in the reverse direction. The IMF and similar agencies promote their free-market policies because they have been 'captured' by private global capitalists who have succeeded in ensuring that national governments (and particularly the American government) require international organisations to reflect their policy preferences and put their own placemen in charge of international agencies to ensure that this happens.

As recent appointments have shown – of Christine Lagarde at the IMF and of Jim Yong Kim at the World Bank – the leadership and direction of those institutions are very much in the hands of western leaders; the Americans have always claimed the right to appoint the World Bank's president and the Europeans have established a similarly proprietary interest in the IMF's managing director.

The influence deployed by these institutions has in the past been a major factor in maintaining a uniform support for the prevailing consensus. That influence has recently come under critical scrutiny, and there is now an increasing acceptance that it has been unhelpful in individual instances, particularly in the case of countries that have been told that they must impose policies of austerity in order to recover from economic difficulties. Following the global financial crisis of 2008, the IMF at least seems to have learnt some lessons; there is, though, perhaps less recognition of the damage they have done in establishing and affirming a general approach to the global economy over a long period.

These formal institutions have been paralleled by less formal forums and gatherings. The annual meetings at Davos, the Bilderberg meetings, the Trilateral Conference and other similar gatherings have all provided opportunities for world leaders, or at least those who share and form part of the prevailing consensus, to reinforce their common purpose and view of what is required. They have accordingly helped to create a formidable defensive bulwark against any challenge to the orthodoxy they espouse. It is probably fair to say that their acceptance of that orthodoxy is more an instance and demonstration of 'group-think' than of any rational process undertaken by individual participants on their own account.

These aspects of the global economy have been both foreshadowed and promoted by efforts to create supranational economies in various parts of the world, reflecting the increasingly permeable boundaries of national economies. Arrangements such as the North American Free Trade Association, the Asia Pacific Economic Conference and the Closer Economic Relations Trade Agreement between Australia and New Zealand are all embryonic regional economies (though they each exhibit different characteristics and have rather different goals), and others will follow suit.

The current negotiations to create a Trans Pacific Partnership involving eleven countries in the Asia-Pacific region are a further instance, and exhibit, in what seems likely to emerge, many familiar features – negotiations conducted in secret, a conviction that free trade must always be beneficial to all parties in all circumstances, a conflation of the two quite separate concepts of free trade and economic integration, and a willingness to elevate the interests of foreign corporations above the rights and interests of the citizens of individual countries. The WTO negotiations to create a new trade round, though limited to trade matters and stalled for the time being, have also provided a substantial impetus towards an increasingly global economy.

In each of these cases, the simple – not to say simple-minded – proposition is that bigger means better, and that sweeping away national controls means removing unnecessary and irksome restrictions on what is claimed to be the self-evidently beneficial movement of goods, services, people and capital across wide areas. The implication is that intervention by national governments is inevitably counterproductive and that the market functions best if it is entirely unregulated, and that the main economic impact of establishing a large and unregulated market across national boundaries is the saving made by eliminating unnecessary foreign exchange and border control costs.

These groundbreaking developments have been reinforced by the reshaping of political structures in the image of international capital. As the global economy began to take shape, multinational investors found it increasingly irksome to have to deal with national governments, each with its own set of requirements, each reflecting the particular interests and priorities of their own voters. They insisted that economies would function more efficiently if those controlling investment capital could deal with authorities that matched their own multinational structure and scale – and that were not democratically elected, but were instead multinational bureaucracies whose goals coincided with their own.

So powerful has been the momentum towards the integration of national economies in the name of greater economic efficiency that no one seemed to notice that the long-term consequence was not only an actual reduction in economic efficiency but also a political loss of a most serious kind – the replacement of democratic governments as the ultimate authority by multinational capital.

The ability of multinational capital to set the political agenda meant that a doctrine that could never have been directly sold to voters in individual countries – the view that markets are infallible, that they must not be regulated or interfered with in any way, that the interests of shareholders and the bottom line are all that matters, and that governments must step aside while market forces have their way – became the dominant driver of the world economy. Nowhere has this been more clearly demonstrated than in Europe.

The EU

Long before it was possible to talk of a single global economy, the most important of the major regional economies was the European Economic Community, or Common Market, which – significantly, as an indicator of its evolution from a purely economic arrangement to a much more political union – then became the European Community and is now the European Union (EU). This is the most sustained and ambitious attempt yet seen to create a single economy over a large range of hitherto diverse economies.

The Common Market began in 1958 as a free trade bloc or customs zone of just six founder countries. But the ambitions of its supporters rapidly outgrew this simple goal. The motivations of those who wanted to go much further and develop a single economy and, in the end, a single political entity comprising the whole of Europe varied considerably and embraced many strands of thinking, both political and economic. Much of that thinking was well-intentioned and idealistic, but what is undeniable is that it coincided neatly with the interests of the great multinational corporations and the purveyors of international capital. Those interests demanded the creation of a large and powerful economy – larger and more powerful than any single European economy – in which elected governments had little influence and multinational corporations were free to deal with a single set of unelected officials, who administered a single set of policies.

This was a huge gain for international capital, as it no longer had to bother with negotiating with national governments. The multinationals had secured a great step forward, but they still faced the inconvenience of having to deal with all the uncertainties and confusions of foreign exchange markets, all nominally at least operating independently of one another. If their victory was to be driven home and made virtually permanent, if not irreversible, the next step was to take exchange rates out of play altogether.

The means to achieve this end was quickly identified. A single Europe-wide currency would cement the gains already made by ensuring that there would be no chance of going back to a Europe in which there was a range of varied monetary policies and conditions. Not only would national governments no longer be able, by virtue of the free movement of capital, to control or even influence exchange rates, but the very concept of exchange rates would be permanently removed.

So, as a 'common market' took shape, and as restrictions on capital movements were removed, it was argued that political institutions would be needed to match the growing power of multinational, European-scale capital. First encouraging and then responding to this demand was very much part of the plan for Euro-enthusiasts. The political landscape, in other words, was reshaped to meet the interests of multinational capital. The European experience demonstrates clearly that economic change will inevitably drive political developments.

The euro disaster

The risks that we run when we fail to cherish our democracy and instead hand the control of our affairs over to small, unaccountable minorities who follow agendas – both political and economic – that they choose not to share with or even bother to explain to the populations directly affected is nowhere better illustrated than by the disaster that is the euro. This is a classic case of arrogance and self-interest trumping common sense and the general interest.

The essence of the case for the euro (and of the European Monetary System and the Exchange Rate Mechanism before it) was, in other words, always a political one. A common currency can only work and make sense if the whole economy is subject to one central monetary policy which must supplant other elements, such as a national fiscal policy, that would ordinarily constitute macroeconomic policy.

In a democracy, a power of this kind could be legitimately exercised only by a democratically accountable government. The unstated conviction of the proponents of a single European superstate was that this logic would mean that a common currency would inexorably lead to the creation of a single European government, if only to provide at least the illusion of democratic control over what would otherwise be government by central bank – a central bank that would do the bidding of international capital.

The economic consequences of such an arrangement pointed to the same outcome. The improbability of the whole of such a diverse economy being appropriately served by a single monetary policy was so great that it could be contemplated only if a sort of Faustian bargain were struck by the participants.

The powerful advanced economies would inevitably dominate monetary policy, which would be framed to suit their interests;

and that would mean that weaker economies would have great difficulty in living with it. In the absence of the ability to deploy an independent fiscal policy or to devalue, their only recourse would be to deflate and accept unemployment. They could be persuaded to accept this only if the stronger countries would implicitly undertake to treat them as – in effect – social security claimants and recipients of regional aid; and that could be made palatable to the taxpayers of the richer countries only if they could be induced to see those in poorer countries as fellow citizens.

That bargain has now – as evidenced by the difficulties that Greece, Spain, Portugal and Ireland and their euro-partners are facing and failing to resolve – broken down. The Greeks, having long struggled with an inappropriate monetary policy, are finding the imposed austerity extremely painful and probably impossible, while the Germans have in effect reneged on their implicit undertaking to maintain the integrity of the euro by bailing out countries that find the going tough.

The blame for the tribulations suffered by the Greeks has, of course, been laid by many squarely at the Greek door. Laziness, lack of discipline, profligacy are just some of the epithets hurled at them, in an attempt to show that they have been the sole authors of their own misfortune. If only they had maintained the rigid financial discipline and rigour of the Germans, it is argued, they – and other similarly irresponsible members of the Eurozone – would have avoided the problems they currently face.

The facts, however, tell a quite different story. Virtually all of the Eurozone governments, admittedly with the exception of Greece, had – until the global financial crisis – maintained a generally prudent stance, either staying in surplus or running deficits well within the 3 per cent limit dictated by the Maastricht Treaty.

There have been occasions when individual governments have, for a short time and for good reason, temporarily run deficits above the 3 per cent limit. And interestingly, these supposed miscreants have included those governments – such as the German government – that have led the charge to tighten the rules yet further.

Even the Greek failure to maintain that discipline is to be explained in terms that do not correspond with the story told by Chancellor Merkel. Greece is as much a victim as a culprit. Greece was never going to live with the monetary regime required by membership of the Eurozone and imposed from Berlin. It was the attempt to do so, without being allowed the usual remedies for lack of competitiveness offered by exchange rate and monetary policy, that led directly and predictably to Greece's current woes.

The same can be said of the similar problems faced by Spain, Ireland, Portugal and Italy. Their problems were not caused by irresponsible government borrowing; the conditions for the crisis were created by excessive private sector borrowing and lending, particularly by over-leveraged banks. The bursting of this bubble led to large falls in output and thus in tax revenue. The Eurozone's government deficits are a consequence of the crisis, not a cause.

The problem, however, is that time and again the measures put in place in order to avert disaster have done nothing to recognise, let alone address or remedy, the underlying issues. Those issues, for as long as they remain unresolved, will continue to throw up crises which seem increasingly likely to drive the European economy into recession and the Eurozone into a failure that will threaten the whole European project.

What are those underlying issues? There are probably two that warrant particular attention. The first, as we have seen, is what might be described as a fundamental flaw in the initial design of the euro which made it unlikely that it could ever succeed; and the second is the determination to continue with economic policies, particularly in response to the global financial crisis, that have made recovery from that crisis more difficult than it should be.

As to the first issue, I was one of a very small number who argued from the outset (as I had argued about the euro's two predecessors) that the euro could not possibly work. I argued this because it seemed clear to me that in a hugely diverse European economy (and that diversity has surely now been demonstrated beyond doubt) it was beyond belief that all parts of that economy could be equally well served by the single monetary policy which a single currency would require.[2] The tribulations of the Greeks and others were absolutely inevitable.

In due course, even the stronger countries – Germany and its more or less satellite economies – which were the immediate beneficiaries of the single currency and the single monetary policy began to suffer a downside. This was because in the longer term, when the periphery of the wider European economy began to slow down – even to close down – even the countries of the central core found that their markets were less buoyant and their obligations to weaker members threatened to increase.

It was precisely because the euro would eventually handicap the whole European economy, as well as individual potential members such as Britain, that I opposed it so strongly. Unfortunately, any such stance was dismissed at the time by most commentators as being simply 'anti-Europe'.

The adverse impact of the euro on the European economy began to come to a head, as luck would have it, just as the second adverse factor – the global financial crisis – burst upon us. In line with, and illustrative of, the economic dominance of Germany in the Eurozone, the measures adopted to help Europe deal with the crisis and escape from recession were largely dictated from Berlin, and reflect a particularly German view of what is required. Those measures focused on the suddenly revealed vulnerability of governments in weaker countries to rapidly increasing public sector deficits, deficits made inevitable by the constraints imposed by euro membership and by the impact of the global financial crisis on the relatively loose policies pursued by those countries within the apparent comfort of the Eurozone.

The reduction of those deficits became the main and essentially short-term goal of German policy. The Germans were increasingly nervous that they would be required to finance any rescues that might be needed; and the German government's own domestic political and ideological preferences (themselves now increasingly challenged within Germany itself) pointed strongly to austerity as the correct response to recession. The consequence has been that the travails of the Eurozone, and particularly of its weaker members, have been exacerbated by the inevitable consequences of austerity. The defeat in the 2013 Italian general election of Mario Monti – installed, as Paul Krugman puts it, as a 'proconsul' by Angela Merkel – is the judgement made on these consequences by Italian voters.

There is a particular irony in Germany leading the charge in demanding that Greece and others should – as their first priority and despite the fact that austerity makes it impossible – repay the debt that Eurozone membership has made inevitable. It is nearly 100 years ago that John Maynard Keynes, as a young British Treasury official, warned that a Germany defeated in war and saddled with the obligation to make reparations could not possibly do so, and that the attempt to enforce the obligation by the victors could only lead to disaster. Keynes held that creditor as well as debtor nations had a responsibility to help to resolve the issues.[3] A failure to follow that wise advice today could again lead – as it did in the 1930s – to social unrest, extremism and conflict.

In most circumstances, an economy that discovers that it has become uncompetitive, as evidenced by a trade or public sector deficit, or in the longer term by falling comparative living standards, will respond with a range of measures that will usually include the devaluation of the currency. A devaluation will have the merit of improving competitiveness across the board and doing so in a fair and impartial way, so that everyone bears some share of the short-term burden of the necessary adjustment. It also has the advantage of underpinning and launching an obvious and well-tested strategy for overcoming problems of lack of demand by promoting growth and expansion.

The devaluation option is not, of course, open to Eurozone members. Without it, they could only grow themselves out of recession – which by definition occurs because of a deficiency in demand – with the aid of a policy framework, in terms of both monetary and fiscal policy, that would encourage greater rather than less economic activity.

That, however, is precisely what was denied them by the proponents of austerity. The insistence that Greece and Ireland, Portugal and Spain, and perhaps eventually Italy as well, should cut spending and reduce demand in order to eliminate deficits has ensured that recession becomes persistent and almost impossible to shake off. As the experience of Spain shows most recently, slamming on the brakes immediately means higher unemployment, falling production, a slump in living standards, decimated public services, social unrest and – most significantly for the proponents of austerity – larger, not smaller, public deficits off the back of lower tax revenues. The Spanish bail-out is the price being paid by the Spanish people for that mistake.

The insistence on austerity is not only economically destructive but it is also fatal to any concept of democracy. If Chancellor Merkel has her way (and who would bet against it?), policies for austerity will be imposed by a single European budget 'tsar' who will have the power to override the budgets produced by national governments if they are deemed not to comply sufficiently with austerity requirements. Little wonder that European populations protest!

Even within its own terms, the policy is doomed to failure. Austerity is meant to provide an escape route from debt, but it has ensured instead that the bail-outs provided to Greece, Spain and others constitute an increased debt burden that they have little hope of repaying while they are going backwards. The consequence of these policies is to create in much of the Eurozone the economic equivalent of a much-enlarged pre-unification East Germany, without the benefit in this case of the huge transfer of resources that the Germans found it necessary to make to their less fortunate fellow citizens.

Even the IMF, one of the three institutions that now constitute the troika that dictates economic policy to Eurozone countries, seems to have revised its view about the correctness of austerity policies as a response to recession. The need for such a revision is clearly shown by a report published by the Center for Economic and Policy Research in January 2013,[4] on the advice provided to EU countries by the IMF in 2008–11. The authors find a consistent pattern of recommendations that focus on reducing spending and shrinking the size of government, in many cases regardless of whether this is appropriate or necessary, or whether it may even exacerbate an economic downturn.

They find that fiscal consolidation was recommended for all twenty-seven EU countries, and that expenditure cuts (which were generally preferred to tax increases) sometimes set targets or limits on public debt/GDP ratios or fiscal deficits below those specified by the Maastricht Treaty. There was repeated emphasis on cutting public pensions and 'increasing the efficiency' of health care expenditures. Raising the retirement age was a standard recommendation, without any correlation to a country's life expectancy. There was also a predilection for increasing labour supply, irrespective of unemployment or labour force participation rates. This included such measures as reducing eligibility for disability payments or cutting unemployment compensation, as well as raising the retirement age.

Labour market policy recommendations were overwhelmingly geared towards measures that would either reduce wages directly or, as in the efforts to increase the labour force, put downward pressure on wages. Such measures included the attenuation of industry-wide bargaining practices and scaling back employment protections.

Little wonder that the IMF felt obliged to abandon advice along these lines, in the face of the incontrovertible evidence that countries such as Greece have been hugely damaged by such policies which have severely exacerbated the problems that were already endemic; but it is also a reflection of recent working paper by IMF economists, published in June 2012,[5] which shows that the multiplier effects of cuts in public spending are much greater – perhaps two or three times greater – than they had thought, and could be as high as two in the case of Greece.

As a result, at its annual meeting in Tokyo in October 2012, the IMF advised against measures designed to cut deficits come what may. They recommended debt forgiveness as the right approach for the Eurozone to debtor countries, Greece for example, and advised that governments that were prioritising the reduction of deficits should at the same time introduce 'automatic stabilisers', such as increased welfare payments and tax reductions, to offset the deflationary consequences.

This amazing volte face is a belated recognition that the economic models used by forecasters who have consistently been too optimistic in predicting post-global financial crisis growth rates are seriously flawed, and it is perhaps just the first indication of a long overdue 'agonising reappraisal'. It is likely to have far-reaching consequences for policy, not just within the Eurozone but – if recent developments in Japanese policy are anything to go by – well beyond as well.

If further confirmation were required, it came with the forecasts published in February 2013 by the European Commission.[6] They showed a worsening economic picture: France's gross domestic product was expected to grow by just 0.1 per cent and Germany's by 0.5 per cent in 2013, both 30 basis point downgrades from three months earlier; while the Eurozone as a whole was forecast to shrink by 0.3 per cent in 2013, compared with a predicted growth of 0.1 per cent in November 2012.

The deepening recession was expected to hit particularly hard in countries that had required EU financial assistance, particularly Greece, Spain and Portugal, which were expected to suffer deeper recessions in 2013. After shrinking 7.1 per cent in 2011 and 6.4 per cent in 2012, Greece was expected to see its sixth year of economic contraction in 2013, suffering a 4.4 per cent cut in economic activity – another downward adjustment from the 4.2 per cent predicted in November 2012. Not only was Greek unemployment expected to hit 27 per cent, up from 24.7 per cent in 2012, while Spain's jobless rate was forecast to grow to 26.9 per cent, Eurozone government debt was expected to hit 95.1 per cent of GDP in 2013, the highest level since the creation of the single currency; and several Eurozone governments – France included – were forecast to fail to meet EU-mandated deficit targets.

The problems are, of course, more than purely economic. In countries such as Greece, Spain and Portugal, there is a rising tide of social unrest, stemming undoubtedly from a sense that the populations of those countries have been betrayed by their leaders. They feel, with good reason, that the post-war settlement which established a balance between the interests of capital and labour has now been fundamentally disowned – a point made by Professor Ha-Joon Chang.[7] He states that after the Second World War a capitalism discredited by the Great Depression was allowed a renewed legitimacy, on condition that minimum provision was guaranteed to help with burdens such as childcare, education, health, unemployment, disability and old age. He argues that the priority given instead to 'balancing the books' has neutered democracy to such an extent that it is not only European economies but European democracy whose legitimacy is threatened.

No attempt has been made by EU policymakers to distinguish between those countries that have prospered and those that have not, or to suggest refinements of the rules that might help those that have not. Those that have already demonstrated by falling into economic difficulties that they find membership burdensome, if not impossible, are now being told that if they want help they must accept still tougher rules within a banking union. This would make it even less possible for them to grow and repay debt, and would require them, of course, to concede what remains of their economic sovereignty.

Even if this proved politically possible (and recent elections in France and Italy throw doubt on this), it is hard to see how such a 'remedy' would do anything other than bury the root causes of the problems even deeper, and make them even more difficult to resolve in the long term. It is the equivalent of plastering over the cracks while the foundations are crumbling. Reality is not averted simply by denying it. The most recent unfolding of the Eurozone crisis suggests not only that the countries already engulfed – the 'PIGS', Portugal, Ireland, Greece and Spain – are doomed to prolonged recession but also that the crisis seems likely to drag a newly identified grouping – the 'FISH', France, Italy, Spain and Holland – under as well.[8]

The way out?

What is the alternative? The first step must be to recognise the reality that Europe as a whole is handicapped rather than benefited by the current breadth of the Eurozone, and that it cannot possibly function well with such diverse membership. There should be a negotiated process for identifying those countries that would benefit from being, or wished to be, released from the burdens of membership, and for helping them to make an orderly withdrawal. Such a process would be complex and difficult, but by no means impossible, and in any case would be less disruptive than the disorderly break-up that otherwise seems inevitable.

Those countries that chose and were able to remain within the Eurozone would no doubt proceed to create what would be in effect a greater German economy. Even so, some of those might well baulk at the prospect of being absorbed into such an entity.

Countries which chose to leave the Eurozone would be able to return to their individual currencies, devalue to the appropriate level, abandon austerity in favour of a strategy for growth, and renegotiate their obligations with creditors on the basis of a credible prospect of improving tax revenues. No one would pretend that this process is without problems, still less choose to start from here, but other countries, such as Brazil and Argentina, have negotiated similar issues and come out on the other side with improved prospects.

The numbers of countries choosing to take this option might swell in due course once the practicality and advantages of opting out of the euro became clear. They could then set about, together both with the Eurozone and actual and potential EU members who are not members of the Eurozone, the task of building a new kind of European cooperation – what might be described as organic or functional cooperation, in which the process of ever-increasing convergence in the pursuit of common interests did not get too far ahead of the political and economic realities.

In economic terms, Europe would be much stronger as an entity if the constituent parts were able to apply monetary and exchange rate policies that were more suited to their needs and in particular to their different stages and rates of development. A Europe made up of economies each enjoying optimal macroeconomic policy settings, trading with each other on special most-favoured nation terms and negotiating trade arrangements with the rest of the world as a single entity, consciously pursuing convergence across the whole field of regulation, co-ordinating and aligning policy development wherever possible, increasingly working together in pan-European deliberative and eventually legislative bodies, would serve Europe's economic interests much more effectively and do more to promote a genuine sense of European identity than the current abortive attempts to impose from above a European superstate that only a tiny elite has ever wanted.

The UK, reflecting the advantages of the decision to steer clear of the euro, has managed to avoid some of the more severe consequences of the euro crisis. This independent stance has been seen in some quarters as a British rejection of the possibility of a unified Europe; but the UK is historically, geographically, culturally, economically and politically inescapably a part of Europe. Despite the reproaches of other European leaders, the British have the chance to plot a course towards a more democratic and realistic Europe which builds on what is possible and abjures the fanciful constructs of an out-of-touch elite. The mere prospect of a referendum should provide a renewed stimulus to new thinking about the shape that a new Europe can and should take.

To acknowledge that there is not yet a United States of Europe, with a single political identity that makes it possible to accommodate without undue strain a range of divergent economic interests, is not to admit defeat but to recognise the need to build a Europe on the basis of democracy and popular will if the result is to be sustainable. The Eurozone crisis may in the end be a blessing in disguise. In the meantime, we should recognise that it is a striking illustration of what happens when a nation's (or a sub-continent's) affairs are handed over to an unrepresentative group of political and business leaders who have little concern for or understanding of the interests and views of the populations they purport to lead.

Chapter 4

The Political Response

The concentration of power

All politics in the end is a response to a fundamental characteristic of social organisation. In every society, there is an inevitable tendency for power to concentrate in a few hands. The power may be expressed in physical, economic, social, religious or hierarchical terms – but at its most fundamental it is power to make choices, the freedom to choose, even at the expense of and against the interests of others.

In any society, those who are stronger, cleverer, richer or luckier, or who enjoy some other advantage, will inevitably acquire more power than others. They will then, with equal inevitability, use that power to enhance their advantage, accreting to themselves differential privileges which will make them yet more powerful, allowing them to entrench that advantage and defend it against attack, and by doing so to reinforce the disadvantage of others. The response that should be made to that intensifying concentration of power is the central and defining issue of politics – and the key characteristic of the response of many in democratic politics has been, traditionally, to resist and counteract it. If it were not for the overriding importance of that objective, why else would we bother with the messy and difficult business of democratic politics?

Not every response, of course, treats it as axiomatic that the concentration of power should be resisted. On the right of politics, efforts are made to find various ways of welcoming or at least of making acceptable the concentration of power and privilege in a few hands. Traditional Toryism takes the view that a hierarchical society, in which everyone 'knows their place', will offer the advantages of stability and certainty, and that the inherent unfairness can and should be offset by the doctrine of noblesse oblige, which requires the privileged to acknowledge and act, at least to some extent, to repay the debt they owe to the underprivileged.

That view is today seen as somewhat old-fashioned. On the right, a different and harder-edged approach has come to dominate, as we have seen, over recent decades. According to that view, it is asserted that if power is concentrated in the hands of the most able then the whole of society will benefit, and that attempts to frustrate this inevitable arrangement will mean that everyone, including the underprivileged, will be worse off. The adoption of this doctrine by powerful elements and its successful promotion in the mainstream of democratic politics is one of the major ways in which the past three decades have represented an important break with the past.

A softer view of inequality, which accepts that it is inevitable but nevertheless recognises that it is fundamentally unfair, maintains that its downsides can be mitigated by ensuring that there should be equality of opportunity, in the sense that everyone should be lined up at the same starting line. If some are then able to go further and faster than others, then so be it. It is not clear what should be done to ensure that those who gain power and privilege in this way are to be made to limit those advantages so that their heirs and descendants do not start their race with a head start, so that power is again concentrated in a few hands.

In progressive politics, on the other hand, there has been an understanding that the concentration of power is a threat to social cohesion and human progress over a broad front, and that if this concentration of power is to be avoided, a conscious effort must be made to ensure that the rewards and benefits of living in society should be fairly shared. This is not, of course, an argument for absolute equality or for saying that we are all the same (as critics often pretend to assume), but merely for ensuring that the concentration of power is not allowed to become entrenched over generations so that large numbers of citizens are kept in positions of more or less permanent disadvantage.

These important issues, and the varied responses to them, have been essential and valuable elements in the political debates that have characterised most democratic societies. This makes it all the more remarkable that at some point in the last thirty years those holding the progressive view seem to have abandoned the debate, and to have acquiesced in the triumph not perhaps of the traditional or patrician right but of a right that has been extreme in its view that the market must in all circumstances prevail, and that the concentration of power that the unfettered market produces should be celebrated and encouraged.

The expectation has been in the past that a progressive government will restrict the growth of untrammelled economic power, especially in sensitive areas such as the media. It will ensure that political power is equally shared – that the democratic process is maintained in good shape and that human and civil rights are protected. It will allow less powerful people to organise themselves so that their collective strength can protect them against the economic force of powerful individuals and groupings. It will guarantee the basic decencies of life to all in society, irrespective of their power or lack of it in the marketplace, so that their life-chances are not arbitrarily restricted. It will develop the cohesion of society so that communities as well as individuals have a role to play and enjoy a stake in its success.

It might be thought that, faced with the challenges posed to democracy by the global economy and 'free-market' policies, a response of this kind would be needed more than ever, and would be rapidly and powerfully forthcoming. This is surely particularly true when the rich and powerful had found a way, through establishing the primacy and supposed infallibility of a global market that would automatically deliver to them an unchallengeable reinforcement of their power and privilege, of escaping the restraints and controls that were surely necessary to protect the interests of the vast majority. But, how much of that expected response can we see in democratic politics today? And how have progressive governments measured up?

The answers are not much and not well. We have seen the emergence of democratic governments which have paid excessive attention to the powerful, both internationally and domestically, and which apparently believe that nothing can or should be done without their support. We see governments that are prepared to endanger the democratic process and civil liberties by placing the interests of big players ahead of those of ordinary people. We see governments that have pursued economic policies that favour the wealthy and the asset-holders but jeopardise the jobs and living standards of those who work for a living; governments that have, in areas such as education, reintroduced unwelcome and unnecessary divisions, have apparently distrusted the idea of community and collective organisation, and have preferred to entrust the functioning of society to the unchallenged marketplace.

The gap between what such governments might reasonably be expected to do and what they have actually done means that a void has developed in democratic politics, a void in that area of political thought and action that was hitherto represented by progressive parties and politicians but which has now been conceded and no longer has substance. This void means that a hugely significant part of the political spectrum is no longer represented in the politics of power. This is more than just a deficiency or an absence. So much of what has been the wellspring of progressive, innovative and reforming policy in democracies across the globe finds that it is not only unrepresented but has actually been supplanted – that, instead of what should be its voice, a different and contrary voice is heard.

Even those political forces which have in the past committed themselves to a fairer distribution of power and wealth have thrown in the towel. A prime example was the New Labour response in the UK to what seemed to be the established neo-liberal hegemony, and the consequently flawed analysis of what was needed to resist and defeat it. The acceptance that British voters had endorsed an all-embracing right-wing agenda led the Labour party to conclude that it would have to accommodate this apparently permanent change by making a wholesale shift of its own political agenda along the spectrum to the right.

Accordingly, much of the neo-liberal agenda was adopted by New Labour, sometimes with considerable enthusiasm. The remnants of any vaguely radical policies were quickly jettisoned and new ones eschewed. When the 1997 election was won, the strategy was seen to be vindicated; little account was taken of the fact that victory had been virtually certain in any case because the electorate – after eighteen years of a Tory government – was determined on change, even if only of personnel.

New Labour failed to grasp that moving their whole stance rightwards was both unnecessary and unhelpful. It confused many voters as to what it was they were asked to support, it failed to convince others who found the Tories more credible exponents of the neo-liberal agenda, and it disappointed many others who looked in vain for a mainstream party that would represent the values and principles that Labour seemed to have abandoned.

Most importantly, the move rightwards disabled New Labour from asserting well-established values, confirmed that most dangerous and insidious of Thatcherite platitudes, that there is no alternative, and left their natural supporters nowhere to go. Little wonder that the disappointment with nine years of New Labour left many voters disaffected with democratic politics as a whole.

The electorates of other western countries experienced a similar sense of confusion and disappointment, even of betrayal. There is a powerful sense of lost opportunity, and a puzzlement that what until recently seemed the prize that democracy should aspire to has been downgraded to the point where it has no value. There can be no more dramatic example of the power of the global economy to shape the political landscape.

Very few progressive politicians have analysed their situation in this way, preferring to tell themselves that they are merely acknowledging what they have persuaded themselves is inevitable and pretending that this central concession leaves intact their political positions on other issues. They have preferred to avert their gaze from the uncomfortable fact that the unchallenged ability of multinational corporations to bypass elected governments has fatally undermined the claim of democratic governments to be able to run the economy in the interests of those who elect them. They would rather not face that issue. Instead, they would rather regard the global economy as an opportunity for putting in place on the one hand a sort of ill-defined and nebulous internationalism and on the other hand for carrying on in domestic politics as though nothing has changed. It is, after all, hardly in their interests to say, 'Vote for us even though there is nothing we can do.'

Why did progressive politics give up the battle?

The advance of the global 'free-market' economy has been so inexorable and all-pervasive that its very comprehensiveness has provided a sort of camouflage. It is not as though fundamental change suddenly appeared overnight – as in an earthquake producing a towering peak or a deep ravine – but rather that the whole landscape has changed steadily and inexorably, so that it is difficult to identify and respond to any particular feature. Rather than confront it, it is easier to pretend that it can be accommodated.

This is partly a matter of genuine ignorance. Surprisingly few progressive politicians understand the importance of the economy – its ownership and control and the way it operates – to the whole of the political process. They are accustomed to thinking of the economy as simply a producer of outputs and of the political process as a difficult but (at least partially) satisfying exercise in allocating the economy's fruits. While they are aware that there have been major economic changes, there is little understanding of precisely what has happened and how, and why it has meant an equally major change in the whole political landscape.

Progressive and pragmatic politicians – at least in modern times – have usually been happier dealing with social issues than with the hard technical questions of economic policy. In particular, virtually no one has any real understanding of the history of economic thought, so the nature of the change that we have seen over the past thirty years cannot be placed in an historical context. As a result, its true significance is lost, and the extent of the defeat suffered by the left is simply ignored. So, though the whole economic policy context has changed, progressive politics carries on as though nothing has happened, preferring to concentrate on other, lesser parts of the political landscape and fretting ineffectually about why its nostrums no longer seem to have any purchase.

Even those who are sufficiently aware to register their concern about what has happened seem unable to establish why it has happened. So, for example, an increasing number of voices urge remedial action in individual areas, for example Third World debt, world poverty, widening inequality in particular countries or the threat to the environment, but very few offer a persuasive and accurate analysis of what links these issues, what causal factors have created all these outcomes, why it is so difficult to counteract them, and what must be done if we are to have any chance of changing them.

Why bother with politics?

The progressive response has not, of course, been universally one of ignorance. There are politicians (who might at other times have been regarded as left of centre) who positively embrace the demise of a large part of the political debate. People of this view have some understanding of the change that has taken place in the political context, but welcome it as confirmation that 'old-fashioned' party politics is now outdated. Politics in that sense, they believe, is an excrescence we are better off without.

Politicians of this persuasion talk of the inappropriateness of 'old' labels, such as left and right. For them, politics is not about understanding that the way society works is a matter of choice, that it depends on man-made rules and processes, and that legal concepts such as property and contract are artificial constructs rather than God-given; rather, the political context is like the natural world – immutable and unchallengeable. The responsibility of the politician is to accept if not the inherent virtue of current political forces at least their unchangeable character, and to make the best of it.

For these politicians, what is important is to elect good people whose hearts are in the right place and who can then safely be entrusted with the task of making good decisions in everybody's interests. This kind of politician tends to be temperamentally unwilling to acknowledge that he or she must at times disappoint people, let alone make enemies.

Politics for such politicians is simply a matter of competence and (if we are lucky) compassion. There is no understanding that we would not bother with the messy and sometimes distasteful business of politics if there were not hard decisions to be made, and if the political process were not on the whole preferable to other means of resolving these issues. There is little comprehension of the fact that a successful society will be one where scarce resources are efficiently and fairly allocated, and stark conflicts of interest are compromised or fairly adjudicated upon. And nor is there an understanding that the meanings of these goals and the ways in which they might be achieved are likely to be fiercely debated and contested in any free society.

Attitudes of this kind are well entrenched in the politics of many countries. A leading example is to be found in the UK, where progressive politicians would in the past have analysed the condition and functioning of society for the purpose of recommending changes they regarded as both necessary and beneficial. New Labour, however, moved away from its ideological base (such as it was) and substituted for political analysis and prescription a simple appeal to the electorate on the basis that they were more to be trusted with the power of government than their rivals. This is a tactic that works well for a time, but is susceptible to being fatally undermined if the trust is forfeited for any reason – for example, the invention of false grounds for an attack on another country.

As to what is to be done by politicians of this kind when they acquire the power of government, little is to be discerned. The promise is not so much to change and improve society as to take the pain out of politics – or even the politics out of politics. The application of reason and good sense, with a modicum of compassion and social concern, will, it is suggested, wash away the conflicts and the difficulties. Politics ceases to be a contest between different ways of looking at what a 'good' society is or could be and becomes instead a choice between the personal qualities of potential leaders. The charge that used to be made against Tony Blair, for example, that he lacked principle, is wide of the mark. It is not principle that he lacked; indeed, it could be argued that he had, as in the case of the moral certainty and religious zeal demonstrated in his decision to unleash war in Iraq, an excess of principle. What he lacked was politics.

The 'Third Way'

The response that has been most commonly made to the 'free market' by those who have traditionally resisted the view that the market must always prevail has been to invent various supposed palliatives for the harsher consequences of a market 'red in tooth and claw'.

So, in the UK for example, New Labour adopted and promoted as its attempt at ideology the concept of the 'Third Way'. This was perhaps the leading example of the attempt to accommodate the 'free market' while retaining a distinctive left-of-centre position on other matters.

The 'Third Way' was developed by theorists such as Anthony Giddens, who argued that neo-liberal economics was now so well entrenched as to be unchallengeable, and was, in any case, by virtue of its efficacy in delivering good outcomes, perfectly acceptable. But he argued that, in parallel with 'free-market' economics, a programme to secure social justice and a fair society should also be pursued.

This is a welcome rejection of the Marxist view that there can be no politics other than that dictated by economic forces. There is, of course, room – even in a global economy where right-wing policies are dominant and democratic governments are enfeebled – for compassion, tolerance, human rights and a concern for some concept of greater equality. The impulses towards these commendable goals are to be welcomed, even where their delivery is gravely handicapped by the overwhelming power of global economic forces working in a contrary direction.

However, the case for the third way, no matter how well intentioned its proponents, remains essentially unconvincing. This is for two related reasons. First, it is surely very difficult to maintain a position which concedes that governments have only a very limited role in the central business of managing the economy but are required and permitted to step up to the plate and supplant the market when it comes to delivering social outcomes. Much of the traditional political debate has, after all, been about the proper role of government. It cannot be convincing to concede the totality of the right-wing case on economic policy, and then change tack suddenly and take the opposing view when the debate moves on to other political issues.

Second, even if the assertion were convincing in principle and the theoretical case for the 'Third Way' could be established, practicalities suggest that the theory cannot be delivered as a matter of real politics. The demands of international capital, and the influence exerted by neo-liberal economic policies, mean that there are strict limits on the ability of governments to stray too far – even if they wanted to – into interventionist policymaking. The result is that steps towards socially responsible outcomes are likely to be only superficial and presentational. Governments might just about be tolerated if they attempt to mitigate at the margins and ex post facto the harsher consequences of neo-liberal economic policies; but by definition, anything more substantial by way of changing the way those policies operate and the outcomes they produce would run headlong into the contrary requirements of those who ultimately control the productive forces that dominate the global economy. 'Free-market' fundamentalism insists that only market values should survive, and that all others are displaced and eliminated.

An example of an attempted resolution of these difficulties was a pamphlet published in 2002 by the Fabian Society and written by Anthony Giddens. In *Where Now For New Labour?*, Giddens attempts to refute the criticisms made by those who have not been persuaded either by the theoretical underpinnings of the 'Third Way' or by its application in practice. Sadly, the argument is not so much disputed or refuted as simply ignored. The flavour is well captured by the following passage in which the author opines that:

Globalisation should not be identified, as each side in this confrontation tends to, with economic deregulation and the spread of world markets. The core meaning of globalisation is increasing interdependence: no matter where we live in the world, we are all affected by events and changes happening many miles away ... The most important factors shaping globalisation are not those to do with finance and markets, but with communication.

So easily are the problems defined away! This resolute refusal to recognise the most obvious characteristics of the global economy is hardly a convincing way of rebutting the argument made here and elsewhere. Unless the issues are properly engaged, it is hard to see that the Third Way can offer much by way of resolution of the real challenges presented by the global economy.

An even more striking example of the willingness of supposedly progressive politicians to accommodate the assumed political realities of the modern world is to be found in a speech delivered by Tony Blair at the celebrations of Rupert Murdoch's News Corp in California on 30 July 2006. Blair is reported to have said that the old divisions between left and right were no longer relevant, and that the modern political debate was 'no longer between socialists and capitalists but instead between the globalisers and the advocates of protectionism, isolationism and nativism'.[1]

Let us leave to one side any mystification that may be felt about his ungenerous characterisation of those who express doubts about the supposed benefits of globalisation. Those who want to oppose or at least criticise some aspects of globalisation do not necessarily do so on the basis of isolationism. Many would see their positions as consistent with openness, freedom and internationalism. They just happen to have some regard as well for democracy, self-determination and values other than those of the market.

What is remarkable about Tony Blair's hymn of praise to, and identification with, Rupert Murdoch and the globalisers, however, is that he seems not only to acknowledge what has happened but to welcome it. Here, it seems, is the most unabashed formulation of what has often seemed a paradox – the support of a supposedly left-wing government for the big battalions, and the willingness of a left-wing government to preside over a shift of wealth and power in favour of the already wealthy and powerful.

If this is what Blairism means, much that is difficult to explain about Tony Blair's policy stances – both internationally and at home – becomes clearer. His attitudes rest on the assumption that the forces of globalisation have produced, in hard practical terms, the best of all possible worlds – an assumption that is surely hard to sustain today in the light of the global financial crisis and the ensuing recession – and that any harshness or absolutism can be remedied by social policy. His impatience with the public sector, his faith in the market and the profit motive, his equanimity when faced with widening wealth and income inequalities, are all seen to come directly from the pages of the international investors' handbook.

We must recognise that neo-liberal economic policies are not there, and have not become dominant, by accident or just for their own sake, or to satisfy some theoretical approach. They are, and are increasingly, applied precisely because they produce certain practical outcomes. Their whole point is that they do produce those outcomes, the very outcomes that proponents of the 'Third Way' then presume to change or at least mitigate. Globalisation is not a game played for fun. The whole point of the 'free-market' economics made possible, and virtually inevitable, by globalisation, is to leave the market dice to lie where they fall – what might be described as a deliberately engineered social injustice. Winners take all.

Chapter 5

Democracy Surrendered

The rise of the global economy has been, as we have seen, of huge economic significance, but has been no less important in political terms. Businesses, however successful they were in the past, always had to take account of the rules set by governments. Now it was governments that had to sue for terms, and would lose out in the competition for investment if they did not comply with the demands of the multinationals.

The world's major corporates could, in effect, set the political agenda in each individual country. The price they demanded for what was seen as essential foreign investment was a menu of measures drawn from the textbooks of right-wing ideologues. That menu included a 'free-market' (or monetarist) economic policy, low business tax rates, accommodating rules about the repatriation of profits, industrial relations laws that reduced the power of trade unions, health and safety legislation that was not too onerous, a regime that allows the externalisation of costs to the environment (or, in other words, the transfer of those costs to the public purse), and labour costs aligned to the lowest international benchmarks.

In addition, foreign investors now understood that they could exercise their power quite irresponsibly; it was, after all, governments – not the investors – that had to answer to their electorates. The investors answered to no one but their shareholders. Most costs could be passed on to taxpayers, who no longer had a voice. And, as voters began to understand that their governments could no longer protect them, confidence in the democratic process began to weaken.

The 'free' market incompatible with democracy

Few seem to have understood – not even supposedly progressive politicians – that democracy cannot coexist with an 'infallible' and unchallengeable market. The whole point of democracy, after all, is that ordinary people can use the political power of democratic legitimacy to offset what would otherwise be the overwhelming economic power in the marketplace of the powerful and privileged minority. If even democratic politicians accept that they are not only powerless to intervene in the market but that it would be literally improper and counterproductive for them to do so, then the powerful are unconstrained in their ability to impose their will on the rest of society. Indeed, the further concentration of power in a few already powerful hands can only become more overwhelming. The protection of the general or common interest supposedly offered by democracy is seen to be valueless.

We can now see the inevitable consequences of that extraordinary concession made by democratic politicians. Unrestrained markets will always threaten, as even Adam Smith pointed out, a conspiracy against the general interest. They will always lead to excesses. As we shall see later, the global recession was the direct and inevitable consequence.

But, long before this begins to dawn on politicians and voters alike, the baleful consequences are plain to see in the constraints imposed on and accepted by most participants in the public debate. So powerful has been the orthodoxy promoted by the masters of the global economy that very few politicians – even those who in principle might be expected to offer a critique of or alternatives to that orthodoxy – have been willing to debate the main principles of the 'Washington consensus'; they have been too fearful of being condemned by the media as being hostile to the market economy.

The consequence is that in most western countries over the last two or three decades there has been virtually no real debate about economic policy. Such debate as there has been has focused on the detail of microeconomic policy – tax rates, tax incentives, changes (usually) from public to private ownership and (occasionally) back again, incentives for investment and so on. The broad principles of macroeconomic policy have remained unchallenged, and the voters have almost never been offered any real alternative to the 'free-market' doctrines which mean in effect that government should not concern itself with this area of policy.

Democratic elections, therefore, have largely been contests between parties who endorse 'free-market' policy but claim to be more efficient on the one hand or more compassionate on the other in its application. To the extent that there has been meaningful debate about the central issues of macroeconomic policy, it has arisen not because the 'free market' has been challenged in any way but because – as in the USA – the proponents of 'free-market' policies have insisted on espousing more and more extreme versions, and have therefore constantly moved the parameters of the debate further and further to the right.

The voters themselves seem largely unaware that their range of choices has been constrained in this way. They seem, however, to have sensed that the governments they are invited to elect have somehow placed the important issues, either unwittingly or by design, beyond the reach of popular debate and decision.

Politics redefined

The role of the market has always been a hotly debated issue in democratic societies, but the nature of that debate has changed significantly over recent years.

In the past, the question debated in most democracies has not been 'whether or not' the market but rather the degree to which the harshness of some of the outcomes produced by the market might be moderated or perhaps supplanted at particular points by other and wider considerations. In most democratic societies, there has been an acceptance that the market economy is the most efficient form of economic organisation as well as being the most compatible with individual freedom and social responsibility; but opinions have varied as to how far interventions in the market are needed to produce better and more rational economic outcomes, and to achieve wider social and environmental goals.

In recent times, though, the area of contention about the market's role has moved significantly. Today's masters of the global economy insist that the dividing line in the debate has now changed, and that the crucial question is not whether the market is to be allowed a significant role but rather whether it is accepted as infallible and unchallengeable. The majority that accepts the great value of the market is now told that it is no longer enough to endorse the market economy and to celebrate its irreplaceable advantages; the market must now be accepted as beyond challenge. In the new orthodoxy, anyone who disputes that proposition is likely to be dismissed as beyond the pale. There is no middle ground; those who do not line up shoulder-to-shoulder with 'free-market' fundamentalists are condemned as necessarily endorsing what is postulated as being the only other option – a non-market or centrally planned and directed economy.

Yet the issue about how the market's huge virtues can be harnessed to outcomes that go beyond the bottom line of individual businesses and accordingly serve wider social, cultural and environmental interests, and the economic interests of the whole community, is surely one of the most important areas for discussion in a democratic society. It is here that some of the most important questions in our society should be resolved.

One of the great features of the market as an economic mechanism, after all, is surely that in addition to its irreplaceable role as an efficient allocator of scarce resources and as a stimulus to innovation and enterprise it responds to whatever signals are provided to it, so that it can be – and almost always is – rigged to produce desired outcomes. Therefore it is potentially an amazingly effective instrument for mediating conflicting interests and arriving at compromise solutions that meet the general will while protecting individual or minority interests.

The true debate today should be between those who support on the one hand an unfettered, unregulated, infallible, unchallenged 'free market' that has historically been the ideal of a tiny minority of extremists, and on the other those who would harness the great advantages of market provision while at the same time understanding its propensity to do harm unless properly regulated. It is essential that this debate takes place for the sake of democracy.

Not just economics – everything else follows

The concession that it is the market that is the only legitimate and effective determinant of economic activity, and that government has only a limited role to play in holding the ring, has consequences that are not limited to the management of the economy. The implications go much wider. If it is conceded that, on the central question of economic policy, decisions can safely be left – indeed, must be left – to the market, then what case can be made for saying that the market cannot be trusted in important but less central matters such as the delivery of health, housing or education? If the market is infallible or at least unchallengeable on the most important issues, then the rest of the game has also been conceded.

And if the fundamental question of managing the economy is to be entrusted to the infallible market, how could it be argued that it is essential that other, less important, matters should be subjected to democratic control? Are democracy and the responsibilities of government to be limited to the detail and the trivia, while the essential issues are decided by business leaders and by unaccountable supposed and self-interested experts?

If, as we have seen, large parts of what was once regarded as the central battleground of democratic politics are no longer debated or contested, and acceptance of economic orthodoxy has become the sine qua non of acquiring the power of government, then it follows that right-wing politicians have an advantage in the political debate. If the rules of the game now provide that the right must win the central debate about key aspects of economic policy, then surely it has a head start in taking on its opponents on other political issues.

This head start means, for example, that right-wing leaders are more easily forgiven mistakes in other areas. Criticism on non-economic issues can be more easily deflected or discounted because 'free-market' ideologues are more or less impregnable on the central issues of running the economy. The effect can be seen across a whole range of policy areas, from privatisation versus public services to direct as opposed to indirect taxation. But one of its main effects is less obvious and more diffuse. It is the loss of intellectual self-confidence by progressive voices and their implicit surrender of positions they once held. If the central issues of politics are no longer debated because it is conceded that the right has won a more or less permanent victory, it can hardly be surprising that there is not much stomach for a fight on other lesser issues.

Thus, even where right-wing governments are defeated and succeeded by governments further to the left, those successors have had great difficulty in detaching themselves from their right-wing inheritance. In the UK, long after the Conservative Party had itself decided that Thatcherism had run its course and even after an apparently landslide general election victory, the New Labour government remained in thrall – on many central economic issues – to the Thatcherite influence. So thorough had been the advance of the political tide of global monetarism that there was no longer a debate to be had, or so it seemed.

It is this loss of intellectual self-confidence, and the perception that the world had changed for good, that explains why the Labour Party in Britain felt it necessary in order to get elected to adopt a programme that was seriously at odds with its own principles and values. It further explains why, even when the Labour government had apparently been mandated by the electorate to implement a programme of change, it manifestly failed to do so. Tony Blair and his cabinet were clearly convinced that any significant departure from economic policy orthodoxy would make election victory impossible and the business of government more problematic. They preferred to restrain such ambitions as they may have had for the sake of gaining and retaining power, even if the consequence was that much of the point of exercising that power was lost.

New Zealand, too, provides an example of the same phenomenon. The election of a Labour government in 1999 was not preceded by, and did not herald, any resumption of a long-suspended debate on macroeconomic policy or any coherent attack on the economic record of the National (right-wing) government. As it turned out, Helen Clark's government did rather better than its British counterpart in moving some parts of the wider political debate further to the left (and, incidentally, by promoting a kinder and more unified society, reaped a political reward for doing so). However, there was no sign of the intellectual self-confidence needed to open up a real debate about how the economy should be managed and in whose interests. The New Zealand Labour government showed itself unable to get itself off the tramlines, even though the warning lights were flashing from a long way off.

This subjugation to the dictates of the global economy has meant that it is not only economic policy whose broad outlines are removed from political debate. Let us take, as examples of apparently discrete areas of policy, the environment or foreign policy. It might have been argued that policy in these areas would be unaffected, whatever might have happened to the former debate about economic policy – but not a bit of it.

On the environment, there has been – to put it mildly – a constant struggle between the wishes of national governments and the electorates they represent on the one hand and the interests of multinational corporations on the other. From property development to the use of chemicals as fertilisers or pesticides, from mineral extraction to genetic engineering, from global warming to nuclear power, the big corporations have leaned heavily on national governments to override environmental concerns in the interests of attracting international investment and supposedly creating jobs and output (for which read profits). The carelessness with which this is done varies according to the political sophistication and power of the country involved. More care is taken in the developed world, for obvious reasons, than in the developing world. But the impetus is the same, as is the difficulty national governments have in resisting the power of the multinationals.

The impact of 'free-market' ideology on the environment is also felt more directly at the national level. Many national governments have been converted to the belief that, even in the face of environmental damage, the market must not be gainsaid, and that the short-term bottom line is the ultimate judge and vindication of environmentally short-sighted and destructive economic activity. For them, the argument that a given activity will produce more 'wealth' in its narrowest definition (and we will look later at the role played in these matters by conventional accounting practice) trumps any other consideration. For the New Zealand government, for example, the mere prospect that overseas mining or oil companies might discover wealth under the ground or under the sea is enough to send environmental concerns packing. It has taken environmentalists a disappointingly long time to wake up to the fact that environmental concerns cannot be looked at in isolation, and that the environment cannot be protected without a willingness to challenge the supposed infallibility of the market.

A similar picture can be seen when it comes to foreign policy. It might be assumed that governments are free to pursue their own foreign policy preferences and goals, irrespective of the role actually, or potentially, played by multinationals in their economies. But a moment's thought will show that foreign policy issues are often closely linked to economic matters. Would many governments, for example, have failed to think carefully about the consequences for trade and investment before deciding on what attitude to take towards the USA in respect of the invasion of Iraq? To pose the question is to point to the inevitable answer.

Even the New Zealand government, which took a cautiously critical approach to the failure to secure UN approval for the invasion, was obliged to tread carefully in enunciating that criticism, for fear of economic retaliation from the USA and, in particular, of a possible free trade arrangement being removed from the agenda. The New Zealand prime minister, Helen Clark, ventured the opinion that the Iraq war would not have taken place if Al Gore had been elected to the US presidency. She was obliged to disown the remark for fear of American reprisals. Similar concerns have often been felt and voiced in respect of New Zealand's courageous non-nuclear policy, which precludes the visit of American nuclear ships to New Zealand ports. Such a stance, it was constantly said, meant that New Zealand was handicapped in seeking a free trade agreement with the USA.

So, the impact of the global economy on domestic policies extends very widely – far beyond the obvious and related issues such as taxation, public spending, welfare policy, health and education, but into every aspect of governmental activity.

The loss of control

The impact of the global economy on local, regional and national communities has had further consequences, often unremarked, which have limited the value of democratic processes and institutions, and have accordingly reduced the confidence felt by citizens in their elected governments. Those anxieties have centred on the loss of control by local communities over their own fortunes as a consequence of the overseas ownership of major national assets and utilities, and a more general concern about the growing power of multinational corporations on both the national and international level.

Canada may be taken as a leading illustration of what can be described as one of the major consequences of globalisation – the 'hollowing out' of the corporate life of individual countries that are not themselves major players in the global economy.[1] Canada is, of course, an extreme example, by virtue of its close geographical proximity to the USA and the consequent pressure to integrate the Canadian economy into the American economy. But the same patterns can be seen in many other economies, including New Zealand, which not only has to contend with the major players, such as the USA, but also with, as its closest neighbour, a bigger economy with the comparative power to seek to become a mini-player in its own right. Where Canada is today, in other words, others will be tomorrow.

The bare statistics of the domination of the Canadian economy by American capital – the high proportion of investment from American sources, the large numbers of Canadian corporations that are subsidiaries of American firms, the volume of Canada's international trade that takes the form of intra-firm transactions – are easily established. The real significance of these statistics, however, lies in what this means for Canada's control, or lack of it, over its own economic fortunes.

The loss of control, as a consequence of the passing of corporate ownership and governance into foreign hands, manifests itself in many different ways. Canadian law no longer governs the affairs, activities and transactions of many of the most important companies active in Canada. Even those requirements of specifically Canadian law that do remain operable are increasingly threatened by international agreements in which the USA has insisted that American corporations, even though not themselves parties to those agreements, should be able to challenge, in specially constituted tribunals, legislation passed by the Canadian parliament or rulings by Canadian courts.

The stocks of many 'Canadian' companies are increasingly not listed on the Canadian stock exchange. Their head offices are no longer to be found in Canada. Their governance structures have been centralised, so that their affairs are run entirely from abroad. Increasingly, their shareholdings are held exclusively outside Canada. Their boards of directors have become smaller and show a higher proportion of foreign directors, and more and more board chairs and CEOs are resident abroad. The result is that critical investment, research and personnel decisions are being taken outside Canada, with the necessary implication that Canadian interests will be given a lower priority within the company. Knowledge of Canadian conditions and interests is less valued. Fewer Canadian-based initiatives are likely to be supported. A similar phenomenon is seen in the transfer of New Zealand corporate headquarters to Australia, and in the increasing tendency to list New Zealand firms, following their sale into foreign ownership, on the Australian stock exchange.

There are also consequences for the wider economy. The loss of corporate headquarters means less likelihood of important support services – legal services, financial advice, merchant banking, software design, public relations, marketing, human resource management, research and development – gathering around a particular company. Those services will instead concentrate outside the country, and will be found where the real decisions are being made. There will be less support and need for higher education, less patronage of the arts, less funding for research, and a smaller market for specialised and upmarket goods and services. Even in matters such as charitable giving, the branch-office or no-office economy will lose out to the pull of the head office. Corporate decisions in such matters are almost always made in corporate headquarters.

Perhaps most importantly, the perception will take hold – painfully but accurately – that there has been a real loss of control by ordinary people over their own lives. The decisions that matter most to them and their living and working environments will be taken increasingly beyond their reach, by people who have little knowledge of them or interest in them. This leads in turn to apathy and disaffection, to a society that is less integrated and feels itself to be less successful.

These aspects of a global economy increasingly controlled from just a few vantage points and centres of power were recognised by John Maynard Keynes as long ago as 1933. He wrote:

The divorce between ownership and the real responsibility of management is serious within a country, when, as a result of joint stock enterprise, ownership is broken up among innumerable individuals who buy their interest today and sell it tomorrow and lack altogether both knowledge and responsibility towards what they momentarily own. But when the same principle is applied internationally, it is, in times of stress, intolerable – I am irresponsible towards what I own and those who operate what I own are irresponsible towards me. There may be some financial calculation which shows it to be advantageous that my savings should be invested in whatever quarter of the habitable globe shows the greatest marginal efficiency of capital or the highest rate of interest. But experience is accumulating that remoteness between ownership and operation is an evil in the relations among men, likely or certain in the long run to set up strains and enmities which will bring to nought the financial calculation.

Ideas, knowledge, science, hospitality, travel these are the things which should of their nature be international. But let goods be homespun whenever it is reasonably and conveniently possible, and, above all, let finance be primarily national.[2]

Power, choice and freedom

The consequences of the loss of democratic choice and debate produced by the global economy are far-reaching. In stark contrast to the much-touted goal of progressive politicians of securing a redistribution of wealth and power in favour of ordinary people, there has been a decisive and possibly permanent swing in the opposite direction. It is the rich and powerful who have seen their power increase, and that increase has seen a corresponding decrease in the power, and therefore freedom, of ordinary people.

This is not just a matter of the freedom to debate and choose different political systems, remedies and approaches. It is also a loss of freedom to act and to govern one's own life. The loss of economic power, accompanied by the removal of the political counterbalance provided in theory by democratic processes and institutions, means a real diminution in freedom for the majority of people.

The failure by democratic governments to challenge the global economy, in other words, has meant a positive decision to allow developments which favour the rich and powerful so that the power of government is in effect turned against the interests of the weak and needy. It represents a real political decision, with real practical consequences in terms of the actual power of ordinary people to make real life choices – to decide where they want to live, what jobs to do, what leisure pursuits to enjoy, how many children to have, where to shop, what schools to send their children to, where to go on holiday, and so on. The outcome is, quite simply, that for many people those choices have been restricted.

Freedom is not an absolute; it is the degree to which one is free to act and choose in relation to the same power exercised by others. If power is concentrated in fewer hands, which then have comparatively more power of decision and choice, then by definition others are less free. Those societies that are part of the global economy can therefore be said to be less free than when they decided – however imperfectly – their own affairs and futures.

These trends are not to be deplored simply in the name of some abstract theory of egalitarianism, but have real consequences for the overall structure, distribution of power and cohesiveness of a given society. Income and wealth inequality have a powerful self-reinforcing effect that is as valuable to the rich and powerful as it is damaging for the poor and weak. A relatively small advantage can – with the normal operation of market forces – rapidly become a much larger one, and so it has proved. Those who have benefited from the shift of power towards the rich have been quick and very effective in entrenching their advantage, by using their economic power to buy educational, health care, housing and more general life opportunity (and essentially differential) advantages. Tomorrow's social divide and a more entrenched economic division have been built before our very eyes.

But there are other losses as well, beyond that of comparative purchasing power. Those with less freedom and power find that they have also lost their voice. They are taken into consideration less and their views are not heard or respected. Their value to society appears to have diminished, and as a consequence their self-esteem suffers. As John Rawls argued, this loss of self-esteem is a major reduction in freedom.

The process by which this has happened is no mystery. As the global economy has extended, and the power of the captains of industry and finance has grown proportionately to that of others (including that of governments representing the interests of those others), so the influence of the newly powerful has also grown. Their voices are listened to more attentively because what they have to say matters more. Their views are more widely and easily accepted, because the price of disagreeing becomes higher. Their values are accepted because they are seen as the signposts to future success. Their account of how to succeed and what it means to be successful prevails over all others because they embody the definition of the success that society appears to value. It is this success, and the norms and values that underpin it, that are constantly celebrated and eulogised in the media, which they control.

An instructive instance of the pervasiveness of these influences is the huge proliferation of business and management programmes and schools throughout tertiary education worldwide. These programmes offer the most highly valued and popular tertiary education qualification and usually follow similar lines, offering a view of how the world works that inevitably suggests the primacy of market and business values, and the importance of business success as a matter of personal achievement and overall economic development. In most western universities today, economics is no longer treated as a social science – a study of human behaviour – but has been moved firmly within the remit of the business and management faculties, where it is treated as subject to inexorable and often mathematical rules. A particular aspect of this trend is the popularity of MBA programmes, which produce a whole generation of business leaders imbued with the same free-market ideology. Very few such programmes attempt to do anything other than produce a constant stream of graduates who have been taught to think and behave in a uniform way.

A similar process can be seen at work in the changing role of universities in western societies. Universities are increasingly seen not as repositories of wisdom and civilised values, underpinning the whole breadth of western civilisation and developing educated and rational societies, but more and more as mere agents of economic development, whose role it is to generate technological progress which can be turned to advantage in commercial terms. Even the universities themselves have largely adopted this role and accepted this reasoning, recognising that this is necessary in order to attract the funding that is needed, thus providing a further example of important institutions succumbing to the overriding drive for supposedly greater economic efficiency.

This trend represents, of course, a complete failure to understand our own intellectual history, and a betrayal of one of the cardinal features of the intellectual revolution that took place at the time of the Renaissance. In most cultures up to that point, knowledge had been treated as pretty much a fixed quantum of fact and belief, often the preserve of a small and usually church-based elite and subject to careful rules as to how and to whom it should be passed on. The great change wrought by the Renaissance was that this view of knowledge altered completely; knowledge was no longer seen as a fixed quantity but as the product of a voyage of discovery that anyone could undertake. Those who undertook that voyage understood that knowledge was limitless and available to everyone; and that when it was gained, it was the property of everyone. It was understood that knowledge shared in this way would benefit and strengthen the whole of society.

It is evidence of the loss of intellectual self-confidence in the West, and the narrower focus now adopted as a result of abandoning these revolutionary attitudes to the gathering and dissemination of knowledge, that we now see knowledge increasingly and exclusively treated as a commodity whose value lies exclusively in the fact that it can be exploited for its economic value in the market.

The loss of faith in democracy

A report published by Democratic Audit in 2012 into the state of democracy in Britain over the last decade warned that it is in 'long-term terminal decline' as the power of corporations keeps growing, politicians become less representative of their constituencies, and disillusioned citizens stop voting or even discussing current affairs.[3] It found evidence that Britain appeared to have moved further away from its two benchmarks of representative democracy – control over political decision-making, and how fairly the system reflects the population it represents, a principle most powerfully embedded in the concept of one person, one vote.

Among the concerns identified by the report and drawn from databases of official statistics and public surveys were that public faith in democratic institutions was 'decaying', there was a widening gap in the participation rates of different social classes of voters, and the 'unprecedented' growth in corporate power 'threatens to undermine some of the most basic principles of democratic decision-making'.

The report found that membership of political parties and election turnouts had both fallen significantly in the last decade: only 1 per cent of the electorate belonged to a political party, while just over six out of ten eligible voters voted in the 2010 British general election, and barely one in three voted in European and local elections. The report's author, Stewart Wilks-Heeg, warned that 'over time, disengagement skews the political process yet further towards those who are already more advantaged by virtue of their wealth, education or professional connections. And without mass political participation, the sense of disconnection between citizens and their representatives will inevitably grow.'

It is surely no accident that, with the rise of the global economy, the dominance of multinational corporations in national economies, and the loss of the power and will on the part of national governments to do anything about it, voter apathy is an endemic problem in the older democracies. Voter turnout in the leading democracies, and particularly in the USA, is notoriously low, and is on a downward trend in most countries.

A striking example of the loss of faith in democratic institutions is to be found in Ireland, a point made forcefully in a recent study by Dr Elaine Byrne, the Irish expert to the EC on corruption.[4] Ireland is a country that has suffered more than most from the global financial crisis and its aftermath, and from the failure of its government to do anything to protect its citizens from the exigencies of the major financial institutions, who have demanded both their pound of flesh and continued austerity. The result has been a massive and painful contraction in the size of the Irish economy, and that has brought about in turn a huge loss of trust in government, which at the end of 2010 had fallen to just 10 per cent. This loss of trust is borne out by collapsing levels of involvement in democratic institutions, such as political parties, and in voter turnout. It has also produced, according to the study, a redefinition of corruption in public life to include the excessive influence of dominant private vested interests in the making of political decisions.

Even in a country such as New Zealand, where there has traditionally been a commendably high participation rate in general elections, voter interest is declining; voter turnout in the 2011 general election had fallen to 74.2 per cent, an historically low figure, and in fact the lowest since the general election of 1887. People may be only vaguely aware that their vote counts for little, but they have been quick to sense that even if they are able to elect the government of their choice, it seems to make little difference. Little wonder that democracy has seemed to lose its value.

Loss of faith in government

A loss of faith in government has, of course, been an inevitable accompaniment of the loss of faith in democracy itself. It is a loss of

faith that seems now to have infected opinion across most parts of the
political spectrum. Even on the left across the western world, there is
a marked tendency to look for salvation anywhere but government.
In the UK, for example, it is almost as though the left has concluded
that – so disappointing was the experience of being in government –
there is nothing more to be gained from that quarter.

The impact of that development is seen most clearly in the outcomes
of the global financial crisis of 2008. It is surely one of the miracles of
the modern world that a private sector meltdown, whose malign
consequences are still with us, and against which the only defence
proved to be the power of government, should have led to calls for a
reduction in the role of government.

It is only to be expected, of course, that in tough times the powerful
should try to shift the burden on to the less powerful, whose diminished
voice means that they are less able to complain. The speed with
which the lessons of the crisis have been reinterpreted in favour of
less government rather than more is testament to the ability of the
powerful to defend their interests – something we shall look at in
more detail later. Whatever the explanation, ordinary citizens have
been left in many countries with even less confidence that their elected
government will be able to protect them.

Much progressive political activism now takes the form of community-
based and often single-issue initiatives of one kind or another – whether
it is support for a local currency, or time-sharing, or various forms of
collective self-help, or the development of local power schemes. The
common factor in all these small-scale projects is their conviction that
ordinary people should take responsibility for changing society, or at
least their bit of it, and that government is not likely to be of any help
but is rather just another part of the conventional power structure –
along with the bastions of capitalism – that has to be overturned.

There is much talk of the need to engage 'civil society' as the
essential element in changing society. Government, it seems, is to
be bypassed as a snare and a delusion. There is an almost romantic
sense that ordinary people possess an innate wisdom and goodness,
qualities that are somehow sullied and rendered ineffectual by the
formal and structured processes of democratic government.

No one, of course, who wants to see a better and fairer society could
object to the impulses that drive these initiatives. But it is distressing
to see the efforts of earlier generations to achieve universal suffrage
and democratic government so casually set aside. Our forebears saw
the power and legitimacy of representative and elected government

as the essential safeguard against the overwhelming power of the capitalist and boss, the one guarantor that the interests of everyone and not just the powerful would be properly protected and advanced.

Community-based initiatives have their value, but as a means of changing society they are too small-scale, fragmented and dispersed to make much impact. Nothing will better serve the status quo than the concession that government should be limited to serving the interests of the powerful, and that proponents of change and defenders of the weak and powerless should look elsewhere.

The state now serves different purposes

The democratic state that exercises its traditional concern for all its citizens, and in particular for those who need its help, may have changed substantially, but the state has not simply ceased to exist The revolution that has occurred under the influence of the global economy has not meant that the activist state has disappeared; it has merely changed its role and focus. It is equally activist now, despite the constant denial of a role for government by 'free-market' ideologues, but it operates in a different interest.

Thus, the modern state is increasingly interventionist in the causes of producing more police and prisons, in providing wider and less accountable powers to security services (especially in the aftermath of the terrorist attack on the Twin Towers), in regulating the labour market and the levels of social support so as to force people to work for lower wages, in affixing a tightly controlled price tag to the steps taken to ensure that basic standards are maintained for the most vulnerable, in making life difficult for immigrants and other non-conformists, in restructuring the agencies that deliver public services, and in redefining the concept of public service virtually out of existence so as to ensure that private interests can pursue profits across the whole economy. As a consequence of globalisation, the state has in other words been recruited as one more soldier to the cause. It is now just one more mechanism for ensuring that the prescriptions of global investors are faithfully followed.

Democracy hollowed out

It may be asked how far the problem of the loss of faith in democracy and government is unwelcome to those who control and dominate the political debate now. The voter apathy that has infected most western countries might be interpreted as encouraging evidence that the real political debate is over – that we have reached the 'end of history', as Fukuyama argued and believed, and that for the first time in the modern era there is no longer any real challenge to the views and interests of the rich and powerful.

It is no accident that the constant mantra of political leaders such as Margaret Thatcher was that 'there is no alternative'. It is very much in the interests of the purveyors of the new orthodoxy that dissent should not only be discouraged but convinced that it is pointless and hopeless. It is distressing that they have been remarkably successful in pursuit of this goal.

This victory is all the sweeter because it can be represented as the proper and defensible outcome of the democratic process. The voters are apathetic, so it can be argued, because they no longer have anything of substance to concern themselves with or to contest. Apathy is, in fact, contentment and an endorsement of the dominant orthodoxy. All the processes and trappings of democracy are, after all, in place. The opportunities are there for the expression of different or contrary views. If they are not taken up, surely that is evidence that those views no longer have traction.

Democracy, we should remind ourselves, is not merely a matter of process – of casting a vote. Democracy is a form of government. To be meaningful, the democratic process must produce for those voting a government that enjoys democratic legitimacy and provides the rights and powers of self-government to those it represents. A democratic government must be one by which the majority consent to be governed, whose legitimacy is recognised by the minority or minorities, and which those minorities believe that they can change. It is this – the substance of democracy – that has been eroded and deprived of meaning.

This is the final irony. When the democratic process has been hollowed out so that there is little of substance left, the mere – perhaps only apparent – existence of that process can be used to silence the critics. A victory won by force or overtly in the face of democratic process would be hard to justify or defend. But a victory that appears to have been secured in accordance with democratic process can not only be justified but celebrated by the powerful.

Chapter 6

The Shift in the Balance of Power

A huge change in the balance of power on a global scale has been brought about, as we have seen, by the dominance of international capital, but it has both powerfully reinforced and been helped by changes that were taking place in any case. Quite apart from the new freedom from political interference that capital has discovered and exploited, other developments have immensely helped capital to take a decisive advantage over labour – by which we mean that vast majority who must work for a living.

The owners of capital have always looked for ways to reinforce the huge advantage they gain from the fact that the law in capitalist economies accords the rights of ownership to the providers of capital. This attempt takes its most fundamental form in the assumption that the market is a natural phenomenon that operates best if freed from all regulation and intervention. This assumption can only be maintained if attention can be diverted from the fact that markets depend entirely for their successful operation on rules and processes created and enforced by laws and governments.

As John Gray points out, the natural condition of markets is that they are highly regulated.[1] This is because, he argues, an unregulated market is and has been so destructive of other values in society, including democracy itself, that it would not be and has not, until now, been tolerated in the ordinary way. It is unfettered markets that are the 'creatures of state power', and they arise because global economic forces have subverted state power to their own ends and overridden all other considerations.

Gray is certainly right in pointing out that contemporary proponents of the 'free market' appear to be completely ignorant of economic history. It is by no means a law of nature that the suppliers of capital should enjoy the exclusive rights of ownership. Whatever nature might or not say on the matter, the current regime that ensures that ownership of wealth-creating capability is vested in the owners of capital rests substantially on human intervention.

The self-same intervention ensures that the counterclaim of labour
to share in the rights of ownership has only ever been – at best –
partially accepted, and then only in particular kinds of organisations,
such as cooperatives, or under employee share-ownership schemes.
Governments have on the whole been resistant to providing any
support or encouragement for such arrangements – which is odd,
given the value so often placed on the profit motive as the supposed
mainspring of human endeavour. If that motivation is so powerful
and beneficial, would it not be a good idea to extend it to as many
as possible? But the rights of ownership are jealously guarded by the
owners of capital; the contributors of labour are restricted to their
role as wage slaves. As a result, labour has had to find grounds other
than ownership to press claims to a share in the benefits produced
by their economic activity over and above the limited price that the
market, left to itself, would accord to labour as a commodity.

Those claims have largely rested on the industrial power of labour
(usually buttressed by trade union organisation) and by the political
power of the wider non-capital-owning community. But it has proved
to be a losing battle, not just because capital has escaped the constraints
imposed by national governments and because those governments
have been persuaded or compelled to reduce legislative protection
for organised labour, but also because the advance of technology has
meant that those able to acquire, own and deploy that technology
have found the balance of power swinging decisively in their favour.

The development and application of new technology is an expensive
business, and so the capability to develop or acquire it rests almost
exclusively with the owners of capital. By definition, decisions in this
area are for the owners and not for the workers. Technology, once
acquired and applied successfully, increases the capital value of an
enterprise and, even if increasingly skilled labour is needed to apply
it, will normally reduce the relative value of labour to that enterprise.

The owners of the technology have the exclusive opportunity,
through the exploitation of new technology, to increase the earning
capacity of the enterprise, and thereby the return on their investment.
That return, which comes to them exclusively, can then be reinvested
in the same enterprise or another one, providing a round of further
reinforcement for the process of increasing wealth.

It is no accident that in the English-speaking developed world the
comparative share and rate of increase in the ownership of wealth
for capital owners as opposed to workers has improved significantly.
New Zealand shows a typical picture: while the after-tax wage share

of GDP fell sharply from 1960 to 2000, and the trend has continued since, the after-tax share of profits held steady. In New Zealand's case, a significant proportion of that share passed into the hands of foreign owners.

The application of new technology thus has the effect of increasing the comparative value of capital inputs and thereby reducing the comparative value of labour inputs, so that the rewards attributable to those different categories of inputs are altered in favour of capital. In addition, there are less direct effects, allowing investors more freedom, for instance, in deciding where production should take place, more control over inventories and their management, and more choice as to what kind of labour to employ. The spread of new technology has also had indirect effects on the balance of power in industrial relations, enhancing an employer's ability to withstand strikes and developing the possibilities of surveillance and control within the workplace, while at the same time producing deskilling and unemployment among industrial workers.

These consequences are intensified to the extent that in many instances the development of technology has the more direct effect of actually replacing labour. While this effect can often be masked by the perfectly legitimate argument that new technology may provide new opportunities for labour, in that it requires new or enhanced skills, it is undeniable that the numbers required and therefore the comparative value of labour in the process of wealth creation are being steadily eroded as technology advances and becomes ever more important.

Those who offer their labour as the sole or main basis of their claim to economic reward have therefore been up against it as the terms of trade have turned against them. In these circumstances, they have needed more than ever the protection of trade union power and the ability, through the democratic ballot, to influence the political process in their favour. But just when they most need those protections, capital has been able to change the rules of the game decisively against them. The protections for labour have been reduced – not extended – as the political power of capital has grown inexorably. In most industrialised countries, the advent of the global economy has coincided with legislative intervention to weaken trade unions or discourage trade union membership.

As the workforce in western countries grapples with these problems, and especially with the rates of unemployment that have occurred in the aftermath of the global financial crisis, we should perhaps remind ourselves of an essay Keynes wrote in 1930, called *Economic*

Possibilities for our Grandchildren, in which he presciently foresaw and warned against these essentially modern developments.[2]

In this essay, written some years before his *General Theory*, Keynes distinguished between unemployment caused by temporary economic breakdowns and what he called 'technological unemployment' – that is, 'unemployment due to the discovery of means of economising the use of labour outrunning the pace at which we can find new uses for labour'.

Keynes took an optimistic view of this issue, arguing that it showed we were making good progress in solving the problem of scarcity, which meant that most people were condemned to a life of toil. He foresaw that technology would make possible vastly increased production at a fraction of the labour previously required. This would mean, he thought, that by the early twenty-first century most people would have to work only fifteen hours a week to produce all that they needed for a comfortable standard of living.

While Keynes was right to predict that developed countries would be much richer and more productive, he was wrong, as we now know, to think that this would mean a working week of only fifteen hours. In fact, working hours have not fallen since the early 1980s, and at the same time 'technological unemployment' has risen. And, as we recover from the current recession, most experts expect this group of jobless as a consequence of technological change to go on growing.

What Keynes failed to foresee was that the lion's share of the benefits from the productivity gains achieved over the last thirty years has been seized by the well-off. The rich and super-rich have become very much richer, while everyone else's incomes have stagnated. The political settlement of these issues imposed on the rest of us by the rich and powerful – by virtue of our (sometimes unwitting) acceptance that the market must rule and must not be challenged – has, without our even realising it, ensured that the modern economy produces its benefits exclusively for those who dominate that market, while the rest of us work longer hours in order to maintain our diminishing share of the wealth produced.

This may in itself offer good reasons for re-examining the constant drive for improved productivity. If the fruits of that improvement go exclusively to a small minority, perhaps the majority should rethink the nature of the bargain forced upon them by the rich. One possible response would be to consider the possibility of natural limits to the relentless drive for more productivity. Ever-increasing productivity means that, without continued economic expansion, unemployment will rise. As Keynes foresaw, the solution would be to accept the productivity increases, shorten the working week and share the available work.

But there is another possible strategy – an approach that has been recommended by Professor Tim Jackson of Surrey University.[3] He points out that there are sectors of the economy where chasing productivity growth makes no sense at all. Certain kinds of tasks inherently depend on the allocation of people's time and attention. He cites as examples the caring professions such as medicine, social work and education. Efficiency in these areas – in the sense of chasing ever-increasing profitability – is surely not the point; the real goal is to improve the quality of our lives. The care and concern of one human being for another, he points out, is a peculiar 'commodity' which cannot be stockpiled or delivered by machines. Its quality rests almost entirely on the attention paid by one person to another.

Professor Jackson's argument reflects work done in the early 1960s by a young economist, William Baumol, working with his Princeton colleague William Bowen. The pair developed an analysis of what became known as 'Baumol's disease'. Whatever advances were made possible by new technology and innovative work methods, Baumol and Bowen reasoned, there would be many undertakings that would essentially demand the same amount of time for their performance. It would still take a pianist the same time to play a Mozart sonata, a barber the same time to cut the hair of the average customer and a primary school teacher the same time to read a story to her class.

This meant, they predicted, that the comparative cost of delivering such services – in sectors such as education and health care – would inevitably outstrip the price of almost everything else; and so it has proved. While technological and other advances have hugely reduced the time and therefore the cost needed to produce goods, the cost in time of producing services has not lessened, with the result that productivity in the conventional sense has not increased greatly in the areas of service delivery. This means in turn that the comparative cost of producing services has greatly increased, since a failure to pay roughly comparable hourly rates would have meant that no one would deliver services at low rates if much higher rates were available elsewhere. 'Baumol's disease' – the propensity of an advanced economy to see the comparative costs of services outstrip other costs – suggests that the future development of an advanced economy is likely to take us away from conventional measurements of productivity and towards a greater emphasis on the quality of life for our citizens. Sadly, our business and political leaders seem very slow to learn this lesson.

The great doubling

There is a further issue that has hardly been recognised or understood by western policymakers but which has substantially shifted the balance of advantage against workers. Before the collapse of Soviet communism, China's movement toward market capitalism and India's decision to undertake market reforms and enter the global trading system, the global economy encompassed just half of the world's population – the advanced OECD countries and some parts (often only small parts) of Asia, Latin America and the Caribbean, and Africa.

That all changed in the 1990s. Workforces in the advanced economies suddenly found themselves in a global market that had virtually doubled in size, and were facing competition from countries that were rapidly developing on the basis of low-cost labour, technological advance and a wave of investment from global capitalists.

Such was the arrogance and ignorance of western leaders, however, that initially they saw nothing other than the prospect of increased returns on investment; even if they had recognised the threat posed by these newly competitive rivals, it is doubtful that they would have lost much sleep, since it mattered little to them whether the labour costs that the global economy enabled them to drive down (at least in comparative terms) arose at home or in the newly industrialising economies they were intent on exploiting.

The fact that the size of the global labour pool was estimated to have virtually doubled from approximately 1.46 billion workers to 2.93 billion workers (something that Richard Freeman called 'The Great Doubling' in his 2005 lecture of the same name)[4] presented global capitalists with a huge opportunity, but it meant at the same time the greatest challenge to western workers since the Great Depression.

The doubling of the global workforce was, initially at any rate, good for employers but damaging for workers, because – since the new entrants to the global economy brought little capital with them – the ratio of capital to available labour fell to only 61 per cent of what it had been, with the result that the comparative value of labour also fell. While the newly industrialising economies will no doubt eventually save and invest so as to contribute to the growth of the world capital stock, it may take three or so decades to restore the global capital-labour ratio to what it was. In the meantime, workers across the globe will find that their value in the marketplace has declined, and that the supply of low-wage labour has shifted the global balance of power decisively in favour of capital.

The flow of capital to countries such as China and India has, of course, increased wages in those countries, but workers in many of the developing countries in Latin America, Africa and Asia have not fared so well. The rise of the new powerhouses has turned many developing countries from the low wage competitors of advanced countries to relatively high-wage but less efficient competitors of China and India.

The doubling of the global workforce has also challenged workers in the advanced countries. First, it creates downward pressures on the employment and earnings of less skilled workers through trade with and immigration from newly competitive economics. And while higher-paid workers in advanced countries might be expected to benefit from, and not to be unduly challenged by, the low-cost imports that then became available, this overlooks the fact that the most successful of the new economies have become hugely competitive in technologically advanced industries, by virtue of the rapid spread of higher education and modern technology, thus negating the economists' assumption that a comparative advantage in high-tech would protect the living standards of workers in advanced countries.

The assumption that only advanced countries have the educated workforce necessary for innovation and production of high-tech products is, in other words, no longer true. Many countries in the developing world now send a higher proportion of their young workforce into higher education than is the case in the West, and China in particular has made a huge effort to increase the number of those graduating with bachelor's degrees many times over.

Multinational firms have responded to this increased supply of highly educated workers by looking for the best candidates in the world and locating facilities, including high-tech R&D and production, where the supply of candidates is sufficient to get the work done at the lowest cost; the development of computers and the internet has enhanced this potential for firms to move work to low-cost areas.

For all of these reasons, we have reached a watershed in the age-old struggle for advantage between capital and labour. It is at least arguable that the battle is over and that all that remains for labour is to sue for terms. If that is so, and labour has a diminishing claim to the benefits of economic progress and increased production, we urgently need a new basis on which to ensure that those benefits are fairly shared. We shall look further at these issues.

Chapter 7

Everything Has a Price:
Or Businessmen Know Best

The dominance of neo-liberal thinking and the economic power of business leaders has had a profound, even if at times unacknowledged, impact on western society. Many of the values that were once thought to be its defining characteristics – conservative values, such as loyalty, honesty, duty and patriotism, as well as more progressive values such as tolerance, compassion, collective enterprise, social responsibility and generosity – have been increasingly abandoned in favour of a more aggressive sense that the only value by which actions and attitudes are to be judged is the pursuit of individual self-interest. It is increasingly accepted that, whatever claims might be made for what are now seen as the old-fashioned values, they can and should be trumped by the imperative of pursuing individual advancement and self-interest.

One of the leading and more obvious consequences of this shift in attitude is the high regard in which business leaders – who are seen to be the prime embodiment of the drive for self-interest – are now held, to the point where they are assumed to have a virtual monopoly of wisdom; and that in turn has allowed them, quite apart from the actual economic power they exercise, to develop a quite disproportionate influence over the way in which we run our affairs in general.

This is such a recent development that I recall a time as recently as the late 1980s (at which time I was Shadow Secretary of State for Trade and Industry in Britain and had a good deal to do with leading businesspeople) when this hugely increased standing had not yet come about. What was remarkable about the business leaders I had the pleasure of meeting and talking to was how little they knew of public affairs. However knowledgeable they were about their own enterprises (and many were very skilled and well-informed in that regard), they were surprisingly unconfident about their understanding of the way the country or the economy as a whole was run, or how society as a whole operated, and, even more significantly, made no claim to knowing much about it.

For many, the world of public administration was completely foreign territory. So lacking in confidence on this score were some of them that they made some young friends of mine very rich by paying them large sums of money for the privilege of being introduced to supposedly important people in government and in parliament who would have been happy to meet them anyway.

All this is, of course, in marked contrast to today's conventional wisdom that businessmen (and it usually is men) are the only people who are competent to decide almost anything. It is assumed not only that they know about business but that their business skills are essential for the resolution of otherwise difficult issues in every sphere of activity. It is not that they are assumed to know everything; it is just that they are believed to know all – little though it may be – that is necessary.

The dominant influence of business leaders is not just a matter of providing role models on the one hand and of aspiration and emulation on the other. The rich and powerful are able to manipulate public opinion to support their world view, as we shall see later, but they are also able to use their wealth and power to have a direct influence on the political process. Governments – even governments whose political stance might suggest otherwise – are unduly susceptible, as we shall see later, to the blandishments of the wealthy.

The message constantly conveyed by the expensive lobbyists employed by the powerful is that wealth equals virtue. Despite the repeated and incontrovertible instances of dishonesty and double-dealing across a wide range of business activities, business success is equated with the notion of reward for virtue. Sometimes this is portrayed in terms suited to the glossy unrealities of the popular magazines or the tabloids, but it is also a hard economic message.

Investors are said to deserve ever greater rewards because of the economic benefits they confer (usually in terms of jobs or output) on individuals and communities. Little attempt is made to quantify in comparative terms what the value of capital investment might be in relation to other inputs such as labour, or even to recognise that other inputs matter at all. It is capital that provides the opportunities for wealth creation and which is duly eulogised; labour is just another cost to be kept as low as possible.

It is not as though the record of our business leaders provides persuasive grounds for confidence in their abilities. We shall examine later what we can learn on this score when we look at the global financial crisis, but even today, and in the more specific focus of decisions made by individual business leaders, the record is not encouraging. As John Kay points out, most of the decisions typically made by one major corporation to take over another proceed on the basis of the ego and macho impulses of the aggressor, and the simple hunger to get bigger, rather than on any detailed and convincing analysis of why the resultant entity will be more efficient, more socially responsible or a better employer.[1]

No one can doubt that enterprising and successful businesspeople are critical to our national future. They should be encouraged and helped to concentrate on what they are good at (and to get better at it). But let us also recognise that there are many other facets of a healthy and happy society that do not lend themselves easily to the nostrums provided by the business manuals.

The belief that businessmen should decide is seen at its most virulent in the constant assertion that economics must be run as though the country is a business. It follows that businessmen alone are equipped to make important decisions about the economy. Nothing could be further from the truth.

This is particularly the case in the middle of a recession. In hard times, a business will survive by cutting costs, laying off workers, suspending investment plans, delaying paying bills – the whole gamut of self-preservation measures. These are all rational steps for a single business to take in its own interests. What makes perfect sense for the individual business, however, is exactly the wrong prescription for the economy as a whole. An economy that responds in this way will drive itself into recession.

A recession is by definition what happens when there is a deficiency of demand in the economy. To try to remedy this condition by imposing policies of austerity, which can only exacerbate the problem by reducing demand still further, is akin to the medieval practice of bloodletting in order to improve the health and strength of the patient.

Yet, so entrenched is the conviction that businessmen know best, and so apparently seductive are the constantly repeated simple-minded mantras that 'you can't spend what you don't have' or 'if you have to borrow you should be declared bankrupt', that we continue to listen to individual business leaders who solemnly assure us that, in a recession, retrenchment is what (like a business) the economy as a whole must pursue. It is this manifestly false analogy that continues to exert a huge influence, even at the highest level, and that drives the imposition of policies of austerity when – as all experience shows – they are the last thing that an economy mired in recession actually needs.

For governments are in truth quite different from individuals and businesses. They have a wider responsibility to the whole economy, and accordingly many more options for bringing about recovery, including adjusting fiscal and monetary policy, and – where appropriate – borrowing to invest, or even printing money if that makes sense in context.

The insistence that a country is just like a business and should be run accordingly is not just an article of faith for businessmen themselves; it is explicitly adopted by some politicians as well. It seems to be the doctrine underpinning the approach of New Zealand's government, where the prime minister is increasingly described as the 'chief executive' and where the emergence of a single global marketplace is not only welcomed and encouraged but is seen to require that countries – just like large corporations – must, if they wish to succeed, operate as a tightly organised business with a clear market strategy.

The attempt to treat the elected government as though it is the board of 'New Zealand Inc.' has the great advantage that it is easily portrayed as almost apolitical and centrist, a simple matter of applying common-sense business precepts to what are otherwise the messy and contested complexities of democratic politics. Few people understand the loss of democracy that this entails, and the advantage it provides to business interests at the expense of other views as to how a fair and balanced society might be run.

The approach has often been adopted, as Naomi Klein pointed out in her influential work on 'disaster capitalism',[2] when it is necessary to deal with the problems faced in the aftermath of natural disasters. The perceived need for quick and decisive action in such circumstances has been, she argues, consciously exploited by neo-liberal free marketeers, who have seen the opportunities to force through a radical programme of deregulation, privatisation and market fundamentalism. Big money knows what it wants and a crisis is the best time to slip it through. To make it all happen demands a centralisation of power, consciously the antithesis of bottom-up, community-led democracy.

Chile, needing to recover from economic and political turmoil under Pinochet's dictatorship, was an early example, and similar changes were brought about in Argentina, Bolivia and Uruguay, then Poland and Russia, following their experiences of similar problems. Those economies were quite consciously reshaped to suit the interests of western capital. We have seen more recently, as countries such as Greece and Spain have struggled to recover from indebtedness and recession, a similar phenomenon; the opportunity has been taken to force through not only policies for austerity but also privatisation on a large scale.

We see a similar syndrome in the national as well as the international arena. In New Zealand, following the Canterbury earthquakes of 2010 and 2011, responsibilities for earthquake recovery have largely been removed from elected local government in Christchurch and handed over to statutory bodies accountable to ministers, while the local authority elected for the wider Canterbury region has been replaced by non-elected commissioners; the motivation for this latter step seems to have little to do with earthquake recovery and much more with allowing powerful business interests to push through measures that will give them control over scarce water resources.

In New Zealand, there is virtually no aspect of national life that would not benefit, it seems, from being run as though it were a business. From public service broadcasting to prisons, from providing health care to protecting the environment, commercial provision, operating on business principles, is seen as preferable to public provision. The extent of this preference has sometimes reached ludicrous proportions.

In 2012, for example, it was reported that ambassadorial posts were to be advertised with a view to opening them up to a kind of competitive process. It was apparently no longer enough to graduate with a good degree and to be accepted against strong competition into the diplomatic service, to have gained years of experience and to have developed special knowledge and skills in foreign languages and international politics, and to have spent a good part of one's life serving one's country in sometimes difficult and even dangerous posts overseas.

Anyone, it seemed, could be a diplomat. Careful analysis, subtle judgement, accurate reporting, the ability to gain the confidence of people of different cultures and politics, are all beside the point. What was needed instead, apparently, was the ability to focus on the bottom line, to secure a proper return on capital, to cut costs and generally to bring the sharp lash of business realism to bear.

But it was not just the diplomatic service that was in the firing line; it was only the latest bastion to fall to the cult of the omniscient businessman. Who cares whether there is any understanding of the complexities of conducting foreign relations, or of the value of a national broadcaster in underpinning and helping to shape a national identity? Who need bother with social, cultural and environmental goals when everything revolves around the short-term return on financial investment? The only people who need to be satisfied are the accountants; the only measure that matters is the bottom line; nothing else is of value or can withstand the apparent conviction that most issues are best entrusted to market forces.

So, private firms are engaged to build and run prisons, and investors encouraged in effect to establish or take over 'partnership' schools (in New Zealand) or 'academy' schools (in the UK). Private consultants and contractors are expensively hired for work hitherto undertaken by the public service, with a view, it seems, not to saving money (since private consultants are an expensive option) but because governments believe that the private sector will inevitably deliver better results.

A 'partnership' school is, like a privately run prison, an example of a public–private partnership (PPP) – or, in the UK, a PFI (Private Finance Initiative) project. The case for such arrangements is that what would normally be funded by the taxpayer is instead financed by private business, with allegedly a saving as a consequence to the public purse.

But a moment's thought would suggest that this is unlikely to be the case. The cost of raising capital for a project will be the same in principle wherever the funding comes from; indeed, the borrowing costs for a government will usually be lower than for a private borrower. Moreover, while the initial capital cost under a PPP is borne by the private investor, that investor will want to cover the cost of capital and in addition earn a return on capital (or profit), and will usually want to secure contractual rights to run the project over the lifetime of the scheme – typically, twenty-five or thirty years.

Not surprisingly, in countries such as the UK where such schemes were pioneered two or three decades ago, it has now been confirmed that they will cost the taxpayer much more over the whole period than if they were funded by more conventional methods. The Treasury reported in 2012 that the 717 PFI contracts, funding new schools, hospitals and other public facilities, with a total capital value of £54.7bn, would ultimately cost £301bn by the time they have been paid off over the coming decades.[3]

Much of this difference was due to ongoing running costs built into the contracts, but the schemes were also criticised for providing poor value for money compared with the interest rates that the government would pay if it borrowed money directly to pay for the schemes. Details of the contracts compiled by the Treasury made it clear that some National Health Service organisations will end up paying almost twelve times the initial sum over what is usually a thirty-year contract. The total annual repayment cost of all PFI schemes in the UK in 2007–8 was £5.78bn, but by 2017–18 that will have almost doubled to £10.1bn.

Successive governments have, in other words, quite unnecessarily and wastefully spent billions, saddling future generations of taxpayers with massive debts, for the sake of an ideologically driven preference for private business as opposed to public provision. And this despite the fact that there is no evidence that anything of value is gained from this excessive expenditure, other than inflated profits for the fortunate contractors. It is certainly not the case that there is a gain in efficiency, since there are many instances of private providers performing very poorly. None of this has dissuaded governments from pursuing PPPs or from bamboozling an uninformed public that they are a good deal in the public interest, and not just a device for pushing business in the direction of the government's friends in the private sector.

But that is only one of the reasons that we should be wary of such arrangements. The insistence on provision being made for commercial rather than public service purposes has a wider explanation than the purely financial. In the case of so-called 'partnership' or 'academy' schools, for example, it is not just the funding that the government would prefer to obtain from the private sector; it is also the policy direction of the education provided for our children that governments have chosen to sell to business – and most of those who have taken up the opportunity have used it to promote their own doctrines, political or religious. It is just one more instance, though a particularly significant one, of the extent to which the market has invaded virtually every area of our daily lives. The view that everything has a market price, and should be traded as though it were a commodity, is now deeply entrenched.

How long before wealthy prisoners are able to buy an 'upgrade' of their cells in the new private prisons, as is already being done in some American states? How about buying the right to drive one's car down a bus lane? We're getting perilously close to that in many western cities. What about the right to shoot endangered species? You can buy that, too, for the threatened black rhino in South Africa. Buying the right to live in the country of your choice? Yes, if you've got the money. And how long before pupils at the new 'partnership' schools are paid, in a ludicrous attempt to improve a measurable criterion, $2 for each book they read – which is what privately run schools in Dallas do to boost performance?

If the market makes everything available at the right price, we lose sight of other – perhaps more important – values. But it will suit some people: those with the most purchasing power will be delighted to find that nothing can be denied them.

Everything has a price

The lesson that everything has a price and that the market price is the only measurement of value that matters is constantly driven home by the media and by commercially driven activity such as advertising. We have become accustomed, for example, to see sport as just another aspect of professional entertainment, with the inevitable corollary that the names of sports grounds or teams have become pieces of property to be sold to sponsors, or that sports uniforms are merely vehicles for the brand names of commercial firms – while sportspeople themselves have become high-priced commodities, to be bought and sold without regard for qualities such as loyalty or shared interests and identity.

Similar developments across the board have prompted questions about whether there remain any values that are not susceptible to market imperatives. Michael J. Sandel, the Harvard political philosopher, explores these issues in *What Money Can't Buy: The Moral Limits of Markets*.[4]

Sandel is concerned that over the past thirty years economic imperatives have begun to crowd out other values. He observes all sorts of situations where traditional mores have shifted in recent years, always in the direction of market morality. In each of these cases, long-held ideas about inherent worth and common ownership have been displaced by the simplicity of market imperatives. This shift in values, he notes, matters more and more as inequality widens: 'The more money can buy,' he says, 'the more affluence (or the lack of it) matters.' And he notes also deeper concerns about how we ought to value what he calls 'the good things in life'.

Why should such developments bother us? Because, he observes, 'markets don't only allocate goods, they also express and promote certain attitudes toward the goods being exchanged', so that 'when we decide that certain goods may be bought and sold, we decide, at least implicitly, that it is appropriate to treat them as commodities', and we thereby reduce or overlook their real value.

We resist the notion that the market should decide who lives and who dies (though the provision of health care on the basis of who can pay for it gets perilously close to that). But market morality carried to its logical conclusion might mean, for example, that we should auction university places to the highest bidders on the ground that we could then be certain that the people who 'value' university education most would get places; and if we followed that interpretation of what the market requires, we would certainly have changed the meaning of the 'value' of a university education.

Michael Sandel points out another seemingly small but quite profound change in society. As recently as a generation ago, economists viewed their job as understanding phenomena such as prices, depressions, unemployment and inflation. It was dismal, as he says, but at least it was science. Somewhere along the way they expanded their portfolio to include the whole of human behaviour. Economists have now become newly confident and ambitious, declaring, for example, that 'incentives are the cornerstone of modern life' and that 'economics is, at root, the study of incentives'.[5] Economists have assumed a role in society that for the past 4,000 years has been held by philosophers and theologians. They claim to have made our lives freer and more efficient, but even if that claim were supported by the facts Michael Sandel says we would be the poorer for it.

Government's role to serve business

One of the greatest paradoxes of modern western societies is that those who most fervently proclaim that government must get out of the way, so that business can get on with making money, are in fact those who have been most successful in recruiting government to deliver to them the essential advantages that allow them to pursue their own interests at the expense of the rest of us. Far from relying on the 'free market' to allow them to exercise their supposedly superior talents, the rich and powerful have increasingly subverted government so that the market is rigged to suit their purposes. This does not, of course, deter them from berating most ordinary people as 'losers' (or, as Ayn Rand would have it, 'moochers') and accusing them – as Mitt Romney notoriously did during the presidential election campaign of 2012 – of expecting the government to support them without doing anything to deserve it.

The context in which this sleight of hand is achieved is worth further exploration. As commentators such as Joseph Stiglitz have pointed out, the wealth of the rich increasingly depends less on augmenting the total of wealth in general but rather on siphoning off existing wealth into fewer pockets.[6] Far from being the 'wealth creators' and 'job creators' of Randian imagination, the wealthy of today make their money from earning a 'rent' from their ownership of assets and by manipulating those assets so as to divert money from others. Their wealth accrues by virtue of what they own rather than what they do or make.

This is partly done by using their existing wealth to buy for them an advantage in the way that a market will operate. They will be able, for example, to exploit a lack of information and expertise – the handicaps under which most people operate in contexts such as financial markets – to sell deals that will reserve the benefits to themselves while exposing their victims to all the risks. If the victims complain and seek redress, they will use their superior resources to ride out the storm and to buy the best legal advice.

It is also achieved by virtue of the techniques developed for 'churning' assets, so that each time a transaction is concluded the ticket is clipped: the foreign exchange markets are just one example. And the financial markets have also been remarkable for the proliferation of new assets of doubtful and often no value, which have been created out of nothing and then traded into the hands of the gullible.

The rich have perfected these techniques to the point where they feel confident about treating government with equal contempt. They have been so successful in persuading everyone, including themselves and the government, that the whole economy depends on their efforts that they are able to insist that their wishes should be met, since otherwise – supposedly – business, and therefore the rest of us, will suffer.

The means by which governments deliver surreptitious favours to business are multifarious and varied. Mining and oil companies are given preferential access to oil and mineral resources, an access which is equivalent to a licence to print money, and are at the same time excused from dealing responsibly with the environmental damage they cause; drug companies and military contractors are given the inside running and negotiate contracts to sell their products at above market prices to the government; other enterprises that wish to utilise publicly provided commodities, such as electricity, are allowed to purchase them at subsidised rates; competition laws are suspended or rendered inapplicable in order to protect emerging monopolies; penalties for breaking the law in terms of misleading the public are set at derisory levels; the laws that protect intellectual property are extended to allow long-standing monopolies to be exploited, in defiance of the offence caused to the claimed 'freedom' of commerce, but reflecting the myth that monopoly is impossible in the infallibly efficient and competitive 'free market'; regulation to prevent the exploitation of dominance in the market so as to destroy weaker competitors is ignored; regulatory authorities are populated with representatives of the businesses they are supposed to regulate; businesses are given privileges not enjoyed by others in matters such as seniority in the order of claims when a business fails; banks are able to borrow at lower rates than others enjoy and have the luxury of guaranteed bail-out if they fail; the interests of those who might claim a share of the profits made by business are deliberately reduced, through so-called 'reforms' of labour laws to remove 'rigidities'; a blind eye is turned by government to the exploitation of the low-paid and to breaches of the laws that should protect them from health and safety hazards; the population as a whole is left unprotected against the damage suffered as a consequence of the activities of large corporations, tobacco and alcohol companies, for example; investment is encouraged by valuable 'tax breaks'; whole industries are subsidised, with the greatest benefits going, as in American agriculture, to the corporate operators who dominate the industry; the list goes on.

So, far from simply holding the ring, as the mythology would have it, governments have been suborned into rigging markets so that big business gets the inside running. Little attention is paid to the consequence that every dollar that is diverted into the pockets of big business is filched from ordinary people. Even if the truth of the matter is revealed, the justification is always that these are the rewards for virtue, and that the less fortunate have no one but themselves to blame. The fact that much-maligned government is an essential instrument for the delivery of profits to big business is conveniently ignored.

The rich have colonised politics

It is not just 'free-market' economists and ideologues who have tried to persuade us that the special virtues of the rich, as witness their success in making money, should confer on them special authority and entitle them to be heard with equally special respect in the corridors of power. The rich themselves have increasingly begun to take direct action by deploying their wealth in order to access political power – often overtly, on the basis that they are justified in doing so because their ability to make money demonstrates that they are peculiarly fitted to make decisions for the rest of us.

In some western democracies, and notably the USA, elected office has increasingly moved beyond the reach of those without personal wealth. Indeed, having a personal fortune, or at least the support of those who do, has become the sine qua non of getting elected to almost anything. Politics in the USA has, in other words, become an arena restricted to those able to spend many millions on campaigning.

In other countries, great wealth is certainly not a handicap – but it is deployed usually with a little more circumspection. In New Zealand, for example, the current prime minister has won two elections at least partly on the basis that his success in making a modest fortune (by international, though not New Zealand, standards) as a foreign exchange dealer equips him to run the country – though whether the short-term (not to say overnight) time horizon of the foreign exchange dealer is a qualification for devising the long-term strategy for a whole economy is at least open to question.

In the UK, too, personal wealth has at least allowed senior politicians such as David Cameron and George Osborne to devote their energies to politics rather than to the more mundane business of earning a living – though, in the case of Tony Blair, the wealth seems to have followed as a consequence of achieving political power rather than the other way round.

The direct deployment of wealth has certainly become a major factor in achieving success in politics, but the rich have also found ways of using their wealth to exploit less direct avenues to power. We shall look later at the particular case of Rupert Murdoch, who has never sought political office but has found other ways of exercising great influence; and we have the instance of another Australian, the mining magnate Gina Rinehart, demonstrating how great wealth can be used, through the financing of advertising campaigns and the purchase of controlling interests in media companies, to ensure that the political establishment does her bidding.

The Rinehart example is particularly instructive. Over recent years, successive Australian governments have presided over the development of a 'two-speed' economy, in which the mining magnates have become hugely wealthy as they have dug up chunks of the continent's barren interior and sold the spoils off to a mineral-hungry world, while the rest of the economy has increasingly suffered from the over-valued Australian dollar that the mineral wealth has produced.

The not unreasonable proposition that the whole of Australia should benefit rather than suffer from the success of the mining companies in exploiting the country's natural resources prompted the proposal that the mining magnates should pay, by way of a special tax, some of their unprecedented profits to the rest of the country. This was strongly resisted by the mining billionaires, who spent millions on advertising campaigns to resist the proposal and to persuade ordinary Australians that it was against their interests as well. So successful was this campaign that the tax was initially abandoned (and the prime minister who proposed it was removed from office), and was eventually reintroduced in a much watered-down form.

Not content with this demonstration of political muscle, Gina Rinehart, Australia's wealthiest woman, then set about emulating her compatriot, Rupert Murdoch, by attempting to take control of a major media company and a television channel so that she could personally and overtly dictate the message they put before the Australian media. We have yet to see whether this strategy will ultimately succeed. What is breathtaking, however, is the blatant and arrogant use of wealth to control the course of political debate.

Gina Rinehart has been quick to defend herself against her critics, whom she accuses of being 'socialists pursuing class warfare'. She advises her employees to work harder and spend less time in the pub; she also urges a reduction in the minimum wage. She herself inherited her Aus$20 billion fortune from her father, Lang Hancock, who discovered huge iron ore reserves in Western Australia before she was born.

Buying the right research results

The rich, as we have seen, have been adept at inserting themselves both directly and indirectly into the political process. They have also been able to exercise a powerful influence by helping to generate and propagate approaches and doctrines that serve their purpose, often indirectly and sometimes surreptitiously.

This has often been a matter of financing think tanks and research centres whose remit is to provide an intellectual infrastructure for 'free-market' economics and social policy. In the USA, for example, David and Charles Koch – two of America's richest men – have used their considerable fortunes to fund an influential but extreme right-wing think tank, Americans for Prosperity, and to lend unpublicised support to many other generators of extreme 'free-market' views.

In the American presidential election of 2012, the Koch brothers were prominent among those many business leaders who took it upon themselves to warn their workforces that a vote for Obama could cost them their jobs. They did not bother with subtlety when they sent 45,000 employees of their Georgia Pacific paper company a list of whom to vote for, warning that workers 'may suffer the consequences' if Obama were re-elected. One commentator (Corey Robin, a political scientist from Brooklyn College) observed that 'When workers are forced to go to rallies in communist countries, we call that Stalinism. Here, we call it the free market.'[7]

A further and well-attested example of the use by wealthy individuals of their financial clout in order to shape the political agenda is the Washington-based 'free-market' think tank, Freedom Works, largely funded now by a multi-millionaire, Richard J. Stephenson, who has succeeded in keeping a low profile. Stephenson is a long-term adherent of Ayn Rand and an early political associate of the Koch brothers. Freedom Works and the Koch-funded Americans for Prosperity have common origins. Freedom Works claims, undoubtedly with some justice, to have played a major part in financially backing the Tea Party movement, and consequently in securing Republican victories (often for candidates supporting the Tea Party movement) in the 2010 elections.

The use of private wealth to promote ideas that serve the interests of the wealthy is not limited to basic ideas about managing the economy or as to the role of government. The lid was recently lifted on the funding that supports one of the most prominent organisations devoted to denying the reality of climate change and to undermining the credibility of climate change science. The Donors Trust, along with its sister group Donors Capital Fund, based in Alexandria, Virginia, is funnelling millions of dollars into the effort to cast doubt on climate change without revealing the identities of its wealthy backers or that they have links to the fossil fuel industry.[8] It has now been established through an audit trail that Donors is being indirectly supported by – guess who – the billionaire Koch brothers, whose company, Koch Industries, is one of the country's largest oil, gas and chemicals conglomerates. Millions of dollars have been paid to Donors through a third-party organisation called the Knowledge and Progress Fund, which is operated by the Koch family but does not advertise its Koch connections.

In many instances, however, 'free-market' ideas have been developed by relatively independent individual thinkers and academics and then gratefully adopted by those with whose interests they coincide. A good example of what is a much wider phenomenon is a theory about tax policy that has been extremely congenial to the wealthy and has accordingly been enthusiastically adopted by governments that wish to apply neo-liberal policies – an informative illustration of how wealth can be used to propagate particular ideas that suit the interests of the wealthy, and then insert those ideas into government programmes.

The Laffer curve is a theory developed by the economist Arthur Laffer; it surfaced when he drew a diagram on a napkin in a restaurant in an attempt to demonstrate that reducing taxes for the wealthy will actually increase tax revenue. This is because, it is argued (though not supported by any evidence), lower tax rates will encourage the wealthy to produce more wealth and will therefore increase the tax base. So, not only will the wealthy be happier (and will no doubt reward the government that makes them so) but the rest of us will also benefit from the extra revenue that can be used for worthwhile projects of general benefit.

The Laffer curve relies on the twin but unproven assumptions that the rich are the essential factor in creating increased output in an economy and that they need incentives to choose idleness over work. But there is little evidence to support either of these hypotheses; as a result, the theory has been widely discredited, not only on a theoretical level but because we have the advantage of an actual instance of its implementation by a direct proponent.

In accordance with Laffer's theory, the Reagan administration implemented a staged cut in the marginal higher rate of personal income tax from 70 per cent to 28 per cent. It is worth noting that not all taxes were cut; payroll taxes were raised so that workers paid more, while capital and corporate taxes were also cut, thus producing a transfer of income from labour and the poor to capital and the rich.

The effect on the budget deficit was striking; it doubled to US$155 billion and tripled government debt to more than US$2 trillion. Reagan's successor, George Bush senior, was forced to raise taxes as the deficit doubled again.

The most recent research casts further doubt on what remains of the theory. In a study by Peter Diamond and Emmanuel Saez,[9] the authors found that there was no correlation between lower tax rates for top income-earners and higher rates of growth; indeed, they found the contrary – that growth had been higher in the USA when tax rates for the wealthy had been higher, between 1950 and 1980, than it had been since, over the period when those tax rates had been cut. Moreover, for OECD countries as a group, growth had been maintained just as well in those countries, such as France and Germany, that had maintained tax rates for top earners at a high level as it had in those, such as the USA and the UK, where the top rates had been cut. The authors argued that the improved growth rate associated with higher top tax rates could be explained by the increased capital investment and investment in public services (for example, education) that is made possible by the increased tax revenue.

The question is why such an utterly failed policy is still recommended by advisers to governments in many western countries. Under Ronald Reagan, of course, it was, very popular with those willing to spend their money on financing his successful campaign to be re-elected, and has accordingly been lauded in many quarters. What is overlooked when Reagan's electoral success is celebrated, however, is that his much-increased budget deficit was funded by borrowing from abroad, and primarily from Japan. Nobody in the USA had to pay for it, at least in the short term. Reagan was able to cut taxes for the rich while living standards rose for the majority of the population because the country went from being a lender of capital to the rest of the world to borrowing substantially from it. The USA is still living with the consequences of that change. The Laffer curve lives on, however, in the pages of the right-wing literature, discredited as it is, because it is so congenial to 'free-market' precepts.

Chapter 8

Mismanaging Our Economies:
The Rise of Monetarism

We have seen that the rise of the global economy and the triumph of 'free-market' or neo-liberal policies have had deleterious effects on both the process and substance of democracy. But, it is sometimes argued, this is a price worth paying for the economic benefits we have gained.

The opposite, however, is in fact the case. One of the most pernicious consequences of allowing power to pass into the hands of a tiny, unrepresentative and selfish minority is that our affairs are then organised in their interests. The arrogance, narrow focus, short-term horizons and indifference to the wider interest that are inevitably manifested by this cabal bent on self-aggrandisement are part of the price paid by the rest of us for allowing this to happen; and while the doctrines they espouse and have carried into effect have made an impact upon not only economic policy but also on other facets of our lives, it is the economic consequences that have most evidently sold the rest of us short.

It is not the case, in other words, that we pay a price in other respects but gain the benefit of well-run economies. The price we pay includes, very importantly, the avoidable mistakes in the management of our economies that are perpetrated by those who have seized control of our democracies.

We shall explore some of these mistakes in succeeding chapters, but we start with one of the most egregious – the insistence that there is very little that can or should be done to improve the way our economy works, and that it is in any case best left to the market. The only business of government, it is said, is to maintain the value of assets, and particularly the currency, by controlling inflation, and that task – being essentially technical – is not really the business of politicians or the concern of democratic processes at all. This simple approach to economic policy is often called 'monetarism' because of its emphasis on monetary policy. It is a doctrine that

I have resisted since it was first adopted, in its modern guise, in the late 1970s.[1]

This supposedly new approach to economic policy was enthusiastically adopted by those who favoured 'free-market' policies and the new opportunities provided by the emergence of the global economy because it was seen to be the correct economic corollary to the political prescriptions of Hayek and Nozick and entirely consistent with the minimalist economic role that was the proper function of the state. The enthusiasm for the monetarist approach to macroeconomic policy advocated by economists such as Milton Friedman was sometimes almost laughable.

A classic example was when William Rees-Mogg – then editor of *The Times* and a recent convert to monetarism – solemnly proclaimed in a leading article published on 13 July 1976 that a monetarist approach to the control of inflation removed all uncertainty from the exercise. He asserted that inflation was like water passing down a hosepipe; the rate of increase in the money supply at any given time would emerge at the other end of a two-year-long hosepipe as the rate of inflation.

He purported to validate this assertion by producing figures showing that an average annual 9.4 per cent increase in the money supply in the nine-year period 1965–73 had – hey presto! – emerged as an average annual inflation rate at exactly 9.4 per cent for the nine years 1967–75, that is, two years later. He seemed not to recognise the fortuitous and accidental nature of such a remarkable coincidence.

Not everyone was as easily persuaded as William Rees-Mogg, but managing the economy was nevertheless thought to be a relatively simple exercise. Early attempts to measure and then control various definitions of money were nevertheless quite quickly abandoned, since the form taken by money – particularly various kinds of credit created by the banks – kept changing (in accordance with Goodhart's Law, which provides that any activity that is measured for the purpose of attracting economic consequences will inevitably be distorted by the fact that it is being measured). It was decided instead that the money supply could be adequately controlled by merely adjusting its price through raising interest rates if the economy overheated – an exercise that could safely be entrusted to bankers and officials, who could be relied upon not to be swayed by the political considerations that might weigh with politicians and divert them from the proper course.

This simple mechanism was not only foolproof; it also, it was thought, had no downsides. Changes in monetary conditions and in particular in the price of money would have, it was confidently asserted, no effect on the real economy, once people understood that the goal was simply monetary stability; it would impact solely on the inflation rate.

Fiscal policy could be safely ignored, provided that decisions on fiscal matters were made within the appropriate monetary framework. The actual level of interest rates and exchange rates would matter little once the real economy had adjusted to the impact on monetary conditions that they were intended to influence. All that the real economy needed in order to prosper was a stable inflation rate – it mattered little what rate as long as it was stable; and since monetary policy would allow any inflation rate to be targeted with precision without creating any adverse consequences for business, the target might as well be nil or very low inflation.

Thus, virtually the whole of macroeconomic policy became compressed into a single goal, the control of inflation using a single instrument – interest rates – and entrusted (often) to a single official (such as, in New Zealand for example, the governor of the Reserve Bank), whose prime qualification was that he was not a politician (but a banker) and therefore did not need to pay any attention to the views of parliament or of the voters. So a major part of policy-making was removed from democratic control, to the point that the decisions made about monetary policy were insulated against public and parliamentary debate, almost as though those decisions were the business of a high priest who could not be questioned by ordinary mortals.

The principal claim made for monetarism was that it offered the only way to beat inflation, and the ease with which inflation has been contained over recent times may be thought to have gone some way to bearing out this claim. It is certainly true that inflation had become an increasingly worrying and difficult phenomenon through the 1970s, and that the introduction of monetarist policies seemed to produce – in the UK, for example, after an immediate and shocking rise – a fall in the inflation rate that has been broadly sustained ever since. But on closer examination the story is not so simple. At the very least, some qualifications have to be made.

First, the fall in the inflation rate in any one country over the period has almost certainly owed a great deal to the fact that inflation worldwide fell substantially over the same period. This may have been a response to the greater openness of world markets, the consequent increase in price competition in those markets, and the success of multinational investors in using low-cost economies as the benchmark for driving down wage rates worldwide. Whether or not that should be claimed as an achievement for the global economy, it was an international phenomenon, and had little to do with monetarist policies in individual economies.

This analysis is supported by the fact that it was argued by monetarist theorists themselves that imported inflation was an important factor in the battle against inflation. Indeed, the international dimension was the key element for a particular school of monetarists who called themselves the International Monetarists and who, through the writings of Terry Burns and Alan Budd, were particularly influential in policymaking throughout the 1980s. They argued that monetary control reduced inflation by producing an appreciating exchange rate, which in turn damped down the price of imports and thereby – because of the need to maintain the competitiveness of domestic production – compelled the price of domestic goods and services to fall into line as well. This, it was claimed, was the elusive 'transmission mechanism' by which monetary control exercised downward pressure on prices.

The second qualification is that a fall in inflation has never been difficult to achieve, provided that it is targeted in isolation from other criteria of economic performance. A government that was prepared to deflate the economy severely enough could always defeat inflation. Such a victory has always been seen, however, as a pyrrhic one. The desired outcome has always been a low inflation rate combined with a sustainable rate of growth and the achievement of other goals, such as full employment.

Monetarist theory maintained that this was eminently possible and, indeed, was not really an issue. Provided that a particular level of monetary growth was maintained, the only long-term effect on the productive economy would be the beneficial one of encouraging investment, and therefore growth, as a consequence of the stability of outlook that would be achieved.

How well did monetarist policy perform against the goal of bringing inflation down while at the same time providing a benefit to, or at the very least not prejudicing, the real economy? Measured by criteria such as rates of growth, unemployment, investment rates and balance of payments, economic performance for the global economy was on the whole variable and unimpressive over the period from 1979 onwards, and provides little vindication for the optimism that was shown.

The explanation for this is that in many economies, as diverse as the UK and New Zealand, the productive sector suffered severely under the monetarist regime of high interest rates and an overvalued exchange rate. In New Zealand, the introduction of monetarist measures led to a severe fall in output, while in the UK, the fall in manufacturing output as a result of a direct and exchange rate-induced loss of competitiveness more than offset the increased output attributable to North Sea oil.

Indeed, the monetarist prescription made it inevitable that in Britain, as North Sea oil output became available, some other aspect of production should decline. The theory predicted that the discovery of a new source of wealth would inevitably drive up the exchange rate, so that other sectors of production were priced out of markets both at home and abroad – and because this is what the theory provided, it was accepted that this outcome was unavoidable. It was never explained why this should be inevitable in Britain but not apparent in the case of Norway, a smaller economy where the advent of North Sea oil was proportionately even more important, but where it was not assumed that there was nothing that could be done to protect the rest of the economy. The Norwegians, in fact, found ways of insulating the domestic economy against the boost produced to overseas earnings by oil exports and import saving.

The reason for the different British experience in this respect was the fact that the attempt to control the money supply necessarily implies a somewhat static view of how the economy operates. Many monetarist economists went so far as to work out the level of demand for money of a given economy (incidentally ignoring the significance of the velocity of circulation, which can vary substantially over time). This approach necessarily fixes a given economy in a given condition. The British economy was assumed, for example, to have a lower demand for money than the German economy, and if this was exceeded increased inflation was inevitable. This assertion, which was unexplained or unsupported by argument, was necessary to explain the fact that growth in the German money supply ran at a significantly higher level than the British money supply, while at the same time permitting the Germans to maintain a stronger growth rate and a lower inflation rate. No attempt was made to explain why this supposedly immutable condition of the British economy should apply – though, as we shall see later, attention was consciously diverted away from the greater competitiveness of German manufacturing industry.

Mistaken monetarist analyses such as these diverted attention, consistently with the western view that we had nothing to learn from more successful developing economies in Asia, from the policies that were pursued in such economies. In particular, we showed no interest in the deliberate creation of credit for productive investment purposes that was a significant element in Japan's industrial development and is currently equally so in China's remarkable economic transformation – and, if only we had the wit to grasp it, had also allowed a depression-riven USA to enjoy an astonishing burst of growth that allowed the Allies to win the Second World War.[2]

In the same way, monetarist economists assumed that each economy had a naturally occurring rate of unemployment which could not be changed by policy. A NAIRU, or non-accelerating inflation rate of unemployment, was ascribed to each economy. In the case of the UK, it was assumed to be relatively high and, more significantly, impervious to attempts to bring it down. In fulfilment of this prophecy, unemployment rose sharply through the 1980s, despite the repeated attempts to massage the statistics downwards. The number of claimants of unemployment benefit jumped from just over 1 million in 1979 to over 3 million in 1986.

The impact on the balance of payments of North Sea oil, providing as it did a major element of import substitution, might have been expected to be favourable. Despite this factor, however, the UK balance of payments remained in substantial deficit throughout the period. The deficit at times reached record levels in terms of its size in relation to GDP. The deficit reflected, of course, the decline of manufacturing and the deterioration in the balance of trade in wide areas of the productive sector. That in turn reflected the loss of competitiveness, which was shown – but ignored – in the various indices used to measure competitiveness.

The level of investment in productive industry was a matter of concern throughout the period. It was repeatedly asserted that a high level of investment was essential to the health of productive industry, but the actual level of investment remained stubbornly below the levels regarded as desirable, and substantially below those seen in competing industrial economies such as Japan and Germany.

One of the reasons for a disappointing rate of investment is a bias inherent in monetarist policy. It became clear over the period that complicated attempts to define and control the money supply were both difficult and ineffective. Reliance was placed more and more on the simple and fundamental instrument of controlling the supply of money by regulating its price through setting interest rates.

The result was that for most of the period interest rates were very high in historical terms. High interest rates were seen as necessary to restrain growth in the money supply, particularly when it became apparent that the asset inflation and property boom of the mid-1980s – itself a classic consequence of monetarist orthodoxy – could not continue.

It was by this time hard to ignore the awkward problem that an instrument of monetary policy designed to do no more than regulate inflation also had a major impact on the real economy, by making investment for productive purposes more expensive. Indeed, the implications of a high interest rate regime are profoundly unhelpful to the creation of new wealth in general. If interest rates are rigged so that they do not effect a fair balance between the interests of lenders and borrowers in the domestic economy, but are used for the quite different purpose of restraining inflation, it is inevitable that the most beneficial course for the economy will be distorted. High interest rates reward the existing holders of wealth. Those with financial assets are offered a virtually risk-free and high return by high interest rates, as opposed to the more speculative and perhaps lower return offered by investment in productive industry. On the other hand, those seeking capital to start or expand businesses find that high interest rates add substantially to their costs and offer a major disincentive to investment.

Nor does the consequent overvaluation of the currency have the minimal effect on the real economy predicted by monetarist theorists. Like interest rates, the exchange rate has a fundamental purpose, which in this case is to fix the international price of a country's production at a level that allows that country to balance its trade while achieving a reasonable rate of growth. If it is used for a quite different and often contradictory purpose – to restrain domestic inflation – it is likely to fail in its central function by pricing that country's goods out of international markets. As we shall see later, the exchange rate is a central determinant of competitiveness, and competitiveness in turn is the key to growth, innovation and productivity. A policy that is designed to produce, through high interest rates, an overvalued exchange rate as a means of holding down inflation cannot help but hurt productive industry – and so both British and New Zealand experience demonstrates. The American experience, resting on a similarly overvalued currency but for slightly different reasons, also demonstrates the damage suffered by the productive sector.

There is, incidentally, a little-remarked weakness in monetarist theory, even when considering its role as purely a counter-inflationary strategy. If the exchange rate is as important a counter-inflationary instrument as monetarists claim, shoring it up through high interest rates and tight monetary policy will only delay the inevitable. The eventual fall in the value of the currency (which cannot be delayed forever, since it will in the longer term reflect what happens in the real economy) will then – if the monetarists are right – necessarily expose the economy to the full rigours of higher imported prices and imported inflation, meaning that the whole exercise would have been in vain and the pain (in terms of the damage to the real economy) quite unnecessary. Inflation, in other words, would only have been suppressed for a time, to emerge at a later date.

The consequence of these difficulties that occur in the real world rather than monetarist theory is that the much-vaunted stability of monetary conditions that is the stated goal of monetarist policy fails to produce much by way of actual stability. As described above, this is partly because of the divergence between the counter-inflationary goals of monetary policy and its impact on the real economy. But it is also because monetary stability, even if achieved over a period, may well require such variations in interest rates and exchange rates (because responses are needed to changing monetary conditions both at home and abroad) as to create highly unpredictable and unstable conditions (in matters such as the level of demand in domestic and international markets) for those operating in the real economy. The tribulations faced by manufacturing in both Britain and New Zealand over the last three decades are testimony to this.

Why monetarist theory doesn't work in practice

Monetarist theory says, as we have seen, that the only purpose of economic policy is to establish conditions of monetary stability and that, once established, this will allow the economy to grow and prosper. The problem here is that in practice monetarist discipline turns out to be nothing more than a means of deflating the economy by using high interest rates and overvaluation to keep some productive resources out of use. If keeping those resources out of use as a precondition of controlling inflation is maintained for any length of time (as is almost inevitably and invariably the case), the resources eventually cease to have any value, even as a margin of spare capacity for the purposes of controlling inflation. The long-term unemployed lose skills and the habit of work and become unemployable; unused plant becomes outdated and pre-existing technologies are overtaken by new developments; markets are lost and cannot be regained. A further range of unused resources accordingly has to be called upon to serve the purpose of exercising a restraint over price inflation. Monetarist policy, in other words, is a recipe for continuing and intensifying nil or slow growth.

The facts also show that concentrating on monetary policy to the exclusion of all else means that the focus of policy is too narrow but its impact is too wide. Monetary measures such as high interest rates reflect a narrow view of the role of economic policy, but they impact on the real, productive economy across a very wide front. Production, investment and employment all suffer under the impact of an overvalued exchange rate, high interest rates and the absence of any government support for the productive sector.

An independent central bank

Monetarism is, as we have seen, an expression of an extreme belief in the infallibility of the market – an article of faith for many supporters of the current orthodoxy. Governments cannot be allowed to intervene in macroeconomic policy since any such intervention will frustrate the market's unfettered operation. monetary policy should be allowed to do its work without interference from politicians. What could be more natural, therefore, than to ensure that elected politicians are excluded from this area of policy by handing it over to an independent central bank?

An independent central bank is seen today as an important weapon in the monetarist armoury. This is not, of course, quite how the independent central bank is presented to the public. The public have been sold the idea that an independent bank is necessary if inflation is to be controlled, on the ground that politicians cannot be trusted to take the hard decisions that are necessary. But a careful study of the recent history of the battle against inflation suggests that it has very little to do with the independence or otherwise of the central bank. Inflation in the 1970s was a worldwide phenomenon, but by the mid-1980s – reflecting world conditions, and largely before the advent of independent central banks – it had largely been brought under control. The claim that an independent central bank is essential if inflation is to be controlled in any case looks less convincing today, with inflation running at a rate that suggests that it is the least of our concerns.

But what is really remarkable about an independent central bank is that it is a major step away from democratic government. The price we pay, in other words, is not just an economic one but is a significant weakening of our democratic institutions. What monetarists identified as the overriding issue in economic policy is now the exclusive preserve, it seems, not of elected governments but of unaccountable officials.

How this has been accepted is even more of a mystery when one considers that the 'independent' central bank is in no sense objective or neutral. It is a bank. Its main clients are banks. It is staffed by bankers. It can be relied upon always to put the interests of the financial establishment ahead of those operating in the rest of the economy. The danger is more than theoretical, as we have seen in the unfolding drama of the dishonesty and irresponsibility of leading bankers worldwide. Our economic policy is, in a very real sense, made in the interests of the holders of existing assets rather than of those who live and work in the real economy where new wealth is created.

That perception is reinforced when we come to assess the reaction of so-called independent central banks to the global financial crisis. The Federal Reserve Bank in the USA, the Bank of England's Monetary Committee, the European Central Bank and even the Reserve Bank of New Zealand have all, in their various ways, shown an unmistakable propensity to give priority to the interests of banks over those of the economy as a whole. They have done all they can to ensure that banks and their balance sheets are protected, with at the same time a remarkable insouciance in respect of the interests of depositors, high levels of unemployment and a recessionary level of economic activity. Therefore we have seen an undue reliance on monetary policy, a reluctance to use fiscal policy, an insistence in a number of cases on policies of austerity – exactly what we have learnt to expect from those with a banker's outlook and with bankers' interests at heart.

This bias seems more extreme the longer one looks at it. Not only have central banks ensured that the productive sector should bear the burden of counter-inflationary measures; they seem also to have deliberately averted their gaze from the factor that really is the primary cause of inflation – the huge rise in bank lending (which we shall look at in a later chapter).

How have we arrived at this remarkable situation? It is not surprising that the bankers themselves should support and welcome it, since it greatly inflates the importance of their role and influence.

Economists, too, will naturally feel that the authority and credibility of their profession have been underpinned by this recognition that it is only the high priesthood that is competent to address these important issues. This view, incidentally, is reflected in the increasing tendency of the media who monitor economic developments to turn exclusively to bank-employed economists for commentary on such matters.

But why have politicians so readily accepted this substantial diminution of their powers? The answer is that it is very convenient for politicians to be able to contract out the most difficult decisions they are faced with. How useful it has been for politicians to pin responsibility on central banks, and to claim that the travails of the economy are caused by the mechanistic workings of the market and of essential monetarist disciplines rather than actual policy decisions. But is it not time that we reminded them of their responsibilities? If they want to exercise power in a democratic society, they should not be allowed to pick and choose which responsibilities they accept.

There is, of course, an important role for an effective central bank. A central bank is essential to maintain a proper prudential supervision of banks and of the financial sector more generally – something that has, as has become apparent, been sadly missing from the scene in many western countries over recent years. A central bank should regulate and enable the banks to interact with other actors in the economy in an efficient way that benefits the economy as a whole. A central bank should be an important source of advice on financial matters. But none of this requires discussion, particularly when it is uniquely entrusted with the power to give expression to a narrow and bank-dominated view of the true purpose of economic policy. Indeed, that fateful decision to burden the central bank with quite inappropriate functions is likely to distract it from its true responsibilities – as the travails of the banks in many countries and the complete collapse of finance companies in New Zealand would strongly suggest.

The growing economic crisis demands that sacred cows should no longer be immune. Even in New Zealand, where the modern fashion for an 'independent' central bank first surfaced, the debate is being reopened. If we want an economy that more faithfully serves the interests of all of us and not just those of a small self-interested minority, economic policy should be restored to the democratic arena.

Surprisingly, it may be thought, Japan may offer the first substantial evidence that this particular logjam may be about to break up. The Japanese government for the past fifteen years, led by parties of both the centre-right and centre-left, has steadfastly maintained policies of austerity and a refusal to use the power of government to provide a stimulus to sluggish economic activity. The role of the Bank of Japan has been central to the maintenance of this rigorous stance, ensuring as it has done that the stability of the banking sector is given priority over those of the rest of the economy.

As we turn into 2013, however, the newly elected centre-right government of Shinzo Abe has signalled its clear intention to acknowledge the failure of these policies and to strike out in a new direction. An important – and unexpected – feature of that new direction is to be the reclaiming from the Bank of Japan of the government's fundamental responsibility to decide the main features of macroeconomic policy. This about-face by perhaps the most committed of the world's major economies to current orthodoxy is an encouraging sign that even the most entrenched articles of faith can be questioned. Much attention will no doubt be paid to the Japanese 'experiment' – and even a small degree of success would, hopefully, produce others willing to emulate Japanese new thinking.

Why monetarism favours the rich and creates inequality

The macroeconomic effect of monetarist economic policies points the way to an important microeconomic and social consequence. The effect of restricting the money supply in order to control inflation is, in the short term at least, to force up the price of money and therefore the value of monetary assets, just as would be true of any other commodity whose price was raised so that its availability in relation to demand was reduced. This interest rate effect is compounded by the appreciation of the currency, so that, for a time at least, each asset is valued – even in domestic terms – according to what the overvalued currency will buy in international markets. This is, of course, particularly congenial to the holders of these inflated assets.

While, in the longer term, most people's experience will reflect the performance of the real economy, and even the wealthy will suffer if that performance is poor, the immediate net result (and major consequence) of monetarist policies is usually a shift of wealth from the poor and dispossessed who do not hold assets, and particularly monetary assets, towards those who do, the already wealthy and powerful. This is partly because of advantages conferred on the wealthy and partly because of disadvantages suffered by the poor.

The process by which the wealthy find the value of their assets inflated by monetarist policies reached its zenith in the UK in the mid- to late 1980s, when house prices in particular zoomed upwards and out of control. Those who owned houses became wealthy; those who did not lost out. The inevitable correction applied to this process in 1988 does not obscure the fact that the asset inflation was an inevitable, albeit unsustainable, outcome of monetarism. A similar asset inflation over recent years has been a feature of both the British and New Zealand experience and, in New Zealand at least, is in the process of reasserting itself with a vengeance.

The experience of the less wealthy and powerful in society under a monetarist or 'free-market' regime is very different. The most significant redistributive factor is the rise in unemployment. This has a direct effect on the unemployed themselves, by reducing their incomes and sense of worth, but it also has a depressing effect on other wages and on the power of labour more generally, as the pool of unemployed drags down the whole labour market. It is this sector of society that must find the resources to transfer to those who benefit from asset inflation, since by definition under a monetarist regime those resources must come not from inflating the money supply but by transfer from some other part of the economy, which inevitably means those who do not own significant assets.

But there is a further aspect of monetarist policy that disadvantages the already disadvantaged. The key element of monetarist policy is that it targets consumer price inflation and is little concerned about the rise in asset values, which works to the advantage of the wealthy. By focusing exclusively on inflation, and requiring that action to control it must take precedence over any other goal of economic policy, the doctrine ensures that unemployment should always remain higher than it should be. This is because, as soon as the economy grows fast enough to promise full employment, the high priests of monetarism profess to see a threat to inflation, by which they mean that in a fully employed labour market workers will be able to demand higher wages.

The automatic response to the supposed threat of inflation is a rise in interest rates, which chokes off any prospect of full employment and depresses wage growth; employers are again guaranteed a labour market in which they hold the whip hand. This is, of course, very congenial to businesses and employers, who can relax in the knowledge that the macroeconomic framework is constantly working to their advantage, and doing so surreptitiously, since who could object to steps taken in order to contain inflation? The result is that millions of workers are forced to struggle against odds that are stacked against them, without even realising what it is that is holding them back and making life difficult. All this is in stark contrast to the equally powerful bias of monetarist policy in favour of high returns on capital and the inflated value of capital assets.

We can now begin to see, in other words, why monetarism has been so congenial to elites in so many western countries. While the policies have meant that the economies in which they live have been less successful as a whole than they might have been, they have helped to widen the gap between the elite and the rest of society – and that gap, that sense of superiority, is of great value and importance to many such people. That, added to the underlying message of monetarism and its related 'free-market' policies, to the effect that successful individuals should be allowed to get on with it without much regard for others, and that government should largely step aside from trying to manage the economy, goes a long way to explaining the support that is offered to (perhaps only dimly understood) monetarist policies by those who suffer under them.

Once again, however, there are signs that even central bankers are beginning to have second thoughts. Mark Carney, who has recently taken over as Governor of the Bank of England, has signalled his interest in a change in monetary policy; instead of targeting inflation, he proposes that nominal GDP growth should be the new measure, offering the prospect – in recessionary times – of a more expansionary monetary policy. It is not clear what would happen if the nominal growth owed more to inflation than to real growth, and, as we shall see later, it is doubtful whether conventional monetary (as opposed to fiscal) policy has much to contribute to recovery from recession, but it is at least an encouraging sign that the old certainties that have dominated policy for decades are at last being questioned.

Chapter 9

Mismanaging Our Economies:
The International Dimension

What's not to like about free trade? Trade is obviously a good thing, and 'free' trade must surely be better than the alternative? In the western or developed world, the 'free trade' label need only be attached to persuade us that the outcome must be an unalloyed blessing. Yet the actual basis for this touching faith has almost never been debated.

Many of the world's most successful non-western economies, and especially those in Asia, have taken a common-sense and pragmatic approach to free trade. In the post-war world, first Japan, followed by Korea, India and now China (which has still not made its currency fully convertible) have recognised the dangers to their nascent industries of allowing them to be stifled at birth by imports from more advanced and competitive economies. It is only as they have developed and grown more able to withstand such competition that they have gradually relaxed the protectionist policies on which they had relied.

But while developing countries have almost always seen the advantages of protecting vulnerable industries against the full force of competition from more powerful economies, the arrogance of the West and its leaders has persuaded us that we have everything to gain and nothing to fear from removing measures of protection and barriers to trade. We shall look later at some of the consequences of this unwarranted optimism.

New Zealand, for example, has approached the global marketplace as a child would a candy store. With astonishing naivety and a conviction that doing what seems to be right will produce its own reward, New Zealand has optimistically and often unilaterally removed tariff and other trade barriers, confident that trading partners would also one day see the light, and that a small, vulnerable and increasingly uncompetitive economy could in any case prosper in direct competition with some of the largest and most efficient or most protected economies in the world. The consequence has been a perennial trade deficit, and the loss of much of the productive base to overseas ownership.

A similar mindset characterised the case for the UK joining the Common Market. The disappointing British economic performance following the Second World War led to a conviction that almost any price would be worth paying if it promised the prospect of increased exports. As a result, the UK abandoned a trading pattern that provided great advantages to the British trading position; by utilising an unrivalled network of trading partners worldwide, the domestic economy was guaranteed access to tariff-free food and raw materials imported at the lowest prices from around the world, while the countries providing these goods offered in return protected markets for British manufactured goods.

This mutually beneficial arrangement, which greatly helped the competitiveness of British industry by keeping costs low, and which at the same time provided a secure basis for the expansion of markets in developing economies, was exchanged for an arrangement in which the price of imported food and raw materials was artificially inflated at substantial cost to the consumer and taxpayer and to the cost structures of British industry, and in which protected and rapidly developing markets around the world were abandoned in favour of competing directly with the most powerful competitors in a single European market.

Typically in such cases of self-delusion, each new step towards free trade nirvana is celebrated and justified by pointing to the increased exports that free trade will bring. No matter that an increase in exports usually owes little to the presence or absence of a free trade agreement and that trading partners on the whole buy goods only because they want them. If trade is going to increase, it usually does so before the conclusion of a free trade agreement. And no matter that, in virtually every case, an increase in exports is more than offset by a sharp increase in imports, with consequent damage to and in some cases actual destruction of domestic industries. The prospects of export growth are so tempting that countries are typically ready to take any risk and make any concession, usually without regard to the impact of increased imports on domestic production.

If free trade were really as beneficial as is claimed, why have perennial trade imbalances in countries such as the UK and New Zealand endured over such a long period? And why has the performance of those economies remained so disappointing? More importantly, have we really understood that free trade arrangements are not just about trade but are often designed to produce an integration of economies?

As we have seen with the development of the EU, a free trade arrangement is usually designed to operate eventually very much like a single economy – and that should sound alarm bells. If the whole of the combined market can be accessed without any restriction from any point within it, why would anyone manufacture anywhere else but the most populous part of the market and the most efficient or low-cost manufacturing centre? And that usually does not include smaller and more marginal economies – just ask Greece, Ireland and Portugal, and to a lesser extent (in the context of Closer Economic Relations with Australia) New Zealand.

And it is not just tariffs that have to be aligned, or removed altogether. Anything that could be argued to upset the 'level playing field' will not be allowed. The EU, in the interests of developing what was originally portrayed as a simple customs union, now extends its rules and regulations into every aspect of the productive economy, and well beyond.

This is not to say that the EU, while paying lip service to free trade, does not regulate trade when it sees this as advantageous to itself. This is particularly true of the agreement being negotiated by the EU with seventy-seven of the world's poorest countries in Africa, the Pacific and the Caribbean, according to which access to the EU for their products is conditional on their allowing free access to their markets for exports from the EU – hardly a bargain between equals, and a virtual guarantee that the poorest countries will always find any attempt at development of their own domestic capability negated by the power of European imports.

And, as others have discovered, the phrase 'free trade' can have a variety of meanings. This is particularly true of the multilateral trade agreements negotiated by the USA with different ranges of partners. The North American Free Trade Agreement (NAFTA) was one such example; another is the Trans-Pacific Partnership Agreement (TPP), currently being negotiated by eleven countries.

These agreements are called free trade agreements but are in fact much more than that; they are a comprehensive effort to integrate a range of economies into a more or less single entity, dominated – in these cases in particular – by the USA. As Professor Jagdish Bhagwati of Columbia University pointed out in December 2011, the TPP's supposed openness has been wholly misleading.[1] Negotiations were quite deliberately initially opened with weaker and smaller economies such as Vietnam, Singapore and New Zealand, which were easily bamboozled into accepting such conditions. Only then were bigger countries, such as Japan, offered membership on a 'take it or leave it' basis.

But Professor Bhagwati argues that there is a wider political purpose in including non-trade matters in such agreements. The fact that the American template for its PTAs includes major items unrelated to trade, items such as labour standards and restraints on the use of capital-account controls that would preclude China's accession, shows, he argues, that the TPP is an aggressive move against China, and that far from being a move to free trade it is better seen as an attempt to exclude China, with the goal of containment rather than cooperation. That aspect of the TPP was explicitly recognised by New Zealand's Ambassador to Washington (and former head of the WTO) Mike Moore, in a television interview in New Zealand,[2] and even more explicitly by the Republican candidate in the presidential election campaign of 2012, Mitt Romney.

For other partners, however, there are other difficulties that seem even more clear-cut and easily identified. A TPP including the USA, for example, would mean for a country such as New Zealand that the cooperative marketing of New Zealand dairy products or kiwi fruit through a 'single desk' would be targeted as an unacceptable distortion of trade. Similarly, a monopsonistic purchaser, such as the New Zealand public agency Pharmac, which by negotiating as a single entity with the major pharmaceutical companies has saved New Zealand hundreds of millions of dollars, would be attacked as inimical to the 'free market'.

As is well established by trading arrangements such as the European Union, whose real objectives go well beyond the simple scaling down or removal of tariffs, governments signing a TPP would find that any attempt by national governments party to such an arrangement to give priority to local suppliers would be outlawed. Such provisions are insisted upon to ensure that the most powerful corporations have unfettered opportunities to sweep the board at the expense of smaller and weaker national providers. And if the model provided by NAFTA and similar agreements is followed, there would be yet more far-reaching consequences in store. A NAFTA-style arrangement would give foreign (usually American) corporations the power to enforce rights against national governments in specially constituted international tribunals, even if those rights were not available to the firms of the country concerned.

These are, in other words, international agreements of an unusual type, where individual corporations, even though they are not signatories to the agreement, have the same rights as governments. Those rights can include exemptions from domestic obligations in fields such as health and safety, or concessions on tax treatment, or preferential treatment when it comes to awarding contracts, or relief from attempts to protect the local ownership of assets. The rights protected by these provisions go far beyond real property rights, and include financial instruments, mining concessions, intellectual property, public-private partnership contracts and even market share. Even if a government wished to change domestic law in these respects, foreign corporations could still enforce their rights against the government under the free trade agreement.

This means that a foreign corporation has far more extensive rights against a national government than any domestic company would ever have. Provisions of this sort, which are becoming ever-present features of what are sold to gullible publics as mere free trade agreements, constitute a major challenge to the powers of self-government in a democracy. They mean that a future government, perhaps elected to change policy in an area such as environmental protection or health and safety (smoking comes to mind), could be threatened with a crippling lawsuit by powerful international corporations unless it backed off.

Nor is it just the government that would be hog-tied. A particular worry for lawyers is that national courts, too, could be overruled or bypassed. The foreign investment tribunals set up under such arrangements have decided that courts are part of a country's government (riding roughshod over any doctrine of the separation of powers) and that governments must ignore court rulings if they conflict with obligations undertaken under the free trade agreement. Even a jury decision in private litigation could be challenged, and lead to a government being threatened with paying millions in compensation.

In a case brought by Chevron, for example, just such a tribunal ordered the Ecuador government, in defiance of their constitution, not to enforce a ruling by Ecuador's Appeal Court that Chevron must pay $18 billion to clean up toxic waste in the Amazon Basin. There has been an exponential increase in the numbers of such cases brought by (largely American) foreign corporations against governments which are parties to agreements similar to the proposed TPP. The issue is still being litigated in American courts. Over $675 million has been paid out in awards made by the special tribunals in cases involving American companies alone.

Ironically, the history of this kind of provision has begun to attract attention because it has come back to bite those who created it. The Germans, some decades ago, began to insert such provisions in treaties with third-world countries, so that the interests of German investors in those countries could be protected. Such was the power of German investment, and the weakness of the recipient countries, that no one took much notice.

Now, however, with the crisis in the Eurozone and the growing investment of formerly third-world countries in Europe, the boot is on the other foot – and European countries are suddenly crying foul at the prospect of being sued by private companies from China or Korea.

The lessons are clear. Free trade increasingly comes at a price, and the price is being paid not just in economic terms by domestic industries which are put at risk by the inflow of imported goods; there is a political price to be paid as well. So-called free trade agreements are increasingly a cover for a significant extension of the powers of major international corporations as opposed to elected democratic governments. The protections apparently offered to citizens by being able to elect governments to defend their interests are being further weakened. Our democracy is the weaker as a result.

The New Zealand experience

New Zealand is a small, open economy, which suddenly decided in 1984 to conduct a far-reaching experiment in applying neo-liberal policies. True to its overnight conversion to free markets and the free movement of capital, New Zealand opened its doors to foreign capital to a greater degree than any other comparable country. A greater proportion of its economy has been sold into foreign ownership than in any other developed country. This has been partly a matter of choice, based on ideological conviction, and partly – though not advertised in this way – a matter of necessity; the proceeds of selling assets into foreign ownership have been an essential factor in balancing overseas accounts that economic failures have condemned to serious deficit.

It might be thought that this sell-off was a once-and-for-all effort to balance the books. The figures show, however, that the process continues apace. By March 2008, New Zealand had sold off NZ$93.3 billion worth of assets, up 900 per cent from 1989. There will soon be little left to sell.

The consequences for the economy have been disastrous. A current account in perennial deficit (eased only temporarily by the slowdown in imports caused by the recession) has been further burdened by the need to repatriate profits across the foreign exchanges to the foreign owners; this is in addition to the interest payments that must be made to that other group of foreigners who help to fill the hole in the overseas accounts by buying short-term debt as a response to New Zealand's very high interest rates. The repatriated profits represent, of course, not only a drain on the foreign accounts but also a very real loss of national wealth that could otherwise be applied to raising living standards and public services.

The four main banks in New Zealand, all Australian-owned, make their own substantial contribution to this outflow of funds across the exchanges. In the aftermath of the global financial crisis, the banks have been able quickly to rebuild their profits to pre-crisis levels, even while the rest of the economy has been languishing; they managed the amazing trick of improving their margins by consistently passing on rises in interest rates quickly and with something added, but delaying any response to cuts in interest rates and making that response only partial. The result has been an increase in profits to NZ$2.78 billion in the 2011 financial year, the highest since they collectively made $3.02 billion in 2008. Every dollar of those billions is repatriated across the exchanges to Australia.

New Zealand's perennial need to rely on overseas borrowing in order to balance its books with the rest of the world has been compounded by a policy recently adopted by those self-same Australian-owned banks. In 2010, they introduced what were called covered bonds – that is, bonds issued on the security of assets owned by the banks themselves. The bonds were offered exclusively to foreign lenders; they could amount to up to 10 per cent of the borrowings made by the banks, and their special feature was that the lenders would take precedence over other creditors, including those New Zealanders who deposited their surplus cash on term-deposits with the banks, in the event of a default. This remarkable innovation, which has been endorsed by the Reserve Bank of New Zealand and is about to be facilitated further by legislation passed by the New Zealand government, attracted virtually no comment or attention, but is yet another striking instance of the price paid for foreign involvement in line with the apparent view that such concessions must be made in the national interest.

Like many other western countries, New Zealand has – perhaps not entirely coincidentally – shielded itself from a public awareness of the outflow of national wealth by abandoning GNP (the gross national product) as a measure of national output in favour of GDP (the gross domestic product). This has the advantage from a presentational viewpoint of including in the total shown to the public the volume of wealth that is produced in New Zealand but is no longer there for New Zealanders to enjoy, since it goes overseas into foreign hands. An increase in GDP is accordingly welcomed as evidence that the country is doing well, despite the fact that an increased proportion of that wealth no longer belongs to it. By such means are the people persuaded that things are better than they are.

The loss is not merely economic. New Zealand also suffers a very real diminution in the ability to control its own affairs. Increasingly, under foreign ownership, decisions over major parts of the economy are taken in Sydney or Los Angeles or Shanghai. New Zealand jobs and businesses depend on people in boardrooms where New Zealand interests are remote from their concerns. The result is a palpable sense that New Zealanders are mere pawns in the plans of powerful people who know little of the country and care even less, and that New Zealand is a poorer place as a result.

None of this has deterred New Zealand ministers from beating the drum for what they describe as 'overseas investment', which they maintain is evidence of the 'confidence' felt by overseas 'investors' in the New Zealand economy but which in reality is merely the cherry-picking of under-priced New Zealand assets by those looking to make a quick buck. There is all the difference in the world, in other words, between overseas investment which brings with it new technologies and new productive capacity, and the purchase of existing assets at knock-down prices so that a high rate of return can be produced by squeezing more profit from them. All too often, those who make the most significant contribution to the increased profits made by new overseas owners are the (often low-paid) employees of the enterprise that has passed into foreign ownership.

A good example of this process at work attracted some attention in New Zealand in 2012 when 1,500 employees of the Oceania Group, the country's largest rest home operator, went on strike. The Oceania workforce was largely female, coloured and part-time; most were paid just a few cents above the minimum wage. Oceania had offered a pay increase of 1 per cent – much less than the rate of inflation. The workers, with very little bargaining power, tried to draw attention to their plight in the only way open to them.

The aged care industry (as we must now call it) in New Zealand was a prime example of the privatisation of what was once a public service. As public services that care for the elderly in their own homes were – supposedly on financial grounds – wound back, the opportunity to make a profit by providing accommodation and care in privately owned rest homes increased. The public purse still provided the funding, so the taxpayer still largely picks up the bill; but the money now goes via a per capita payment to private companies rather than public employees.

The expanding industry offered a tempting investment opportunity to private investors. Two New Zealand-owned companies, ElderCare and Qualcare, had built a strong market position; and Oceania achieved its dominant position in the New Zealand industry by buying both of these firms.

Oceania is a group of private equity investors which was set up under the aegis of Macquarie Bank, the Australian banking entity popularly known as the 'millionaires' factory'. The new Australian owners knew little about care of the elderly, and were motivated by the prospect of making a good return on their investment. But they had miscalculated. The new venture offered a smaller return on their investment than they had hoped, perhaps because they had paid too much. They found themselves instead owing a large debt to Macquarie Bank.

The investors demanded that this position should be corrected. Since the operation's income was largely predetermined by the amount paid to them by the government, the only way of squeezing out a higher return was to cut costs – and that meant making real-terms cuts in the wages of an already low-paid workforce. With costs cut, and the debt repaid, rich pickings were in prospect.

That exercise was reasonably successful, at least from the view-point of the investors. But the profits used to reduce the debt were squeezed out of the workers, and no doubt also meant a lower standard of service to elderly customers who have little power to insist on better. Those profits – tens of millions of dollars produced from the funding provided by New Zealand taxpayers – are now being paid across the foreign exchanges into the pockets of Australians, thereby adding to New Zealand's balance of payments burden. But Oceania's involvement, as an instance of 'overseas investment', is welcomed by New Zealand's government and business leaders, who are determined to see only the inflow of foreign money and to overlook the deleterious downsides.

The sale of public assets

The painful and unmistakable lessons, in both economic and political terms, from selling off assets to overseas owners have nevertheless been resolutely ignored by western governments. The New Zealand government, again, offers a striking example of the determination to proceed with the sale of public assets despite the clear lesson offered by direct experience that the inevitable outcome is that those assets will pass into foreign hands, with consequent increased burdens for the balance of payments and a serious further loss of control by New Zealanders over their economy.

The New Zealand government decided in 2012, in the face of opposition consistently expressed by nearly four out of five New Zealanders, to sell up to NZ$7 billion worth of publicly owned assets; this is on top of the extremely high proportion of the New Zealand economy already in foreign hands. The reasons advanced for continuing this seriously flawed policy have not been clearly spelled out. They certainly include the fact that raising extra cash from the proceeds of the sales will help the government to reduce its deficit in the short term, even though the evidence is clear that the loss of the valuable income streams from the assets that are sold will simply create indebtedness problems for future governments (and taxpayers).

In 2012, after all, the New Zealand government could borrow at 3.45 per cent for ten years to fund its deficit, but was preparing to sell assets that generated an average return of at least 7 per cent after tax (and probably a good deal more) on their likely value. This is so self-evidently a poor bargain that there must be some other explanation. That explanation is probably that the government wishes to help some of its friends in the financial services sector by bringing, at least for a short time, new assets to be traded on New Zealand's capital markets, with all that this might mean for increased capital gains and commissions for market operators. Those who bemoan the smallness and shallowness of New Zealand's capital markets do not seem to recognise that a major reason is the transfer of foreign-owned New Zealand assets to markets overseas.

The reason often advanced for the sale of public assets into private hands is that this will produce a more efficient management of the assets, and therefore a better return. While many intuitively accept this argument, it is supported more by the mythology created by 'free-market' ideologues rather than by any actual practical experience.

Professor David Hall of the Public Services International Research department at the University of Greenwich Business School has extensively researched this issue. He makes clear that there is little basis for any expectation of improved performance from privatisations. And, as reported in an article by Brent Sheather, he says that 'there is no clear proof that the involvement of the private sector delivers higher efficiency or productivity or a lower cost of capital'.[3]

Professor Hall looked at the performance of PPPs in the EU. He investigated whether they 'provide a way of financing or running private services which is better for the public and the services', and concluded that, contrary to many expectations, the private sector cannot borrow money more cheaply than government; in fact that the opposite is true.

He also concluded that 'the empirical evidence shows that the private sector is not more efficient than the public sector'. PPPs, he found, always start with the handicap of a higher cost of capital, which can only be offset by lower operating costs, supposedly the result of greater efficiency but usually meaning higher prices for consumers. These conclusions have also been reached in reports from the OECD, the IMF and Martin Wolf in the *Financial Times*.

Professor Hall also draws on an analysis of British privatisations by Professor Florio from the Massachusetts Institute of Technology,[4] which meticulously examines all the companies privatised by the Thatcher government and finds no evidence whatsoever of efficiency gains but clear evidence of regressive redistribution; that is, wealth and income passing from the poorer to the wealthy. This is on top of a study by the New Zealand Treasury that found that there was 'little evidence of systemic underperformance' in New Zealand's publicly owned State-Owned Enterprises.

Professor Florio shows that in almost all instances of privatisations, the assets sold were underpriced, there was a large rise in management salaries and, most important of all, privatisation made little difference to long-term trends in productivity and prices. Little wonder that chief executives and senior management of enterprises to be sold are always enthusiastic about the idea, since they stand to benefit from high salaries, huge bonuses and share-ownership schemes.

An insightful account of the privatisation of public assets in the UK is provided by James Meek in an essay published by the *London Review of Books* in September 2012.[5] He identifies the genesis of the modern experiment with privatisation as the 'reforms' carried out in Chile by the regime of General Pinochet under the guidance of advisers such as Milton Friedman. After initial scepticism, this lead was taken up enthusiastically by Mrs Thatcher's government. The motivation was a combination of ideological hostility to the concept of public ownership and the desire to reward powerful private sector supporters with the prospect of making substantial private profits from hitherto publicly owned assets.

In assessing the outcomes, one of the ironies (as James Meek points out) is that the British electricity industry was 'rescued' from public ownership in the hands of the British taxpayer only to end up in the hands of foreign owners, the most important of which is the publicly owned French enterprise, EDF. While the overwhelmingly largest part of Britain's electricity is now owned by foreigners, the supposed disadvantages of public ownership remain in being for much of that industry, only now in French rather than British industry.

In a scathing review of the history of British privatisation, Meek identifies one of the signal failures of the safeguards that were supposed to protect British consumers from the pricing policies of rapacious new owners. The regulators put in place a regime that allowed the new owners to raise prices only in line with inflation. What they had not bargained for was the scope for cost-cutting that was gratefully exploited by the private owners; and reduced costs, of course, meant that it was the workforces that lost jobs and had wages held down so as to allow large profits to be made by the new – largely foreign – owners.

The conclusion we must reach is that in the new global economy the allegiance owed by national governments that see themselves as merely players in that much larger entity is to the major operators – the huge multinational corporations – rather than to the people and communities they are elected to represent. Free trade and the sale of national assets to foreign owners are pursued not for their own practical merits – which are largely non-existent or at the very least outweighed by the downsides they produce – but because they are required by 'free-market' ideology and by the interests of the powerful operators in the global economy.

Chapter 10

The Rise of Powerful Rivals and Other Models

The rise of China

Those powerful interests which have dominated and controlled the development of the global economy for the past three decades have typically exhibited an arrogance that has led them to assume that their dominance is unchallengeable and that they can accordingly focus on extending their operations on a global scale while neglecting the western economies that have been the base and source of their power. Foremost among the developments that were not foreseen was the rise of newly developed economies with the potential to challenge and eventually displace the most powerful economies in the western world. The prime challenge of this kind has come from China.

I first went to China in 1978 as a member of a British parliamentary delegation. We were the first western politicians to be invited into China following the fall of the Gang of Four. It was like visiting the moon; the country was unlike anything I had ever seen. Literally everyone wore drab-coloured Mao tunics. The only cars were heavy black Soviet-made limousines that ferried senior party officials around Beijing; otherwise, everyone rode bicycles.

There were no shops, apart from the handful of Friendship Stores that were open exclusively to foreign dignitaries and diplomats. Other than these, the only signs of commerce were the mounds of cabbages and pumpkins piled up on street corners and brought to makeshift markets by peasants from the countryside.

There was no colour anywhere, apart from huge red banners proclaiming the Five Modernisations. It was impossible to escape the blare of loudspeakers broadcasting party propaganda on trains, in streets and from poles in the fields. When we ventured out of our state-run hotel (also restricted to foreign visitors) in the evening, we would attract large crowds who had never before seen a white face.

The way that Chinese society and the Chinese economy operated was so different from anything I had ever encountered that it provided no real basis for comparison with what I knew. The country and people were immensely rich in cultural heritage, but China in 1978 showed nothing that was remotely recognisable as part of a modern economy.

I returned to China in 1995, and thereafter visited it once or twice a year for a period of eight or nine years. The transformation since 1978 was astonishing. Vast new infrastructure projects were being undertaken: popular wisdom had it that 20 per cent of the world's cranes could be found in Shanghai over this period. Huge areas of traditional housing were swept away to make way for motorways and new industrial and commercial development. I recall travelling into Wuhan from the airport along a newly opened, multi-lane motorway and my taxi having to avoid peasants walking towards us with donkey carts, so unfamiliar were they with what a motorway was.

That transformation has continued apace. The rest of the world has been astonished by the speed with which China has taken its place as a major economic power. At a time of recession for the rest of the world economy, the country has maintained an annual growth rate over recent years averaging at or near 10 per cent.

China has now overtaken Japan as the world's second largest economy, having supplanted Germany in third place five years ago, and it is on track to overtake the USA by 2030 – and possibly well before that. China has become the world's largest producer of manufactured goods, surpassing the USA. It is already by far the world's largest car manufacturer, with a total production nearly twice that of Japan, and two and a half times that of the USA.

In just a decade, China's share of world trade has grown from 4 per cent to 10 per cent. China became the world's largest exporter, overtaking Germany, in 2009. China's foreign exchange reserves now total US$2.454 trillion, even after huge overseas investment over recent years. That means that the Chinese economy is sitting on a massive war chest that allows it to buy up major assets, from mineral reserves to new technology to farmland, all around the world.

It is not just on the production side that the Chinese economy has achieved a new dominance. China is now the world's largest car market and the biggest energy consumer. Inward foreign direct investment totalled US$105 billion in 2010 and Chinese outward foreign direct investment now totals US$261.5 billion; both totals are growing fast.

The scale and speed of Chinese economic development is impressive enough, but future development may be even more significant. China accounts, of course, for a fifth of the world's population, but Chinese GDP per capita is at present only about one-fifth that of Japan, once purchasing power parities are taken into account. This provides some idea of the potential for future growth that Chinese leaders will have in their sights.

While the economic development is the most eye-catching aspect of the transformation, the student of politics will also find much to marvel at. China has succeeded where the Soviet Union failed, by finding a way to combine a centrally directed economy and a monolithic political structure with the innovation and enterprise that only a market economy can provide.

Mao Tse-tung recognised the Soviet failure – the extent to which the Soviet economy had succumbed to sclerosis and Soviet society had become stultified. His solution to the problem of maintaining rigid central political control while stimulating renewal and innovation was the Cultural Revolution – an attempt to ensure that the party organisation was never allowed to become a dead weight; but the cure proved to be worse than the disease.

Following Mao's death and the fall of the Gang of Four, however, Deng Xiaoping initiated a new approach, in which the Chinese Communist Party maintained its central political control and set the broad framework of macroeconomic policy, but within that framework allowed private enterprise to flourish. It is a version of private enterprise that we are unfamiliar with in the – a version that is self-consciously an arm of government policy but which, in return for complying faithfully with that policy, is free to pursue its own interests.

In the West, of course, dominated as we are by the Anglo-American model of capitalism, a close relationship between government and the private sector is regarded as anathema. The western view has been that the best thing government can do for industry is to 'get off our backs'. Government intervention is almost invariably seen as unhelpful; second-guessing an infallible market, it is said, will always produce worse results than if it had been left to itself.

Regulation of the marketplace is seen as unnecessary and sure to be self-defeating. And even those traditional spheres of governmental responsibility and activity, such as infrastructure investment, or the provision of public services such as education or prisons, are increasingly being colonised by private investors and providers.

In western countries, such as the UK, the goal of government is to 'shrink the state'. In the USA, the Obama administration struggles to identify, let alone apply, lessons from the global financial crisis. In a small economy such as New Zealand, which has experimented for nearly three decades with an extreme 'free-market' policy, there is no disposition to recognise its failures. Blind faith is still reposed in the magical ability of the 'free market' to deliver salvation.

There can hardly be a starker contrast than with the approach followed by the Chinese government. To explore that contrast, and to ask the obvious questions, is not to endorse or commend all or even any of what the Chinese have done and are doing. But it is surely prudent to recognise that the Chinese have achieved an economic performance that is already world-beating and is likely to overwhelm us if – as is probable – it continues to develop, and that they have done so while pursuing a very different political and ideological approach from our own. No dispassionate observer, comparing the West's recent history and immediate prospects with those of China, could possibly say that we can have nothing to learn from the Chinese.

So how have the Chinese done it? In many respects, there is no mystery. A government that has virtually guaranteed stability and continuity is able to take a long strategic view. A government that sees little need to curry favour with voters or with particular interest groups has been free to pursue a single-minded objective – the economic development of the country. A government that can take decisions irrespective of the civil or property rights of individual citizens has been able to plan solely in accordance with those economic goals.

They have used that freedom of decision and action to be quite ruthless, and have accordingly attracted severe criticism from trade partners. A case in point has been their policy on the foreign exchange value of their currency. The Chinese renminbi is still not fully convertible, and its value is accordingly established by the direction of the Chinese government. By pegging its value to the US dollar for a long period, they have been able to take advantage, in terms of the competitive pricing of their exports, of the fall in the dollar's value.

There can be little doubt that the renminbi is substantially undervalued and that this is a deliberate element in Chinese trade policy. The size and persistence of the Chinese trade surplus is incontrovertible evidence of that undervaluation. The situation is reminiscent of the German and Japanese trade surpluses before the Second World War, which Keynes and others correctly characterised as a powerful and aggressive assault on the economic power of the

USA and the UK. Keynes was clear that the creditor countries were as much to blame as debtor countries for the trade imbalances that threatened world peace.

Manipulating the currency is just one example of government intervention in economic policy and in wider strategic matters. It is safe to say that, in marked contrast to the western attitude that the national interest can safely be left to market forces, the Chinese government has a well-developed strategic view regarding where the national economy can and should develop, and literally every economic actor in China is required to comply with that strategy.

The domestic programme of infrastructure development is highly planned, therefore. Transport, physical and electronic communications, energy supplies, scientific research and education across the board are all integrated parts of a wider strategy. They are all publicly funded as part of a coherent programme of economic development. That programme is given practical effect as a matter of national priority; individual interests that might conflict with that priority are simply swept aside in a way that would be unacceptable in a western democracy.

The Chinese government takes full responsibility for macro-economic policy. It determines monetary policy (principally interest rates) and controls exchange rates and capital flows in and out of the country. It relies greatly on fiscal policy, principally public spending levels and taxation, to control inflation and to target sustainable growth rates. It exercises close control over the Chinese banking system, and directs it to create large volumes of credit which is then channelled into investment in new productive capacity. It pays particular attention to the competitiveness of Chinese production – the key to their export success and growth rates – which, of course, is an area where controlling the international value of the currency is of great importance.

This is all quite different from the attitude of western governments. In line with the general antipathy to allowing or recognising either the actuality or possibility that governments might be able to help strategically in identifying what is needed for economic success, macroeconomic policy is almost totally ignored in western countries. What passes for macroeconomic policy (and the term itself is almost regarded as a dirty word) is limited to delegating to unelected and therefore unaccountable bankers the responsibility for fixing interest rates as part of a narrowly focused emphasis on controlling inflation. Everything else is left to the market.

The Chinese government goes much further. It has a clear industrial strategy; unlike the West, where 'picking winners' is widely
dismissed as futile and counterproductive, the Chinese have no
doubt about where those winners are needed. Huge public resources
are put into developing leading-edge technology – and if they cannot
wait to develop it themselves, they buy it or perhaps even steal it.
The essential building blocks for future development are therefore
clearly identified and targeted, and are then either supported from
the public purse or entrusted to private firms, which are required to
meet the goals set for them.

The labour supply is a further element which is clearly recognised
as a governing element in future economic development. Great
attention is paid to the skills needed by the labour force in a modern
economy – not only to the higher-level research and technological
skills but also to the general level of education of the workforce
as a whole. The Chinese government understands that economic
development depends at least as much on the general level of
education in the workforce as it does on the achievements of the
best educated. It is well aware, too, that it has so far brought into the
sphere of a modern competitive economy only about 10 per cent of
its potential total workforce.

The Chinese have, in other words, a virtually inexhaustible source
of cheap labour waiting for the chance to become more productive.
The Hong Kong economy of the last quarter of the last century
offers a telling example, on a much smaller scale, of how valuable
the constant underpinning and renewing of a developing economy
through a supply of cheap labour (in their case, by virtue of illegal
immigration across the border with China) can be. Low wage rates
and therefore competitiveness can be maintained at the bottom
end of the labour market, even while growing development and
competitiveness are raising living standards and wage rates at the
higher end. The Chinese government will be well aware of this
trump card in its hand.

In planning the future course of Chinese economic development,
the Chinese government takes, in other words, a coherent long-
term strategic view which is quite foreign (and almost repugnant) to
western governments and business leaders. They control and direct
(to a degree that would be unacceptable in the West) a population
that is well-educated and hard-working, and represents a fifth of
the world's population. They have an immense potential for further
development, in terms of a huge supply of cheap but well-educated

labour, unmatchable competitiveness, substantial natural resources, a well-directed and financed research effort, and a large and growing war chest of foreign exchange reserves.

Within this established framework of consistent and centrally directed strategy and policy, the Chinese are content to encourage the natural entrepreneurial instincts of their population. Chinese businesspeople are free to make profits wherever they can, provided they do so in compliance with government policy. The individual successes of Chinese enterprises owe much to the stability and support provided by government; and they in turn repay the government by rewarding government strategy with economic success.

It is a fair bet, however, that Chinese leaders do not take it for granted that these advantages will produce the outcomes they want. If the Chinese are to achieve the living standards they want, comparable with those in the West, they are going to need access to a much larger share of the world's resources than they currently command. The resources they need now and will need even more in the future if they are to achieve their goals are in most cases finite – minerals and agricultural land, to name but two examples.

The best time to achieve that access and guarantee it into the future is to buy it now, when assets in most western economies are relatively cheap and when China itself is cash-rich. But Chinese leaders will calculate that it is not enough to sign trade deals or conclude contracts to buy the products they need. If their future development is to be guaranteed, they need to do more than acquire access just to the products, the minerals or the food supplies; what is needed is control over and ownership of the means of production.

Without that degree of control, and relying only on contractual arrangements with those who currently own and control the relevant resources, they will find themselves ultimately in a competitive bidding process with other advanced countries who will also be bidders for scarce resources. China's goals can only be achieved, in other words, at the expense of others. A greater share of the world's finite resources for China means a smaller share for others.

To recognise this is not to criticise. China is entitled to compete, and compete hard, with western countries for what the Chinese will see as a fairer distribution of the world's resources. But we should be under no illusion about this being the Chinese game plan.

It should come as no surprise, therefore, to see a huge Chinese effort around the world to buy up not just outputs but the means of production of key strategic assets. This phenomenon has even attracted the attention of novelists. *The Man From Beijing*, a recent novel by the Swedish crime writer Henning Mankell, takes as its theme a high-level Chinese attempt to buy, in effect, a poor African country.

Real life provides substance to underpin this fantasy. Chinese outward foreign direct investment is rising fast, and will go on rising. Nearly 20 per cent of the US$227 billion total Chinese outward FDI was made in 2009, all the more remarkable in view of the overall fall in global FDI in that year. It is targeted at industrial capacity – particularly high-tech capacity – in the USA. Government-owned Sovereign Wealth Funds and State-Owned Enterprises, as well as private companies with undeclared links to government, are the principal actors.

It is even more obviously focused on mineral resources in Australia, where Chinese investment has increased dramatically. The Australians have become increasingly wary of such investment; for example, a Chinese bid to gain control of the world's largest deposit of rare earths was blocked in 2009 by the Australian Foreign Investment Review Board. China already controls 95 per cent of the world's rare earth reserves; rare earths are an essential element in much modern electronic communications technology.

And it extends beyond Australia (where Chinese purchases of Australian farms have risen tenfold) even to a small economy such as New Zealand, where Chinese interest in food production has risen significantly. Some Chinese efforts to buy up not just dairy products but also dairy farms and production processes in New Zealand have attracted considerable attention and aroused public anxiety.

A Chinese bid to buy sixteen New Zealand dairy farms in 2011 offers an instructive example. What distinguished the bid (which was not initially approved because of doubts about the good character of the bidders, but was subsequently approved when a different Chinese corporation took up the bid) was the comprehensiveness of what was proposed. The purchase of the farms was part of a process which would take dairy production from the Chinese-owned farms to be processed in Chinese-owned factories in New Zealand, and then transported directly to be marketed to Chinese consumers.

The farms would remain physically in New Zealand, and some local labour would be employed; but to all intents and purposes that element of New Zealand's dairy production would have been integrated into the Chinese economy. The farms might as well have been relocated to Zhejiang province. Ownership of the land and of its production, decisions about what that production might be and where it might be sold, the wealth it produced for its owners, all would have passed into Chinese hands.

Anxiety about the activities of Chinese firms in such instances is, of course, increased by the close but murky connections between the Chinese government and its strategic goals on the one hand and the purely commercial objectives of Chinese companies on the other. Such connections between government and commerce are not unknown in the West, but most international trade deals attempt to establish level playing fields, and therefore outlaw supposedly commercial proposals which are in reality subsidised means of achieving governmental objectives.

Yet it is clear that the huge increase in the number of Chinese firms bidding successfully for major infrastructure projects around the world is a function of the interest that the Chinese government takes in securing such contracts. The suspicion must be that some firms are set up specifically to obtain overseas contracts as a means of extending Chinese influence, particularly in developing countries.

A company such as the telecommunications and IT giant Huawei, which has set itself the goal of becoming a world leader in the field, has made huge strides in that direction. It is headed by a former senior officer in the People's Liberation Army, and it is reasonable to assume that it has close links to the senior echelons of the Chinese government. So seriously have these concerns been taken by some western governments, such as the USA and Australia, that Huawei has been excluded from participation in sensitive contracts for fear that national security might be compromised. A report from the USA Permanent Select Committee on Intelligence in October 2012 warned against doing business with Huawei and another Chinese telecommunications firm, ZTE, on the grounds that to do so would risk malicious cyber-attacks on American interests and accordingly jeopardise American security.[1]

Chinese firms are often able to offer favourable prices and financing arrangements because their commercial operations are in effect guaranteed by cheap funding, which, in turn, is guaranteed by a virtually inexhaustible government purse. Chinese firms are already by far the biggest international infrastructure contractors, with strongly entrenched dominant positions throughout Africa and in Eastern Europe in particular.

The Chinese government is able to combine these contractual arrangements with claiming a position as significant aid donors to poor countries, particularly in regions such as the South Pacific. A relatively small investment of aid in poor countries can buy a disproportionate degree of influence. They see trade, aid and influence as complementary elements in a single integrated drive to ensure that China will have the access and control it needs to claim a much greater share of the world's resources.

The West should make the necessary adjustment in its thinking, in other words, so that it is understood that a bid for a strategic asset by a Chinese firm may not be just a matter of a private firm taking advantage of a commercial opportunity. It may be part of a much wider picture in which the firm and its bid are to be seen as elements in a government-directed strategy to secure national goals.

These factors should be taken into account in assessing the influence exercised in the global economy by an essentially totalitarian government, able single-mindedly to pursue its own self-interested objectives. That government represents not only one-fifth of the world's population, but the economic power that is as a consequence placed in its hands is potentially enhanced by the development of a sizeable zone of economic influence in which the economies of other, smaller countries could in effect be absorbed into the greater Chinese economy and be directed from Beijing.

None of this means that we should regard Chinese development as unalloyed bad news. Our concern should be to understand the Chinese situation and the nature of their policy objectives, so that we can make sensible and prudent responses in our own interests. We should focus on protecting and advancing those interests, and on encouraging the Chinese to develop in a direction which creates mutual benefit rather than conflict.

The signs in this regard are not entirely discouraging. By contrast with the experience of the Great Depression, when American protectionism helped to drive the world economy into reverse, the Chinese economy has remained – through the current recession – dynamic, open and increasingly market-driven. That continued buoyancy has been helpful in avoiding a repetition of the earlier experience.

Moreover, the Chinese have their own reasons for changing course, at least to some extent. The Chinese economy is at present seriously unbalanced. Odd though it may seem to westerners accustomed to concerns about a damaging emphasis on consumption rather than exports, the Chinese have the opposite problem.

A Chinese refusal to allow an appreciation of their currency so that their extreme and unfair competitiveness is reduced is likely to present them with an inflationary problem, which will do the job for them. One way or another, we are likely to see a rebalancing of the Chinese economy, towards domestic consumption and away from exporting, over the coming years.

At the same time, the Chinese face a problem that is familiar in the West but takes a more virulent form in China. Western countries recognise that care for the elderly in the future will become, as the elderly constitute a higher and higher proportion of the population, increasingly expensive; in China, that problem is greatly exacerbated by the impact of the 'one child per family' policy of recent decades. A smaller workforce in future years will have to shoulder the burden of looking after an increasingly long-lived older generation.

The future may not, in other words be as clear cut as we assume, and we should not forget the example of Japan. I recall spending time in Japan in 1980, at a time when the Japanese economy looked very much like today's Chinese economy, albeit on a smaller scale. The air was thick with predictions that Japan would overtake the USA as the world's largest economy by the turn of the century. We now know that those predictions came to nought – and it may be that China, as it emerges from the rapid growth of its initial development phase, will also find the going increasingly tough. With Chinese wages and raw material costs rising fast, and major firms such as General Electric reviewing the comparative advantages of manufacturing in the USA rather than China, it may be that the era of easy growth for China may eventually come to an end.

This suggests that we should concentrate on trying to ensure that China is increasingly drawn into global efforts to regulate the world economy, by reforming the international monetary system and dealing with trade imbalances, and to achieve environmentally sustainable development. Chinese membership of the WTO may be a useful pointer to such future cooperation.

Most importantly, we need to make sure that competition for the world's scarce natural resources is conducted with as little conflict and misunderstanding as possible. We need to strike a balance between accepting China's legitimate claim to a fair share, and our own right to continue to own our own assets and manage our own affairs.

While China is the most successful and significant of the new Asian powerhouses, the Chinese have not necessarily been the pioneers. Japan had achieved similar success, on a smaller (though still substantial) scale, and countries throughout Asia – India, of course, Korea, Taiwan, Singapore, and increasingly Malaysia, Indonesia and Thailand – have all begun a rapid transformation. In most of these cases, economic success has been achieved by building a powerful partnership between government and private enterprise – something that runs counter to most current western opinion as to the best way to produce economic efficiency.

Nor is Asia the only region where rapid growth is being achieved at a time when the established western economies are languishing. Brazil, Russia and South Africa are also making impressive progress, notwithstanding both actual and threatened global recession – and they, too, have depended less on finance from western financial institutions, following western prescriptions less slavishly than might have been expected twenty years ago.

If we lift our eyes from the purely economic, and consider other and wider social and political goals as well, we can see further examples of how less-developed countries have achieved success while at the same time defying the prescriptions that are thought to be sacrosanct in the West. South America is an area where much damage has been done to individual economies by the so-called 'disciplines' imposed by neo-liberal doctrines. Perhaps as a consequence, we can now see a number of regimes enjoying wide popular support for policies which give priority to sharing resources more equally, raising living standards for the poor, strengthening public services and defying the power of multinational corporations. The recent re-elections of the governments of Chavez in Venezuela and Correa in Ecuador followed the re-election of Bolivia's Evo Morales in 2009, the election of Dilma Rousseff in Brazil in 2010 and Cristina Fernández de Kirchner in Argentina in 2011.

The successful pursuit of policies that are affronts to the basic tenets of neo-liberalism in such countries has done little to shift opinion among western business and political leaders, who prefer to avert their gaze from the evidence before them; but the rise of successful economies and healthier societies which pay little attention to the supposed triumph of western ideology is at the very least a profound shock to the Fukuyama prediction that history is now behind us.

Chapter 11

Mismanaging Our Economies:
Ignoring the Evidence

The rise of China and other rapidly developing economies has not been the only development that our leaders have failed to recognise or understand. They have imposed upon us a virulent form of self-delusion about both the correctness of their doctrines and the success that they are claimed to guarantee. Our leaders have been so concerned to convince the populations of western countries that they are uniquely successful managers of our affairs that they have themselves fallen victim to the constant barrage of propaganda they have produced to this effect.

It has long been claimed that the global economy operating on 'free-market' principles has delivered to us unprecedented prosperity and well-being. Yet, long before the global financial crisis demonstrated the hollowness of these claims, the truth was that the prosperity supposedly produced for all was limited to a minority of countries – especially bypassing the poorest – and to an even smaller minority of people. Even in supposedly successful western economies, large numbers of ordinary people have been able to maintain nominal living standards only by working longer and on the basis of having more than one member of the family in employment.

Yet, despite decades of underwhelming economic performance and declining competitiveness that deny the glowing accounts of the publicists, we still seem to be locked into an ideological deep-freeze. In many western countries, particularly the English-speaking ones, we continue to live well beyond our means, making up the gap between what we earn and what we spend by borrowing from overseas and by selling off our assets to foreign owners. We have been doing this for decades, but the price we pay for this indulgence is getting increasingly steep. We have to pay an interest rate premium to foreign lenders, if they are to continue to lend to us, and we also have to pay to foreign owners – across the exchanges – the profits on the assets we no longer own, with the result that perennial trade imbalances become even harder to manage. More and more of our national wealth goes overseas. We have less and less control over our own economy, as the proportion we actually own diminishes.

Our leaders have refused to acknowledge that this has now become a long-standing and deep-seated trend. The consequence is that they have equally failed to consider even the most obvious remedies for this state of affairs. It must be concluded that the maintenance of their own personal advantages over the rest of us has become more important to them than the welfare of the societies they claim to lead.

Ducking the real issues

It seems not to have occurred to our leaders that the world has changed, that we cannot just assume that we are entitled to a higher standard of living than others, and that we cannot avert our gaze from the fact that other economies now – and will increasingly – perform more efficiently than our own. We arrogantly believe that there is some law of nature that guarantees our superiority over 'lesser breeds', and that if our actual productivity and competitiveness levels do not provide this for us, then we can seek short cuts to produce the same result.

Our leaders long ago concluded that western economies could not compete as manufacturing economies with newly industrialising countries. This did not displease them greatly, since it much reduced the bargaining power of unionised workforces and made it even easier for them to direct western economies to suit their interests. They were, of course, anxious to take advantage of those low costs to boost the profitability of their own investments, but unwilling to share those advantages with workers in western economies. Instead, they looked for ways of avoiding – in their home bases – competition with low-cost countries.

The UK, followed closely by the USA, has been the major exponent of this approach. The alternative they found to direct competition in manufacturing was the creation of a whole new industry. Financial services became the new Eldorado; here was an area of economic activity where only those who already had capital could hope to prosper. It was by definition a course that less-developed economies could not easily pursue themselves.

So the exploitation of the huge markets for manufactured goods was abandoned to the newly efficient economies of the developing world, a favour that they have succeeded in turning to great advantage.

It was exchanged for a monopoly in financial services – an industry which turned out to have the immensely valuable characteristic, for a time at least, that it rewarded those of little talent by allowing them to write their own rules and to create money and money's worth out of nothing, simply on their say-so. We shall see later how all this turned out. Suffice it to say that the financial services industry as a creator of real wealth has proved to be much less effective and satisfactory than manufacturing.

In one sense, though, we should not be surprised at the course that our leaders have taken. It has long been the characteristic of developed economies that they become, as they mature, more concerned with maintaining the value of assets than with competitiveness. The first and leading exemplar of this phenomenon was the UK, but that path has been faithfully followed in due course by the USA. A kind of economic sclerosis takes over; the preoccupation is with using existing power, including military power, to provide physical as well as legal and policy protection to the wealth that has been accumulated (and often concentrated in fewer and fewer hands) in previous generations.

The focus is no longer on the creation of new wealth, in other words, but on maintaining the value of previously acquired wealth, and on entrenching it beyond reach of challenge. This becomes the main purpose of the most powerful people, and that order of priorities has an obvious influence on everyone else, including the best and brightest. The cleverest minds look for economic opportunities in increasingly esoteric activities, where the competition from more efficient economies can be avoided. The whole range of financial services, the professional services, insurance, retailing, consultancy, therefore become the new sources of wealth. Risk aversion, subdued innovative impulses, conservatism, and over time a failure to understand how successful manufacturing economies actually work, become the characteristics of such sclerotic economies.

Interest rates are therefore manipulated to serve the interests of lenders rather than borrowers. The exchange rate is allowed to rise as a counter-inflation measure, without regard for the competitiveness on which the profitability, market share, innovation and investment of the productive sector in the real economy depends. Inflation is treated as the only goal of macroeconomic policy, though – of course – asset-inflation, a rise in the value of existing assets, is welcomed.

Those responsible for formulating policy in these areas seem, either knowingly or unwittingly, to allow their own preconceptions and self-interest to skew their response to the loss of competitiveness.

As we shall see, rather than use the most obvious and effective remedy of lowering the exchange rate, which would (from their viewpoint) have the unwelcome effect of requiring them to make their own contribution to the resolution of the problem by reducing the value of their (largely financial) assets, they prefer to transfer the burden to wage-earners alone by demanding that they should resolve the competitiveness problem by accepting lower real wages. It is safe to assume that this skewed policy has been a major factor in growing inequality in western economies.

Under these influences – these priorities of the masters of the global economy – the West has accordingly wasted three decades believing that our problem is inflation, whereas our real issue is that we (or at least major parts of us) have become basically uncompetitive. We have steadfastly ignored the fact that the world has changed, and that rapidly developing economies such as China, India, Korea, Taiwan and Singapore are now super-competitive economic powers, determined to build on that huge advantage by holding down their exchange rates and becoming ever more competitive.

They have rapidly built the strength of their productive sectors and have earned huge trade surpluses, which have allowed them to buy up the assets (including our own) that they will need for further development. Many of them already enjoy living standards, without our realising it, that are better than ours, and they pay wages and salaries that are higher.

We, on the other hand, are arrogant (and stupid) enough not to bother with understanding how they have achieved their success, and to believe that manufacturing is irrelevant; that we can prosper even while conceding to our most dangerous competitors the huge advantages of mass markets and technological progress. We overlook the evidence that shows conclusively that manufacturing is the most important source of innovation, the most substantial creator of new jobs, the most effective stimulus to improved productivity and offers the quickest return on investment.

We are convinced that competitiveness does not matter, and that we can – in defiance of economic rationality – continue to push up our exchange rates or hold them at overvalued levels with impunity. By focusing on inflation, to the exclusion of other objectives, and using interest rates and an overvalued dollar in the attempt to control it, we make it inevitable that our lack of competitiveness gets worse.

The result is that we dare not grow – even in a recession – for fear of balance of trade constraints, and are reduced, for as long as we can find willing lenders and buyers, to financing our unsustainable consumption by overseas borrowing and selling off what little remains of our assets.

New Zealand goes much further than mere benign neglect of the factors that determine the competitiveness of the economy. Policy-makers have quite deliberately defied rationality by using high interest rates so as to drive up the value of the New Zealand dollar. The result has been a New Zealand economy that is caught in a vicious circle. Overvaluation brings about a loss of competitiveness which generates slow growth, poor productivity and inadequate investment; this in turn produces a perennial trade gap which has to be financed by overseas borrowing, which demands high interest rates to attract lenders and which then drives the currency higher – so that the circuit starts again.

New Zealand is not the only country to demonstrate a complete lack of understanding of the crucial role of the exchange rate in determining competitiveness. The USA has spent recent decades allowing an overvalued dollar to damage American manufacturing and production more generally, relying on the world's willingness to hold US dollars in order to make up the consequently inevitable gap in their trade. By the time the global financial crisis had revealed the truth, it was in many senses too late.

The UK has pursued a policy of overvaluation for many genera-tions; it has become such an endemic feature of the British economic scene that most policymakers seem completely unaware of it. As a British MP in the late 1970s, I took a particular interest in exchange rate policy, and was amazed to discover that it was one of the few topics on which it was not possible to require ministers to answer parliamentary questions. And when Alastair Darling, the former British Chancellor of the Exchequer, wrote his memoirs in 2011, he managed to give a 300-page account of his stewardship without making a single reference to the exchange rate. It has without doubt become the black hole or blind spot in western economic policy – or, to change the metaphor, the elephant in the room that policymakers would prefer not to see.

Whereas a country such as Singapore focuses on indices of compe-titiveness as the prime determinants of macroeconomic policy, most western countries pay so little attention to the issue of competitiveness that we hardly bother to measure it at all. The nearest we get to monitoring competitiveness is the occasional article in *The Economist*, for example, in which purchasing power parities are compared and a generally reassuring conclusion is drawn. Sometimes, the exercise descends into farce when what is measured is the comparative price across a range of economies of McDonald's hamburgers.

Yet purchasing power parities are a completely misleading and inadequate means of measuring competitiveness. This is because what matters to competitiveness is the cost structures in the export (usually manufacturing) sector of a given economy, which will often be very different from costs across the rest of the domestic economy. What matters is not how cheaply we can buy a hamburger for immediate consumption in the domestic economy but what price we charge in export (and international) markets for high-quality manufactured goods. The movement of costs in the exporting sector will follow a quite different trajectory – because of the economies of scale and the possibility of reinvesting the profits offered by large export markets – from that of costs elsewhere in the economy. To place reliance on purchasing power parities in order to reassure ourselves about how competitive we are is simply evidence of our lack of seriousness in addressing the issue.

People are told that the economy's problems are all their fault, and are nothing to do with the government. They are told that they insist on spending too much (mainly on imports) and saving too little. But economics is a behavioural science. People act the way they do in response to the stimuli provided by economic policy. Why not spend rather than save when each overvalued dollar or pound buys more foreign goods than it should? Why invest when the return on productive investment in the domestic economy is inadequate and uncertain? 'Failure to save' is merely a restatement – not a cause – of the problems. It is the direct consequence of monetary policies that have stimulated asset inflation, made investment for productive purposes unattractive, and encouraged spending on artificially cheap imports.

Why the exchange rate matters

There is never any shortage of opinion to the effect that any disadvantage to export competitiveness from exchange rate overvaluation is adequately offset by cheaper imports; many commentators seem to assume that by some miracle of natural law the one perfectly offsets the other. There is little understanding that making exports dearer and imports cheaper (even if those imports include raw materials, capital equipment and fuel) is a foolproof recipe for destroying the productive sector of the domestic economy.

There are those who discount the impact of exchange rate overvaluation or volatility, and there are always some who actually see advantage (because, for example, they are importers) in an overvalued currency. They will often be heard to argue that it is the economy that must adjust to the exchange rate rather than the other way round. But this is special pleading, wish-fulfilment and ignorance on a grand scale.

The truth is that the exchange rate is the single most important determinant of international competitiveness, and – as we shall see – competitiveness is in turn the single most important determinant of productivity and profitability, and ultimately of living standards. This is because the exchange rate converts all domestic costs into prices in the internationally traded goods sector. There is no other factor that has such a direct, inevitable and comprehensive impact on the ability to compete in international markets.

There are those who argue that, in today's global economy, price competitiveness matters little, and that the competitive edge that makes the difference is in product quality and meeting the customers' needs. What this argument overlooks is that a lack of ability to compete on price will eventually and inevitably lead in the longer term to poorer quality and a reduced ability to satisfy the customer. It is, in other words, difficult and eventually impossible to match the foreign competition in quality terms if a lack of price competitiveness means that the profits that are needed to reinvest in improving quality are simply not available. The domestic producer and 'wannabe' exporter then has the difficult task of trying to sell into international markets goods that are not only more expensive but inferior in quality as well.

If the currency is overvalued or appreciates, those selling against international competition both at home and overseas either have to raise prices and risk losing market share or have to hold prices and accept reduced margins. Reduced profits (either because of lower sales or narrower margins – or both), if sustained over any length of time, mean less reinvestment, less growth, less employment, less research on product development, less new technology and equipment, less market research and development (especially overseas), and less to spend on skill training, marketing and after-sales service – all the factors that govern success in the internationally traded goods sector, where the real prospects for growth lie. For the economy as a whole, it means the inhibition of growth and investment, and an increasingly restrictive balance of trade constraint. Even the most

successful exporters (New Zealand's dairy exporters, for example)
find that the cream is blown off the top of export earnings by the
overvalued currency, so that even in the good times they have less to
spend and invest than their competitors do.

A brief period of overvaluation or exchange rate volatility is bad
enough. A deliberate policy of creating or allowing overvaluation
as a permanent or constantly recurring condition, however,
produces much more serious and longer-term damage. Profitability
improvements that might result from a temporary fall in the currency's
value are treated as windfall gains, and are spent as consumption
rather than reinvested for the long term. If farmers, manufacturers,
exporters and investors know that a good year or two will inevitably
be followed by an upswing in the currency's value that closes the
brief window of opportunity, how can we expect the sustained
investment in new capacity, skills and research that is needed to
improve economic performance? And as the private productive
sector invests less in new developments, governments – even those
who eschew 'picking winners' – become increasingly keen, not to say
desperate, to try their luck in funding research into what they hope
will be technological breakthroughs that will miraculously transform
the outlook.

If these trends persist for any length of time, there is then a second-
order range of consequences. Talent and resources turn away from
productive activity and are diverted elsewhere. The economy's best
people move away from the potential growth points – that is, the
sectors selling into large international markets. Bright graduates
cease to go into productive industry; they prefer to try their luck in
asset speculation, finance and retailing – anywhere that is protected
from foreign competition. In many cases, those resources of people,
capital and ideas literally get up and go elsewhere. People look to non-
productive assets such as housing as the place to make their fortune.
Capital moves to wherever it is possible to make a quick buck, rather
than to long-term investment in increased capacity in terms of both
quality and volume. Successful businesses move overseas or are sold
to overseas buyers. Corporate headquarters move to foreign capitals.

In the longer run – a generation or more, which is by now the
experience of most western countries – the culture itself changes.
Borrowing, in the belief that the world owes us a living, becomes a
way of life. We lose faith in saving, investing, and producing goods
and services for sale as a way of providing for ourselves. A mindset
that rejects wealth creation as either possible or even desirable, and

a culture that is diverted to other goals, such as screwing a larger slice for oneself of a cake that fails to grow, are entrenched in society as a whole. It is hard to think of a strategy that is more inimical to the interests of western economies and societies. Yet this is the direct consequence of the strategy adopted by our narrowly focused leaders.

Can policy influence the exchange rate?

But, it may be objected, even if we suffer from the endemic over-valuation of the currency, there is surely nothing we can do about it. The rate for a given currency – floating as it is – will be decided by the foreign exchange markets, and not by the policymakers. The answer to this is a resounding 'No!' There is no such thing as a clean float. The view that foreign exchange markets take of our currency will be influenced by many factors, most of them inevitably within the control of our policymakers.

Take the New Zealand example. The legendary Japanese house-wife or Belgian dentist, who typically indulges in the 'carry trade' by borrowing cheaply at home in order to take advantage of New Zealand's high interest rates, knows nothing of the impact of their actions on the New Zealand economy. They know little and care less about the performance of that economy. What persuades them to buy New Zealand dollars is the virtual guarantee that the New Zealand authorities will go on, as they have done for decades, paying them an interest rate premium. And, because so many are attracted by that risk-free windfall, and the demand for and price of the New Zealand dollar therefore go up, even short-term investors can usually expect a capital gain as well. The syndrome occurs only because it is encouraged by policy – a policy that could easily be changed but is not.

If policymakers chose to focus on competitiveness, to recognise the role of the exchange rate in that context, and to avoid policies that artificially force the exchange rate above its justifiable level, this alone would bring about a revolution in the rate's behaviour. If high interest rates were no longer pressed into service as the central mechanism for controlling inflation but policy addressed instead the excessive bank lending for non-productive purposes, which is the real engine of inflation, this would be a major step forward. The mere realisation that the object of policy was no longer to offer an interest rate premium to overseas lenders would immediately lead to a fall in the exchange rate.

It is, of course, also true that governments in the UK or New Zealand, for example, which proclaim that their prime goal is the maintenance of confidence, thereby signal to the purveyors of 'hot money' that they can enjoy the advantages of high interest rates without risk of the currency depreciating. A government that gave priority instead to the performance of the real economy, in matters such as full employment, profitability and investment, would no doubt be gratified at how little confidence really mattered and how rapidly its absence would help a depreciation of the currency, with consequent gains to competitiveness. In addition, there is no shortage of measures that could easily be adopted – measures designed, for example, to insulate the domestic economy against excessive inflows of money from overseas or to provide differential interest rates – that would help to bring the exchange rate down. What is missing is not the means but the will.

The impact of overvaluation

As we have seen, an economy that lives with an overvalued exchange rate will become uncompetitive and will suffer low growth rates and declining output, productivity and living standards, at least in comparative terms. These have been the characteristics of many western economies over recent decades.

Perhaps the most obvious and persistent evidence of an overvalued exchange rate, however, is an endemic imbalance in the current account. Countries such as the USA, the UK, Australia and New Zealand have lived for years with current account deficits, to such an extent that they are now assumed to be unremarkable and simply part of the natural order of things.

By definition, however, a trade deficit has to be financed in some way or another. The usual consequence is that both individuals (persons and corporations) and governments have to borrow or sell assets to cover that proportion of the cost of imports that is not covered by exports. In each of these cases, therefore, both governments and countries take on increased debt, and this will in turn see the balance of trade problem worsen, as increased interest payments to lenders and repatriated profits to new overseas owners have to cross the foreign exchanges.

This, as both economic analysis and practical experience tell us, is exactly what has happened to many western economies. It is well established that a trade deficit on the one hand will inevitably total to the same sum as the private sector deficit and the government deficit combined: they are accounting identities.[1] So, when a lack of competitiveness means that trade cannot be balanced as a consequence of the value of imports exceeding the value of exports, the resulting trade deficit will inevitably create a combined private sector and government deficit of the same size as the trade deficit.

Rather than tackle the trade deficit by focusing on the need to improve competitiveness (in which exercise the exchange rate is by far the most important determinant), however, western governments – unwilling to concede the true position which is that their economies are fundamentally uncompetitive – engage in lengthy and unsuccessful campaigns to adjust private sector saving and spending levels, and in even more damaging efforts to reduce government deficits by cutting expenditure, apparently unaware that such measures are less than helpful to the basic problem of uncompetitiveness. The fall in the level of economic activity, as a consequence of falling tax revenues and the higher cost of unemployment, is not only a deterrent to investment and innovation but – paradoxically it may seem – means that government deficits tend to increase.

On the other hand, reflating an economy that is basically uncompetitive is also fraught with difficulties. Increased domestic demand in an uncompetitive economy only helps to suck in more imports, worsening the trade deficit, increasing overseas debt and putting credit ratings at risk, with the consequence that the increased debt will then cost more to finance. It was exactly this dilemma that led the British Prime Minister James Callaghan to tell the Labour Party conference in 1976 that 'you can't spend your way out of recession'.

The statement is a nonsense, of course. There is no remedy for recession that does not involve spending more. Callaghan's statement would have been more accurate if he had said, 'we can't do what is required to escape from stagnation because our fundamental lack of competitiveness means that spending more would make our inflation and balance of payment problems even worse'. The problem he was trying to describe was really one, in other words, of competitiveness rather than anything else.

He was not alone in trying to deny, or perhaps in being ignorant of, the UK's lack of competitiveness at that time. Most commentators prefer to avert their gaze from what is staring them in the face. But in the end, the facts cannot be denied; whether a currency is overvalued or not is best resolved by asking whether the consequences typically to be expected in instances of overvaluation are to be found in the economy under consideration. Those consequences include slow rates of growth, high unemployment, low rates of investment and productivity growth, persistent trade deficits, a perennial need to borrow overseas, a propensity to sell off assets – including national assets – into foreign ownership, high levels of import penetration, a weak export sector, and low rates of return on investment and therefore of profitability. Does this sound familiar?

There is only one sure-fire way to tackle the problem of uncompetitiveness and its trade deficit consequences, and that is to tackle the root cause. A trade deficit arises because the country concerned does not and cannot sell enough of its produce into international markets at a price that earns a profit, and that problem arises because the costs of production in that country are too high. The solution, therefore, has to be to get those costs down.

Where costs are too high in international terms, western countries have typically tried to get them down by forcing down wage rates through a range of measures which have often included cutting benefits, reducing the ability of trade unions to defend wages, and tolerating unemployment. Even if these measures succeeded, that success could be achieved only over such a long time-frame as to make them practically ineffectual, and – because the burden of adjustment is placed exclusively on working people – at a social cost that would make the downsides more debilitating than any gains.

This approach, though ineffective in achieving its stated purpose, has nevertheless been favoured by policymakers and those who control our economies, because it is politically congenial to them to diminish the claims of labour on the economy. It is for this reason that those same interests have been hostile to a much more obvious analysis and remedy.

At any given moment, the cost structure of a given economy in international terms is, in the last analysis, a function of the exchange rate. A lower exchange rate will reduce those costs across the board in the most immediate, effective, fair and comprehensive way available. It is a measure of the reluctance of our policymakers to accept this simple truth that they have expended so much effort over such a long period on trying to reduce labour costs and to improve competitiveness by exhorting and encouraging productivity to rise – something that is virtually impossible if the start position is that the economy is basically uncompetitive. There is, in other words, only one reason that costs in an economy are too high. It is because our policymakers choose, by denying the obvious remedy, that it should be so.

Excuses for overvaluation

The exchange rate's significance is often dismissed because it is asserted that, even if the attempt to bring down the currency's value were made and succeeded, it would be ineffective to improve competitiveness. This is because it is argued that any advantage to competitiveness from a devaluation would be quickly eroded by inflation, and that it would in any case bring about an unacceptable fall in the standard of living, which would be politically unsustainable.

Neither of these propositions is true; both are lazily asserted in defiance of the available evidence. My co-author on an earlier occasion, John Mills, has shown conclusively in a recent book that devaluation does not cause living standards to fall, but the reverse, nor is it followed by higher inflation.[2] Mills establishes these points by looking first at the economic arguments and then at the empirical evidence.

A lower exchange rate will immediately reduce all domestic costs, of course. Exports immediately become more competitive and therefore easier to sell, with the result that a bigger market share is easier to achieve and sales increase. The sales that are made are also more profitable. The increased demand for the goods of the devaluing country means an increased level of activity in that country, with more employment and investment, faster growth in productivity and higher profitability. Wages, too, can be allowed to grow in domestic terms, and the balance of trade constraint is loosened to allow for the growth that is stimulated by the increased demand for exports and the increased purchasing power in the domestic economy.

It is true that the price of imports will increase, but – in an interesting reversal of the usual argument that cheap imports will hold down domestic prices – importers will be under pressure to keep their prices low so as to compete better with newly competitive domestic production, as orders are switched from foreign to domestic suppliers. Taxes and interest rates can both be set at lower levels for the same outcomes, factories working at less than full capacity can increase production and unused resources of labour can be drawn back into use, so reducing the rate and cost of unemployment. For all these reasons, the benefits of greater competitiveness quickly and substantially outweigh – by providing a real stimulus to growth – the immediate cost-reducing impact of a devaluation.

Sceptics will say that these outcomes are all very well on paper but that in practice a country that devalues will suffer a fall in living standards. This contention can only be made by those who refuse to look at the evidence. John Mills has analysed ten significant devaluations over an eighty-year period, ranging from the 24 per cent British devaluation in 1931, through the 28 per cent American devaluation from 1985 to 1987 and to the 18 per cent British devaluation of 2007–9. He is able to show that in almost every case real GDP per head increased significantly in the period following the devaluation – and even in those few cases where GDP fell for a time, it was owing to factors such as the global financial crisis rather than the devaluation.

Furthermore, in the aftermath of devaluations, and contrary to almost all predictions, inflation did not soar. This was particularly striking in the case of the British devaluations of 1931 and 1992 (following the British exit from the Exchange Rate Mechanism), where, despite dire warnings, inflation was unaffected.

Productivity and competitiveness

Nothing is more revealing of our failures of analysis than the repeated and increasingly pathetic attempts by our policymakers to use microeconomic intervention and exhortation to remedy our problems. Our political and business leaders have consistently turned their backs on the obvious and easily accessed remedy for problems of loss of competitiveness and have concentrated instead on increasingly fruitless efforts to talk up and otherwise encourage improvements in productivity. This is not to say that better productivity is not desirable; but it is very difficult to achieve at a time of declining international competitiveness.

The first point to make is that levels of productivity – as a guide to international competitiveness – do not exist and cannot be measured in a vacuum. Despite the West's economic travails, it remains the case that, by virtue of our head start in industrialisation, most western factories are more efficient and productive in absolute terms than those in, say, China. But that tells us nothing about competitiveness. Chinese goods are more competitive because their exchange rate correctly sets their domestic costs at a level in international terms that more than compensates for lower productivity.

This is not to say that low productivity growth is not a real problem in western economies; but the bad news is that this is not a brilliant new insight. If talking and worrying about low productivity growth was a cure, we would have solved it long ago. The difficulty has never been in identifying the problem; it has been in knowing what to do about it. And the evidence is that we have learned nothing from our past failures.

It is not as if we have not tried the usually touted solutions. Privatisations, tax reforms, removing 'labour market rigidities', holding down wages, strict adherence to monetary policies; all have been tried – and none have worked. And we are constantly told that we should eschew a lower exchange rate in favour of improving productivity, as though the latter was not largely and causally dependent on the former.

If we really want to address the problem of low productivity growth, so as to justify our predilection for high exchange rates, we need to do more than wring our hands and repeat the failed nostrums of the past. If we really want to solve our problems, we need to take a broader view. A broad economic failure is likely to have an equally broad economic cause. But that is the one possibility that our policymakers and business leaders have resolutely refused to contemplate.

If low productivity growth is both a consequence and a cause of poor economic performance, should we not at least be asking whether our economic policy settings over recent decades have been correct? Are we so locked into a mindset that says there is no alternative to the policies that have produced such poor results that no one is prepared even to ask whether there has been a failure of our macroeconomic policy?

Productivity is a function of many factors, almost all of which cost money. To improve productivity, western firms need to spend on new skills training, new technology, new product development, new equipment, new market development, new research and development. The truth is that they haven't done so because our productive economies have not been competitive or profitable enough to allow adequate investment in productivity growth.

Some recent research at Victoria University in New Zealand about productivity throws some interesting light on these issues. It shows that, as expected, the New Zealand firms that are able to export are the most efficient and productive in that economy – typically, it is only the most competitive enterprises that will venture into export markets.

Less expectedly, however, the research also shows that those export firms did not increase their productivity any faster than others. They remained at a higher level of productivity than their domestic competitors, but exporting did not seem to widen that advantage. They did not, in other words, 'kick on' to take advantage of bigger and more profitable markets overseas, as similar industries in developing economies have succeeded in doing.

The researchers asked themselves whether this showed that exporting was not the stimulus to greater efficiency that it is sometimes claimed to be. This would be surprising and would call for some particular explanation, since the experience of other more successful economies shows that the advantages of scale derived from accessing major international markets for manufactured goods, especially perhaps technologically advanced goods, does produce a measurable benefit to unit costs, efficiency, margins and market share.

The conclusion must be, therefore, that there has been something in New Zealand's economic environment that has prevented these expected benefits of exporting from being delivered to New Zealand exporters. The obvious explanation is surely that the burdens of high interest rates and of an overvalued dollar that reduce price competitiveness and cut profit margins – both characteristics of the New Zealand productive environment for nearly thirty years – have meant that New Zealand exporters were simply unable to invest in the productivity growth that was needed to improve competitiveness against overseas rivals. They were, at best, hanging on by their fingernails. An increasing number, as the statistics show, simply gave up and moved their operations overseas.

New Zealand policymakers, like most of their western counterparts, have been persistent in their efforts to talk up a better economic performance, even in the face of repeated failure. A good example of an initiative designed to produce a miraculously better performance was a major international conference, sponsored by both the government and leading universities in 2001 and in which I was asked to lead one of the working parties, designed to unlock the secrets of more successful economies.

It turned out that there were few mysteries to divulge. The explanations for economic success were all too obvious and commonplace. Ireland, for example, in whose apparent prosperity there was a great deal of interest, was the beneficiary of EU largesse, which created an asset bubble that eventually burst. Australia, as has become increasingly clear, has the great advantage of being able to dig up its barren interior and sell the product to a mineral-hungry world.

Other explanations are equally obvious. Developing economies, China and India now, for example, and Japan and Korea before them, do well if they can access mass international markets and exploit economies of scale by combining cheap and plentiful labour with rapidly growing technological expertise, while holding their exchange rates at competitive levels.

And wealthy mature economies that focus on reinvesting in new wealth creation, such as Germany, will do better than those, such as the UK and now the USA, that give priority to the protection of existing asset values and to consuming more than they produce.

Developed economies that suddenly benefit from a new source of wealth, such as the discovery of oil, will do badly if they simply spend the proceeds through allowing the exchange rate to appreciate – as the British and the Dutch did, and as the Australians may be in the process of doing with high mineral prices. Those such as Norway, on the other hand, that invest the proceeds in new assets so that they go on producing wealth after the initial benefit has dissipated, can enjoy a long-term benefit to economic development.

Yet, despite these commonsense conclusions, the effort is still made to seek the magic elixir that will propel western economies back into the top league of productivity growth and thereby justify our insistence on overvalued currencies. We still believe that one more jobs summit, one more nostrum from the latest management guru, one more ministerial exhortation to improve productivity, one more brilliant new piece of research will do the trick.

Western governments remain convinced that 'supply-side' measures, such as encouraging research and development through tax breaks, funding large-scale research projects from the public purse, organising and reorganising support in various forms for private enterprise, will make up a deficiency in the private sector's willingness and ability to help themselves. They are unwilling to concede that this deficiency is evidence that the market is somehow failing to stimulate the innovation and productivity growth that are needed.

It is one of the ironies of the policy stance currently adopted by western governments that they have so little understanding of and confidence in the market's operation that they are apparently unaware that – while loudly condemning any government intervention – their own insistence on manipulating both interest rates and exchange rates for inappropriate purposes has so distorted the market's normal functioning that it is unable to serve its proper purpose.

We have been unwilling to face an obvious truth: that economies are such large, complex and multifaceted fields of activity that it is very unlikely that single, focused initiatives – even if worthwhile – will make much, if any, difference. Of much more importance in determining whether economies perform well or otherwise, and whether or not they are stimulated to innovate and develop, is the broad macroeconomic context in which they operate. It is that context we should focus on; but that is precisely what we are not prepared to do.

Chapter 12

Hubris and Nemesis:
The Global Financial Crisis

Any claim that western leaders know how to manage their economies was surely dealt a fatal blow by the crash of 2008. The uncertainties and confusion created by the global financial crisis – a crisis that was manifestly building over a long period but was almost entirely unforeseen by most western political and business leaders – must surely have undermined the primacy of neo-liberal ideology; and while, contrary to any rational expectation, the 'Washington consensus' remains the dominant ideological force in the West, it is hardly surprising that countries in the developing world are less convinced than they were that western investors and financial institutions have all the answers. The ideological debate remains alive and well in these countries, where the balance of advantage seems increasingly to rest with views other than those that are still hardly challenged in the West.

The economic fallout from the crisis was, of course, immediate, extensive and severe. It was felt in the shock delivered to our financial institutions, in the balance sheets of our major corporations, in growth rates around the world. More damagingly still, it took its toll far from the City of London or Wall Street – on the jobs, homes and lives of perhaps billions of ordinary people in all parts of the globe.

But among the many casualties has been the belief – virtually unchallenged for thirty years – that the market's presumed infallibility solved the problem of how to run the economy successfully. That conviction has surely been shaken to its core. The simple confidence that the market could always be relied on to deliver the best outcomes can no longer stand in the face of the meltdown produced by market forces that were allowed to run riot. The widely accepted assertion that markets, left to themselves, are self-correcting cannot survive the crisis. We now know that this is self-serving nonsense, and that the natural tendency of the unregulated market is to lead to excess, irresponsibility, inefficiency and eventually collapse.

Even Adam Smith accepted that markets could and would become the means by which dominant market operators were empowered to act against the general interest. And Keynes warned that this tendency of markets more generally was exacerbated in the case of financial markets.

This was because, he maintained, of the inherent instability of financial markets and their excessive reliance on opinions and sentiment – not to say guesses and hunches – rather than on real things with well-established values. We have seen exactly what he meant. An unregulated market in financial assets was permitted to create and put a price on new kinds of assets which had no more than a speculative value. As long as those assets – futures, securitised debt, credit default swaps and so on – were accepted at face value, they could be offered as security for debt, which could then be used in turn to underpin the creation of a new swathe of assets.

Those who manipulated these money-making mechanisms must have felt as though they were living the alchemist's dream. Those who watched from the sidelines – including our political leaders, who might ordinarily have recognised their responsibility to provide some safeguards – could only marvel, lost in admiration and envy, dazzled by the riches being generated. And as long as the asset values kept growing, the fact that they were underpinned in real terms only by debt mattered little.

It seemed to be a fail-safe operation: no great skill was required, and the mechanisms and processes – novel and untried as they were – were apparently supported and validated by complex mathematical models. Even substantial operational errors, such as the gross overvaluation of assets, could be quickly washed away by the rising tide of asset values right across the waterfront. Even the unskilled could make fortunes – to say nothing of the opportunities offered on an unprecedented scale to fraudsters: Bernie Madoff, for example.

But it needed only a scintilla of doubt to creep in about the value of these new assets for the whole ramshackle structure to come tumbling down. When the confidence bubble burst, assets lost their value, but debt did not. The result was, as we have seen, the collapse of the financial infrastructure and financial institutions of many of the world's major advanced economies.

The financial sector was the first victim. The banks came under pressure when their investments linked to the American housing market lost value, but no one could be sure how much money each institution stood to lose. The banks found themselves facing the crisis with little in the way of capital to bail them out when the bets went wrong. They had sanctioned borrowing at levels that were only sustainable if the value of share portfolios and property continued to rise. When they took fright at the fragility of their supposed assets and stopped lending to each other, as they did in August 2007, the wider financial system ground to a halt.

Governments, too, were caught out. They had assumed that buoyant tax receipts were permanent and would sustain increased public spending. Instead, the finance crisis deepened, the banks began serious retrenchment and house and share prices fell. The Lehman Brothers bankruptcy in September 2008 triggered the biggest slump since the Great Depression.

The emergency seemed to require governments to arrest the slide by bailing out the banks, but they wrecked their own finances in the process. Not only was bailing out the banks a hugely expensive exercise but the recession meant much lower levels of output, which in turn reduced tax revenues. Individuals and corporations, banks and eventually governments all fell back into debt. This indebtedness, particularly of governments, which was essentially a consequence of market failure, eventually and paradoxically became regarded as the original cause rather than a consequence of the global financial crisis.

Learning the lessons

A fallacy that did not, or should not, survive the global financial crisis is the argument that risk can be quantified according to reliable mathematical formulae. A great deal of modern economics has been driven by esoteric work aimed at providing an apparently reliable basis on which risk can be quantified. It was on this basis that much of what are now recognised as having been worthless assets were happily traded from one interest to another, each trader taking a profit as the asset appeared to grow in value as it passed from hand to hand. The huge superstructure of debt and valueless assets, built initially on the sub-prime mortgage market, eventually came crashing down.

A further lesson is that decisions taken by business leaders alone are a poor guide to a successful economy and society. Business leaders have been so eulogised over recent decades that many people were persuaded that more and more decisions affecting our lives should be handed over to them, and that they could be more trusted in many cases than our elected leaders. We now know that business decisions are invariably taken for reasons of self-interest, and take little account of wider or longer-term interests. Those countries, such as the USA and the UK, which most enthusiastically accepted that societies should be run in the business interest, are those which have on the whole suffered the most severe consequences of business failures, with the greatest damage to social fabric and environmental sustainability.

Another casualty of the failed neo-liberal experiment is the self-serving contention that increasing the wealth of the rich so that inequality widens will produce a better economy or a stronger society. The 'trickle-down' theory was often used to support the proposition that if the rich got proportionately richer the rest of us would benefit in absolute even if not comparative terms from the lift in economic activity that the increased wealth of the rich would produce, through increased investment and employment. This theory has been discredited in the absence of any credible evidence to support it, and in the face of evidence to the contrary, which shows that in countries where inequality has widened the most the living standards of the poor have actually declined.

A few of the immediate global lessons to be learned from the deficiencies of unregulated markets were applied quickly, albeit belatedly and partially. The first priority was to understand what had gone wrong and to ensure that it did not happen again. The new regulatory regime for financial markets and institutions introduced by President Obama when he was elected was a recognition that we should never again entrust our economic future to unregulated markets. His example was followed with various degrees of reluctance by other, but by no means all, governments. The British government, for example, presiding as it did over some of the most serious market failures, was slow to react. President Obama at least seemed to understand that we cannot correct and prevent egregious errors by handing back control to those who committed them in the first place. Effective regulation is now surely the name of the game.

Yet we see the failure to learn these lessons repeatedly perpetuated in the belief that the first priority of the policymakers must be to protect the banks at all costs. The determination on the part of many governments to respond to the recession by cutting back the role of government is all the more surprising when it was the public purse that had to be opened, at the taxpayer's expense, in order to save the global economy from the consequences of the private financial sector's irresponsibility.

Rather than sheet the responsibility and the burden home to where they belong, however, governments have spent billions on helping the banks to shore up their balance sheets, with the perhaps unintended result that the banks have continued to pay out massive bonuses to their employees. It is the taxpayer that must now pay the burden, not just in repaying borrowings made to deal with the crisis but in suffering the cutbacks in public services and the loss of jobs that are the inevitable consequences of current policies.

It has even been a struggle to compel the banks to accept tighter rules about capital reserves and lending ratios. While President Obama has introduced tighter regulation of American banks, the British government has been extremely slow to recognise the need to do anything, and other governments have also dragged the chain. While individual voices have been raised in support of measures such as a Tobin tax on financial transactions, governments have so far given them little consideration, and those that have – like Sweden – have found that they are easily evaded if other countries do not follow suit. In view of this timidity in dealing with the banks, we cannot be surprised that no one apparently stopped to wonder why, if the taxpayers put up the money, they did not acquire the ownership interest – and, even more pointedly, why it did not occur to anyone that, if banking so obviously relies in the last resort on underpinning by the public purse, we should perhaps recognise that banking is in essence a public function.

In addition, we should surely now recognise that bankers should not be trusted with the most important decisions in economic policy. No policy measure was more widely welcomed than the handing of monetary policy over to 'independent' central banks. We now have good reason to know that their decisions are not only likely to be wrong but will certainly be self-serving – no more reliable or impartial than those of casino operators, who will always set the odds in their own favour. If we are truly to grapple with the lessons set out above, we need to restore the main decisions of economic policy, including the effective regulation of markets, to democratic control.

The responsibility of government

Many commentators and practitioners, however, have increasingly jibbed at accepting the longer-term and wider lessons to be learned from the meltdown. They have been keen to see government intervention to correct past errors as merely a case of dangerous times requiring exceptional measures. The central task, they believe, is to right the ship; it should then be allowed to sail on as before. They impatiently await the opportunity to return to what they see as business as usual, so that governments can safely be put back in their boxes.

This is to misunderstand what has happened. The current role of government in correcting and counteracting recession is not an unfortunate aberration. The recession has revealed an abiding truth – that the market can deliver its unmatched benefits only if governments are there when needed to make good its deficiencies and act against its excesses.

The plunge into recession has illustrated beyond peradventure what happens when market operators become so powerful that governments are unable to restrain market excesses. But the response that is now needed to limit and shorten recession delivers a further lesson – that governments must bear a responsibility not only for allowing the recession to develop but also for the measures needed to counteract it. Governments can and must act to correct market failure in ways that the market left to itself cannot. Economies are robust things: they would recover sooner or later without intervention. But – as all but the most purblind should surely have recognised – it became the responsibility of governments to hasten the recovery process, and thereby limit the misery that recession inevitably brought about.

The reason for this is that governments, uniquely, have the ability to counter the inevitable tendency of recessions to feed on themselves. For most actors in the economy, the demands of self-interest mean that in a recession they spend less, invest less, cut costs, employ fewer people. Each individual decision taken by companies or businessmen may be – indeed, usually is – rational and justified, but the cumulative effect for the economy as a whole is that recession is intensified.

There are those who wish to resist this line of argument. They are reluctant for ideological reasons to accept that governments should ever have a special role and responsibility. They argue that governments should act (if at all) as though they were individual people or companies. According to this view, governments in a recession should also cut costs, spend less and lay people off, as though they were just like households or businesses.

But if governments behave like everyone else, the economy is condemned to a deeper and harsher recession than need be. Those holding this view are so blinded by an ideological hostility to the very idea of government as to deny Keynes's statement of the obvious – that governments have a unique responsibility to act countercyclically.

Only governments have the capacity and the duty to act against market logic. Only governments have the resources to override what would normally be market-based self-interest and to substitute for it the wider interest in getting the economy as a whole moving again. Only governments can afford to live with increased indebtedness, and then have the capacity to repay that debt when the economy escapes from recession and tax revenues accordingly become more buoyant.

The damaging consequences for the economy when governments fail to perform this role have been underpinned not only by recent experience in the Eurozone and elsewhere but also by a revision of economic policy undertaken – as we have seen in the context of Eurozone austerity policies – by the IMF. The IMF has now concluded that the multiplier effect of contractionary policies, especially involving cuts in government spending, is much greater than was previously thought, and these policies make it much more difficult to escape from recession. This, coupled with the volte-face in favour of government-financed intervention and stimulus through measures such as investment in infrastructure undertaken by the new Japanese government at the outset of 2013, suggest that lessons may at last be beginning to be learned.

There is also an increasing recognition that an undue emphasis on immediate deficit reduction may be ineffective even in terms of its own objective. If policymakers are willing to live with the damage that is done to public services, it is always possible to cut a deficit in the short term; those who are adversely impacted tend to be those who are most reliant on those services and to have – as a corollary – voices which are least likely to be heard. But, as the former American Treasury Secretary Lawrence Summers points out, immediate cuts in public spending will often have the effect of simply suppressing the deficit, and ensuring that a backlog of essential spending, particularly on infrastructure, builds up.[1] The effect, in other words, is just to defer public expenditure, so that the burden of making up the shortfall is passed on to the next generation.

The orthodoxy that requires austerity and debt reduction as a response to recession received an even more serious setback when a paper produced in 2010 by the highly regarded economists Carmen Reinhart and Kenneth Rogoff was shown to be vitiated by fundamental errors and defective methodology,[2] such as the arbitrary exclusion of data, including figures for New Zealand which, if included, would have substantially altered their conclusions. That paper purported to show that countries where the debt to GDP ratio exceeded 90 per cent experienced a sharp fall in economic growth when that supposed watershed was reached. The paper provided the intellectual support for the Republican insistence on cuts in public spending in the US, and for similar policies pursued in the Eurozone and in the UK.

The discovery – eventually conceded by the authors – that they had made some obvious errors and that the correlation they postulated between high debt levels and low economic growth was by no means established served only to add to already existing doubts concerning their hypothesis;[3] those doubts concerned, among other issues, questions about the direction of causality in any such correlation.

This most recent development has further undermined the credibility of an approach that has in any case been substantially disproved bypractical experience, not least in the UK. George Osborne's decision to treat the reduction of the government deficit as the top priority of policy, and to implement austerity policies in order to achieve it, has produced some literally counterproductive consequences – a repeated failure to escape from recession, an increased government deficit and a loss of the prized top credit rating. The chancellor remained, however, one of that dwindling band who refuse to recognise the truth of what is happening.

Government intervention, in other words, whether to underpin the liquidity of the financial sector or to stimulate demand in the real economy, is certainly necessary if recovery is to be hastened, but it is – importantly – more than a singular response to a singular problem. It is a statement of a wider and ever-present relationship between governments and markets. Markets function best – indeed, only function properly at all – if government is ready and willing to second-guess and lean against market outcomes. What is required of governments to save and support financial markets in a recession is equally required, in differing ways, if markets across the whole economy are to function properly.

There are, of course, those who would at this point throw up their hands in horror. For them, the debate is about absolutes. According to such people, there is only one alternative to the unfettered market and that is state-directed economic centralism. They do not see that to recognise and correct the deficiencies of the market is the best guarantee that a market economy can sustain itself efficiently and beneficially.

A perverse response

What has been extraordinary, if not unexpected, in the aftermath of the global financial crisis has been the speed with which most of the world's most powerful leaders headed back to familiar territory – not to say, political prejudices – and not only embraced again the very nostrums that had brought about the global financial crisis in the first place but used the crisis as an excuse to press for a smaller state and a decimated public sector, even though that threatens a renewed dip into recession.

So, we find that right across the western world, the prime focus of governments has been to cut public spending, as though it was excessive government spending rather than the failure of financial markets that had caused the crisis of 2008. There is, as a result of the irresponsibility of those engaged in those markets, a real problem of indebtedness, but it is perverse to draw the conclusion that retrenchment by governments is the right response. To reach that conclusion represents a triumph of ideology over common sense.

But, say the 'deficit hawks', the deficit needs to be funded, and the money markets will lend for that purpose only if they see strenuous efforts to get the deficit down. But this is to allow prejudice – a visceral dislike of public spending per se – to displace rationality. As Paul Krugman points out, our policymakers run scared of the bond vigilantes on the one hand and seem on the other to have a naïve belief that the confidence fairy will somehow convert policies that are intended to produce retrenchment into a recipe for recovery. And, since it was only very recently that the financial sector was totally dependent on public finance for its very survival, how is it that their fantasies are again so soon able to dictate terms to the rest of us?

This has not deterred governments from countries as far apart as the UK and New Zealand from identifying a political goal – a reduction in the size of government – in preference to the economic goal of recovering from recession. Even those, for example the American and Australian governments, that have been more sympathetic to putting recovery first have been deterred by the force of the political pressure mounted by their opponents from implementing full-scale recovery programmes.

The success of the right in this regard has been particularly significant in the USA. Unable to secure enough popular support to prevail in elections, they have used their power in the media to shape and to a large extent control the debate. The techniques they have employed have been effectively analysed by Thomas Frank in his recent book *Pity The Billionaire*.[4] He lays bare the stratagems, the tricks, the lies that, at a time when public opinion might have been expected to revolt against the manifest failure of the unregulated market, have persuaded many Americans that it is the private entrepreneur who is the victim and the regulator the criminal.

He describes the skill, ruthlessness and sheer willingness to exploit human weakness demonstrated by those who have manipulated opinion so successfully. Glenn Beck and Rush Limbaugh, luminaries of the American extreme right, are – he argues – prime examples of the hugely influential commentators who, through their radio and television shows, fan the distortions and hatreds that shape large swathes of American opinion.

The doctrines developed and espoused by another luminary of the right, Ayn Rand, received a sudden new prominence through the selection of Paul Ryan as the Republican vice-presidential candidate in 2012. Ryan is a self-avowed devotee of Rand, and in particular of her best-known work *Atlas Shrugged*. The novel is in one sense little more than a Boy's Own fantasy of an individual hero standing up against the forces of evil, but it also attempts to convey a serious political message (at great length and tediousness) that the successful individual is all that matters, and that other entities – governmental and social – and less successful people (whom the author derides as 'moochers') should not be allowed to restrain the freedom of the successful. It is astonishing that such a poorly written and poorly imagined piece of fiction should now be treated by some serious political figures as a guide to a successful future.

It is not just in the macroeconomic context that the extreme right has tried and often succeeded in denigrating the concept of government. They have had similar success in attacking and limiting the role of the public sector and of public service in maintaining standards of health delivery and education, which have become even more important to populations at a time of recessionary cutbacks.

A telling example of such an attack was highlighted by Dr Gabriel Scally, a senior NHS doctor in the UK.[5] In announcing his retirement from the NHS, he gave as his reason that the reorganisation of the NHS planned by the British government was, he believed, part of a planned enfeebling by the government of public services generally. He was quoted as saying that, 'I think there's a very deliberate policy across all of the public sector to roll back the achievements that have been made in this country since the Second World War, including the NHS, and that financial austerity is being used to pursue an agenda aimed at dismantling the state.'

This is not the only assault made by the current British government on the fundamental concept of a national health service. Under the government's franchise plan for the NHS, shareholders and equity investors will use the service's logo as a Trojan horse to prise open the budgets of other countries' health systems, but prospective customers will be buying neither NHS services nor the NHS model of care. How has this happened?

Since 1948, the British National Health Service has been the model for universal healthcare that is free at the point of use and available on the basis of need. In 2012, the British parliament effectively ended the NHS by abolishing the government's sixty-year-old duty to secure and provide healthcare for all. From 2013, there will be no NHS in England, and tax funding will increasingly flow to global healthcare corporations (though, in contrast, Scotland and Wales will continue to have a publicly accountable national health service).

NHS hospitals and services are being sold off or incorporated; land and buildings are being turned over to bankers and equity investors. Private companies, often with little or no experience of delivering health care, are taking billions from taxpayer funds for leasing out and part-operating PFI hospitals, community clinics and GP surgeries that were once publicly owned.

Strangled by PFI debts and funding cuts, NHS foundation trusts have compounded their problems by entering into joint ventures. A process that began in 1990 with the introduction of the internal market and accelerated under the PFI programme now takes the form of franchising, management buyout and corporate takeovers of public hospitals. There is no public accountability. Commercial contracts are redacted so that crucial financial information is not in the public domain, and is withheld on the grounds of commercial confidentiality.

The belief that markets distribute resources more efficiently is the basis of changes in which the UK led the way, starting with gas, water, telecoms and railways. By 2004, the whole of Whitehall was committed to putting corporations in control of what had formerly been publicly administered services. Now that it is the turn of the NHS, the loss of public control will mean higher cost and fewer services. The American corporations which are now part of England's new healthcare market, and helped design it, will mean that billing, invoicing, marketing and advertising will add greatly to administrative costs, compared with the low level of just 6 per cent in the former (and much-maligned) NHS bureaucracy.

One shocking and unwelcome outcome of these changes can be seen in the report by Robert Francis QC and published in February 2013, following his inquiry into the scandalous failures of the Mid-Staffs hospital.[6] The report found that the Department of Health had 'put cash over patient care', and that this was the principal cause of the unnecessary deaths of up to 1,200 patients. The report, which is likely to be followed by further inquiries into similar failures at other hospitals, made a total of 290 recommendations and pointed the finger at local health authorities and the trust board – but did not blame any one individual or organisation for the 'disaster' at the hospital. Sir David Nicholson, who was in charge of the local strategic health authority for Stafford between 2003 and 2006, and is now Chief Executive of the NHS, admitted that the 'whole system' failed patients at the hospital, but remains in post.

Throughout the western world, and despite the obvious failures of unregulated markets, private ownership and the profit motive are still regarded as the best guarantors of economic efficiency. So, a country such as New Zealand, consistently with the commitment of successive governments to the 'free market' as the driver of economic efficiency, has persisted with a twenty-five-year history of privatisation. Like so much else in the neo-liberal agenda, repeated privatisations have done little to raise the level of performance, and in all too many cases privatisation has meant only profit-gouging by private owners, who have then sold back the enterprises – inadequately invested and saddled with debt – into public ownership. Both the New Zealand railway system and the New Zealand national airline are cases in point.

There are further lessons to be learned. For example, we should surely now recognise that fiscal policy is, for most purposes, more effective than monetary policy – most importantly, in times of recession. We have been told for decades that monetary policy is all that is necessary, and indeed all that is effective, both in controlling inflation and in setting the real economy on a sustainable course. But we now know that using monetary policy to ward off or recover from recession is no more effective than pushing on a piece of string. This is surely the lesson to be learned from our experience with quantitative easing, which has been helpful up to a point but which has done little to stimulate the economy in the way that a fiscal stimulus can.

This lesson from practical experience (and from Keynesian analysis) is being learned – painfully and slowly – but will continue to be resisted by those who are unwilling to admit that it is not the banks, as the agents of monetary policy, but governments, as the initiators of fiscal policy, who hold the key to recovery, and who must act if we are to hasten the end of recession.

There are lessons to be learned on the global scale as well. We now know that gross imbalances in the world economy are likely to make it topple off the high wire. The growing gap between rich and poor nations is bad enough from a moral viewpoint. But the imbalance between surplus and deficit countries is equally damaging as a strictly economic phenomenon. The surpluses drive us toward recession because they represent resources that are hoarded rather than spent, while those countries with deficits are likely, as Keynes pointed out, to try to control them through deflating their economies, thereby reinforcing the deflationary bias. To the extent that others are willing to finance the deficits (as, for example, China's financing of the American deficit), this simply encourages uneconomic production and an excessive reliance on credit in the deficit country, meaning that the world economy wobbles perilously on an unsustainable foundation.

A related lesson is that the freedom to move capital at will around the world has exacted a heavy price. The total removal of exchange controls, as we have seen, meant that international investors could ignore and, if necessary, blackmail national governments; this became a major factor in allowing market operators to escape and defy any attempt at regulatory controls. We have to make up our minds whether we trust accountable governments, with all their imperfections, or the unrestrained and totally irresponsible market. Our recent experience surely makes this a no-brainer. What we now need is a new international regime, negotiated between governments, to regulate exchange rate volatility, international lending practices and the obligations of international investors.

The successful resistance to the Multilateral Agreement on Investment (the MAI) in 1998 was a natural response to the attempt to commit governments across the globe to what was in effect a blueprint for guaranteeing the rights of international investors to do as they pleased, whatever national governments might think. But that experience should not close our minds to the possibility of an international agreement that would address a different and more beneficial purpose – regulating the activities of foreign investors so as to protect the interests of national governments and peoples.

Is it not clear that we need new forms of international cooperation to restrain the irresponsible and excessive flows of 'hot' money and the volatility of exchange rates, to provide better prudential supervision of international lending and to require greater responsibility of international investors to the communities in which they invest?

Chapter 13

Our Leaders Are Ignorant of How Our Economy Works

Where does money come from?

One of the most startling aspects of our recent economic history has been the revelation that those who control our economy know so little about how it actually works. In particular, it seems that, even though they run a monetarist macroeconomic policy that focuses exclusively on money, they are almost completely ignorant of what money is or where it comes from.

This is despite the fact that our recent experience has demonstrated conclusively that it is governments in the end, not banks, who are the funders of last resort and who therefore stand behind and underpin the value of money. If there was ever any doubt about this, it must surely have been put to rest by the collapse of the banks in many parts of the world, and the taxpayer-funded bail-outs that governments have had to organise. Why, then, are political leaders still so reluctant to recognise that is they, not the banks, who must ensure the stability of our financial system?

The reason is that they are still prisoners of the same intellectual straitjacket that created the crisis in the first place. Despite all the evidence to the contrary, they are still convinced that the major decisions in the economy should be taken by banks – or the private sector more generally – rather than governments. Even when they have spent billions on bail-outs, and the billions have disappeared into the banks' balance sheets, they still somehow expect that the banks' self-interested pursuit of their shareholders' interests will revive the economy as a whole.

Old habits die hard. Privately owned banks have been allowed to develop a virtual monopoly of credit creation for more than 200 years. It is such a familiar feature of our landscape that it has been scarcely remarked, even when bank credit became by far the most significant element in the rapid growth of the money supply – and therefore the greatest factor in inflation. The banks' impact on monetary policy, and the exclusive focus on that monetary policy, was itself a huge abdication of responsibility in favour of private interests. But just to make absolutely sure that the banks would not only monopolise credit creation but would also control monetary policy itself, governments surrendered the task they had been elected to fulfil by handing monetary policy over to an 'independent' central bank.

Our politicians are still at it. We are told that we must give the banks some 'breathing space'. That is after they have walked away with billions of our money. It does not seem to have occurred to our political leaders that it was not the interests of bank shareholders and the survival of banks as institutions that mattered. The focus of policy should have been first the security of deposits, second the maintenance of an appropriate liquidity and flow of credit in the economy as a whole, and third a rethinking of whether the banking function should remain a private monopoly or should be seen properly as a public responsibility – as, de facto, it has become. If governments – for which read society as a whole – have had to put up the money, why should we not call the shots?

But while the banks have skated through the global financial crisis and its aftermath without conceding any of their privileges, the tribulations of banks worldwide have made it inevitable that their role in the global economy should increasingly come under the spotlight. The continued exercise by the banks – irresponsibly and at times dishonestly – of an inappropriately unaccountable power, and their failure to learn any lessons from their fall from grace, means that they have done little to avoid such scrutiny.

The revelations that many of the world's leading banks have been guilty of dishonestly rigging markets and misleading investors have already claimed one victim, in Barclay's Bank, and seem likely to involve many more. Not surprisingly, the British government is establishing a full-scale review of the banking sector, and few would now bet against the pressing of criminal charges. But it could be argued that these scandals are not just a reflection of the criminality of a handful of bank leaders but arise inevitably from the role that banks in general have been allowed to play.

Most people still see banks essentially as institutions that provide a safe repository for our savings and from time to time lend us money either on overdraft or on mortgage. But this is seriously to underestimate the power that banks wield in our economy, and the extraordinary nature of the concessions that allow them to do so.

The central feature of banks, which seems only dimly understood even within the banking sector itself, is that they are private commercial enterprises which have been granted a unique and virtual monopoly over the creation of money. By far the largest proportion of the money in the economies of all advanced countries is not notes and coins but bank-created credit. That credit represents no more than bank entries by bank officials; its status as money rests entirely on the suspension of disbelief – or, to put it another way, on our willingness to accept that it is money because the banks say it is money.

The mechanism by which this is brought, though seemingly a mystery even to many bankers, has over recent times been well analysed by an increasing number of campaigners who are determined to lay bare the role that banks have been allowed to play in our economy. A good example of the detail and rigour of that analysis is the submission made in 2011 to the Independent Commission on Banking by Professor Richard Werner of Southampton University, Ben Dyson of Positive Money, and Tony Greenham and Josh Ryan-Collins of the New Economics Foundation.[1]

In that submission, what the submitters term 'fractional reserve banking' is identified as a principal cause of the difficulties that the banking sector has inflicted on the economy as a whole.[2] The key feature of fractional reserve banking, they explain, is that banks in creating credit effectively create new money in the form of new bank deposits. They point out that this is not a new revelation. As the Bank of England's 2007 Q3 Quarterly Bulletin put it, 'When the banks make loans they create additional deposits for those that have borrowed the money.' The Governor of the Bank of England, Mervyn King has been equally direct in conceding that banks create credit and therefore money on a huge scale.

In a 2012 report entitled *Banking Vs Democracy*,[3] the campaigning group Positive Money argues that the banking system has more spending power than the democratically elected government, yet has no accountability to anyone. The government has simply surrendered one of its most important powers, the power to create money and control the money supply, to private commercial firms – which have ruthlessly exploited their power in their own interests.

Banks create this money without regard to how much is needed for the economy and society as a whole to operate effectively, and they put over 90 per cent of this money towards non-productive activities that do not contribute to the growth of the economy; virtually no attempt is made by governments or anyone else to ensure that much of this money goes into productive investment. It is this power to create money that causes inflation and insidiously transfers wealth from savers and those who hold their wealth in cash (that is, the poor and those on medium incomes) to those who are rich enough to hold their wealth in other assets (such as property and financial assets). The banks' monopolistic power to create money also means that whenever additional money is needed in the economy only private banks can provide it (other than in those extreme situations when governments 'print money' and are roundly criticised for doing so). In effect, virtually the entire money supply must be rented from the banking sector, at great cost to the economy and to individual people and businesses.

This unprecedented gift of huge economic and commercial power to private interests at no cost is bad enough, but there are other major costs as well. Society may now be acutely aware of the direct cost to the taxpayer of bailing out banks, but less is known about the subsidies and other concessions they receive. First, because of both implicit and explicit government guarantees, banks are able to borrow money at an interest rate lower than would otherwise be possible. Second, by giving up the power to create money (at least in most circumstances), governments forgo an important source of revenue, which results in higher taxes, lower spending or a bigger national debt than would otherwise be the case. Conversely, the banks benefit financially from the power to create money, and make huge profits for themselves and their shareholders as a result. These hidden subsidies more than outweigh any taxes paid by the banks.

Unlike pension funds and other holders of the public's savings, banks are not required to disclose how they will use their customers' money. For example, as 97 per cent of the money supply in the UK is effectively held with banks, the economy is shaped by the investment priorities of the banking sector, rather than the priorities of society. Just five banks hold 85 per cent of the country's money, and these five banks are steered by just seventy-eight board members whose decisions decide the directions taken by the British economy.

The banks' power does not arise by accident. Lobbying is, of course, a fact of political life across the board, but it is clear that the resources of banking sector lobbyists far exceed those from other sectors and therefore are likely to weigh disproportionately with political leaders. This may well explain the easy ride and relative freedom from effective regulation that the banks have enjoyed in the UK and elsewhere.

The close relationship between the banking sector and its regulators should be a cause for concern, especially given the record of the last few years. The UK's Financial Services Authority sat on its hands while the City's excesses became increasingly corrupt and criminal – not entirely surprising, since the FSA is funded by the banks themselves, a prime example of self-regulation and its inadequacies. And, it should be noted, the revolving door between the banks and their regulators turns very fast: one of those who passed effortlessly through it was a former prime minister, Tony Blair, who now consults for one of the world's largest investment banks at a salary approximately twelve times more than he earned as prime minister.

A few economically simple changes to the banking system, Positive Money argues, would restore some level of democratic control over the economy. They recommend that banks should be required to ask for permission from their customers before they lend out their money and to disclose how that money will be invested, so that members of the public can refuse to fund activities of which they do not approve. And they recommend that the power to create money should be removed from the banks and returned to a democratically accountable body.

Views similar to this are increasingly respected and shared by well-regarded commentators who have not in the past had much time for this kind of analysis. The *Financial Times*, for example, recently published an excellent article by Martin Wolf, the influential chief economics commentator of the FT and member of the Independent Commission on Banking in 2010–11.[4] Martin Wolf is quite explicit in his conclusion. 'The job of managing money needs to be delegated to an independent institution,' he says – that is, taken out of the hands of the banks.

In describing the banks' ability to create new money, he says that the central bank alone can guarantee the 'moneyness' of the public's bank deposits. The commercial banks cannot do so because, as he acknowledges, most of the money they create is not based on actual deposits – a factor that has increased in significance as a result of quantitative easing. He then asks why there should be objection, in principle, to the creation of money by the central bank rather than by private banks, and concludes that the job of managing money should be delegated to an independent institution, albeit one that cooperates in times of crisis with private institutions.

Here, in other words, is a call by one of the most respected commentators that the exclusive power to create money should be removed from the hands of the banks and made more accountable. Similar comments have been made in the *Independent* and even *The Economist*. Indeed, an unnamed journalist at *The Economist* explains how there has been 'a massive burst of credit creation. Total credit in the American economy passed $1 trillion in 1964; by 2007, it had exceeded $50 trillion.'[5]

The writer goes on to make the point that this 'massive burst of credit creation' was really an explosion in the money supply, as a result of money creation by banks when they make loans. This rising money supply goes hand in hand with a rising mountain of debt, and so 'this debt explosion showed up not in consumer prices but in asset prices, notably in property. The cycle was self-reinforcing: banks lent money to people to buy property, causing prices to rise, making banks more willing to lend, and so on.'

As a number of economists have pointed out, the famous Fisher equation, which explains the relationship between money supply and prices (MV=PT), should now be changed by replacing M, money supply, with C, for credit supply. Credit is now, after all, used for over 99 per cent by value of all transactions; those who rail against the creation of a few hundred billion through quantitative easing in the UK completely ignore the creation of over £2 trillion of credit money by the high-street banks, largely for non-productive purposes. As Professor Richard Werner points out, most of the money and credit that is created is now used for financial transactions and purchasing financial assets (including property), rather than actually trading in the real economy.

One of the most surprising, and encouraging, developments in this area in recent times was the publication by the IMF in August 2012 of a paper called 'The Chicago Plan Revisited'.[6] The Chicago Plan was a proposal at the height of the Great Depression from a number of economists, including Irving Fisher, that recommended the separation of the monetary and credit functions of the banking system, by requiring 100 per cent reserve backing for deposits.

Irving Fisher claimed in 1936 that this proposal would provide much better control of what he saw as a major source of business cycle fluctuations, the sudden increases and contractions of bank credit and of bank-created money. It would, he argued, eliminate bank runs, dramatically reduce public debt and at the same time reduce private debt, since money creation would no longer require simultaneous debt creation.

The authors of the IMF paper reported, as they concluded their study, that they supported all of Fisher's claims. They went further:

> by validating these claims in a rigorous, microfounded model, we
> were able to establish that the advantages of the Chicago Plan go

even beyond those identified by Fisher ... One additional advantage is large steady state output gains due to the removal or reduction of multiple distortions, including interest rate risk spreads, distortionary taxes, and costly monitoring of macroeconomically unnecessary credit risks. Another advantage is the ability to drive steady state inflation to zero in an environment where liquidity traps do not exist ... This ability to generate and live with zero steady state inflation is an important result, because it answers the somewhat confused claim of opponents of an exclusive government monopoly on money issuance, namely that such a monetary system would be highly inflationary. There is nothing in our theoretical framework to support this claim. And ... there is very little in the monetary history of ancient societies and western nations to support it either.[7]

One further instance of a growing acceptance that reform is necessary is the review of the structure of EU banking carried out in 2012 by an expert committee chaired by Erkki Liikanen, governor of Finland's central bank.[8] The Liikanen report suggests the ring-fencing of the trading activities of banks so that proprietary trading and either assets or derivative positions incurred in market-making would be assigned to separate legal entities. The report argues that 'the specific objectives of separation are to ... limit a banking group's incentives and ability to take excessive risks with insured deposits' and to 'prevent the coverage of losses incurred in the trading entity by the funds of the deposit bank, and hence limit the liability of taxpayer and the deposit insurance system'. This and related recommendations echo similar conclusions reached on these points by the UK's Independent Commission on Banking, of which Martin Wolf was a member.[9]

Irresponsible banking

Support of this kind for the reform of the monetary and banking systems could and should mean a total reappraisal of the role played by banks and their ability to create money. The current failure to understand this fundamental aspect of our economy leads to serious errors in formulating economic policy. The overwhelming role of credit-creation by the banks in inflating the money supply should be our central concern in controlling inflation, particularly when the vast majority of that credit is created and lent for non-productive purposes, such as house purchase.

Because we don't understand this inflation-engendering pheno-menon, we grapple with inflation using seriously inadequate and inappropriate instruments such as interest rates, which are not only slow-acting and poorly focused but do great damage to the rest of the economy. A more accurate analysis of inflation-producing pressures in our economy would lead to more effective measures to restrain them and at the same time encourage a more productive and competitive economy.

But it is not only this aspect of the banks' operations that should cause concern. Over the last two or three decades, the banks have used their ability to create money to invent a whole range of new financial instruments of dubious value which they are then able to sell to gullible investors; so profitable was this trade that it became much more important to banks than their traditional role.

One of the most extreme forms of this casino capitalism is what is described as high-frequency trading (HFT) – the use of complex computer systems that spot market patterns, buy millions of shares and hold them for micro-seconds before selling them on. These techniques, in the wake of the global financial crisis, have attracted heavy criticism, in the American Senate, in the Australian stock exchange, whose head denounced them as 'inherently dangerous', and in the European Parliament, where plans to impose severe regulation of such activities have been introduced.

These criticisms have, however, been rejected by the British Treasury and the City of London. The reasons are not hard to find. HFT gene-rates huge profits for financiers and stock exchanges. The price paid, however, is substantial instability and risk of failure. But HFT also reveals a deeper problem: the extreme short-termism of financial markets, and the priority given to trading rather than investment and jobs.

John Kay's report, published in July 2012, was scathing about these aspects of City culture, but attempts at reform are likely to be frustrated by lobbying from finance.[10] A majority of the members of a 'high-level stakeholder group' – one of the two panels advising the Treasury on the issue – have links to the HFT industry. Those lobbyists represent a bias inherent in the merchant-style capitalism that has dominated British policy for centuries – a preference for short-term profit over long-term investment in real productive capacity.

It was the prospect of unlimited profits created out of nothing (to say nothing of the huge rewards and bonuses paid to individual bankers) that led in due course to the global financial crisis. And when that irresponsibility inevitably ended in collapse, it was that same mentality that led bankers into the realms of fraud and criminality. In a world where anything goes, the rules are made to be broken and personal fortunes are there for the taking, who can wonder that bankers could not accept that the ordinary rules applied to them? We have reaped what we have sown.

Following the revelations that Barclays Bank, and almost certainly other leading banks, had conspired to rig the Libor rate, which sets interest rates in large parts of the world, evidence has now emerged that HSBC and Standard and Chartered have been involved in money-laundering on a massive scale. This aid provided to criminals, drug traffickers, sanctions-busters and possibly terrorists should not perhaps surprise us, coming as it does on top of a charge sheet that includes, as Charles Ferguson pointed out, 'selling defective mortgage securities during the housing bubble; creating and selling securities to bet on their failure, bringing the world to the brink of collapse; colluding to manipulate interest rates; hyping your failing company while secretly selling your own stock; cooking the books, and assisting fraudsters like Bernard Madoff'.[11]

Will Hutton was equally condemnatory.[12] He describes investment banking as 'an organised scam masquerading as a business'. He accuses its practitioners of systemic amoral behaviour and extreme avarice, and declares that if the regulators had done their jobs properly many of them would be serving prison sentences or otherwise disgraced. He describes their activities as 'a tax on wealth generation – the beast that is devouring British capitalism'.

He makes the point that, so focused are City managers on their own extravagant bonuses, that they do not have the time or inclination to monitor the real-time positions, measured sometimes in seconds, that are taken by underlings, with the result that rogue traders can lose banks billions, as has happened on more than one occasion.

We need to pinch ourselves to remember that the targets of these excoriating condemnations – people who have committed fraudulent and probably criminal acts which must be punished and prosecuted – are those who until recently were regarded as the leading figures in the global economy, people whose judgements could in no way be questioned. These were the people who proclaimed that the unregulated market delivered the best of all possible worlds, who declared that there was no alternative, who congratulated themselves on discovering the secret of unlimited wealth, who enjoyed the adulation of political leaders and governments, and who stuffed their own mouths with gold.

Even since 2008, the charade has continued. The attempt has been made to persuade politicians and public opinion alike that lessons have been learned, and that effective regulation at the international level is now being put in place. But, as a report from Andrew Haldane of the Bank of England has shown,[13] the principal measure of bank resilience prescribed for and by regulators around the world – the capital ratios calculated according to principles laid down by the Basel Committee on Banking Supervision – have no value whatever in predicting the probability that a bank will fail, and therefore provide no opportunity for averting such an outcome. On the other hand, Haldane found, a simple measure of the bank's leverage ratio – the relationship between a bank's core capital and its total assets – would provide such guidance.

As John Kay pointed out in the *Financial Times* on 11 September 2012,[14] the most likely explanation of this is to be found in Goodhart's law. This proposition was first set out in the 1970s by the economist Charles Goodhart, and provides that any measure adopted as a target loses the ability to regulate behaviour, since people change their behaviour to meet the target. That is why the risk-weighted measure of Basel, which is a regulatory target, proved to be less reliable than the leverage ratio, which is not. The Basel arrangement simply stimulates the creation by the banks of instruments that transfer assets from one risk category to another; it encourages them, in other words, to reverse-engineer products to meet the demands of rating agency models.

The British government claims that the dangers arising from risky speculation by banks will be curbed by requiring the separation of investment banking from retail activities. But, while this would be a useful reform, it would be quite inadequate to deal with the problem. Barclays, a single bank, holds a derivatives portfolio of about £43 trillion, about thirteen times the size of the British GDP. Even a small fall of about 4 per cent in the face value of that portfolio would wipe out Barclays' total capital.

Prem Sikka explains the limitations of the policy and what more needs to be done.[15] He argues that, even after separation, investment banks will continue to apply to speculative activities the funds they obtain from retail banks, pension funds and insurance companies. They will continue to shelter behind limited liability so as to leave innocent bystanders with any losses. Separating retail from speculative operations will work only if unlimited liability for investment banking is ended, so that those who take excessive risks bear full liability for their mistakes.

We can see that calls for the separation of the banks' retail activities from their own investment business are now coming thick and fast. One of the most startling aspects and consequences of the current intermingling of these quite separate activities comes in the form of proposals from a range of banking authorities across the world for settling in advance the question of who should bear which liabilities in the event of a banking collapse – whether of a single bank or on a much wider scale.

A good example of such proposals is the 'Open Bank Resolution' currently being proposed by the Reserve Bank of New Zealand. As the Reserve Bank explains, the current options in the event of a bank failure are limited – liquidation, government bail-out or takeover by another entity. The post-global financial crisis history of the impact on government finances of bailing out failed banks has obviously reduced the appetite for such operations in future, and in most such cases there will not be a long queue of institutions willing to take over the failed entity.

Liquidation, however, would immediately threaten the security of customers' deposits – a political risk that governments would be reluctant to take. The Reserve Bank argues that in these circumstances the main priority would be to keep the failed bank afloat and functioning. They therefore propose that the failed bank should close for just twenty-four hours while a statutory manager is appointed and an assessment made of the bank's financial position. A calculation should be made of the proportion of customers' deposits with the bank that would be needed to cover the bank's liabilities, and that proportion should then be frozen. The bank would then re-open, but the frozen deposits would be retained for the statutory manager's use so that the bank's financial situation would be stabilised. Any unused portion of the deposits could then be returned to the depositors. Similar processes would be applied to shareholdings in the bank.

This proposal that depositors should take what is popularly called a 'haircut' may make sense as a measure to protect the bank and ensure its survival; but it is nevertheless an astonishing assault both on the property rights of depositors and on confidence in the banking system, and it arises entirely because banks are entitled to use their customers' deposits for their own trading purposes. Other authorities around the world, including – according to some reports – the EC, are apparently contemplating similar measures.

There can surely be no stronger instance of the case for urgent and fundamental reform.

I view the whole post-global financial crisis scenario as one of chickens coming home to roost. In 1986, I led for the Opposition in the British House of Commons when the Financial Services Bill was in committee. I warned throughout those lengthy proceedings and the detailed scrutiny of the legislation that self-regulation of financial markets and institutions was extremely dangerous and would not work. Twenty-seven years later, we have seen the consequences of ignoring that advice. Effective regulation of the banking function must now be a priority. For the future, investment banking should be totally separated from commercial or retail banking, and the banks' monopoly of the creation of credit must be ended.

Chapter 14

The Role of the Media

We have become familiar over recent decades with the power wielded by those popularly (or perhaps unpopularly) known as the media barons – those who control the press and broadcast media. We are now adjusting to the development of new forms of media, the internet, social media and electronic communications more generally, and the huge influence that they wield over individual lives and social organisation. The power of those who own and direct these media of communication, old and new – not least over the political debate – is immense. The fact that much of what is generally known as 'the media' is in the hands of the same people who dominate the global economy and who have sidelined democracy is, and should be, of great concern.

The influence of the media over the political debate has long been a cause for concern. While voices are occasionally raised to deny that this influence exists, most people – both within the media and beyond – concede that the attempt to sway the voters is made and is effective. In countries where there is no free press, of course, the influence is clear and direct. Dictators have always found that control over the media is an important aid to gaining power and an equally important aid to retaining it. They are not mistaken.

In democracies, it is no less true that control of the media is an important, if not actually decisive, element in the achieving and maintaining of power. The media's ability to influence political outcomes is scarcely denied and is sometimes, occasionally notoriously, even celebrated. It was the Murdoch-owned newspaper *The Sun* that famously proclaimed, on the morning after the Tory victory in the 1992 general election in the UK, that 'It was the Sun wot won it!' It is perhaps surprising that a similarly blatant claim was not made by the Murdoch-owned Fox News for the role it played in the re-election of George Bush.

The journalist Martin Linton published a study of the impact of the Murdoch press on voting patterns in the 1992 election, in which he argues that the voting intentions of readers of *The Sun* were significantly influenced by the political line then taken by the newspaper.[1] While these findings have been treated with some scepticism (sometimes for fear that it will play into the hands of the right-wing press and induce progressive politicians to become even more accommodating to the media barons), it is not surprising that the deliberate slanting of news reporting and of political messages should have their effect. If they did not, it would be unlikely that the media would spend so much time and effort on a futile exercise, and it would no doubt also attract the critical attention of those advertisers who spend billions with those self-same media.

Politicians of the left have long been resigned to fighting the political battle with the odds stacked against them by virtue of the right-wing (and sometimes quite overt) bias of much of the media. My own experience as the director of the Labour election campaign in 1987 bears this out. The Labour campaign, which surprised many commentators by its professionalism and effectiveness, was nevertheless handicapped by comparison with its Tory rivals – as I observed at the time – by the fact that my counterpart, Norman Tebbitt, was able to launch any news story of his choice, particularly in the last week of the campaign, by making a couple of phone calls to sympathetic editors in Fleet Street.

Owning mass-circulation newspapers and television channels is expensive and is therefore inevitably the preserve of 'big business'. The proprietors of these media, while sometimes exerting pressure surreptitiously, are unlikely to allow these outlets to express views either directly or indirectly (through the slant placed on news reporting) that are at variance with their own. No one should be surprised, therefore, that the media on the whole reflect the essentially pro-business and pro-vested interest views of their proprietors.

There was a brief moment when the advent of new (and, it was expected, cheaper) technology offered the hope that the press at any rate would become accessible to those with little capital, and that a rash of small-circulation papers would help to offset the influence of the mass-circulation giants. Those hopes have proved to be misplaced. There has indeed been a proliferation of titles, but many of them are absorbed almost immediately into the large conglomerations, and few of those that remain can hope to match the power of the media moguls.

The importance of television in our lives was at one point thought to offer hope that the power of the press barons would be offset by a range of different views presented on the screen. The fate of public service broadcasting in most countries and the powerful position acquired by private owners such as Murdoch (or in Australia, say, a Packer), however, has dashed these hopes; the television channels are just as likely to present the financial establishment view as the major newspapers, since their owners are in many cases the very same people.

Similar hopes are again held for the spread of the internet and social media, which are seen as alternative outlets for views that may differ from those of the media establishment. The internet does indeed offer the prospect of views other than the orthodox, and those enjoined by the powerful, gaining currency and being disseminated. The use of the internet during recent elections in the western world has allowed the expression of views on a substantial scale that did considerably more than reflect the tightly controlled debate sanctioned by the party machines. There is undoubtedly more to come by way of using this resource to free up the political debate.

It is right, too, to salute the role of these new media in arousing public awareness and allowing political opposition to be organised against repressive regimes; the 'Arab spring' owes much to these means of communication, which have proved difficult for dictatorships to bring under control. But we should also recognise that in a country such as China the internet is on a much shorter and more effectively restrictive leash.

Moreover, in terms of its ownership and control the internet is not as diverse as it may seem, and is therefore less likely than its supporters hope to provide diversity in generating news and information. The process of merger and takeover, leading to the concentration of ownership that is such a feature of the global economy, is equally marked in the case of the press, and now of media and internet companies. And it is now beyond doubt that the major operators in this new world of modern communications, sadly and perhaps inevitably, are the new giants of global communications – Google, Facebook, Apple, Amazon, Microsoft and others. Perhaps despite themselves, their interests as major global operators and those of their major shareholders will be reflected in the way they behave and in the view of the world they present.

Whatever hope may be held for the internet, there are apparently inexorable trends in the opposite direction in almost all developed countries. Democratic governments have on the whole expressed unease about these trends towards the concentration of media ownership and the tolerance of cross-media ownership, but none has summoned up the political will or power to do much about it.

This is not surprising. Multinational media companies are for this purpose just a subset of multinational corporations as a whole. Governments that find it impossible to resist the demands of inter-national investors in general are hardly likely suddenly to discover the courage to stand up to that particular group of international investors who have the power to destroy them through their ability to manipulate public opinion.

As the inexorable process towards concentrating power in a few hands continues, it ensures that rival or different viewpoints are choked off and excluded. Not only this, but such is the profitability of the new multinational media that they have available financial resource on such a massive and growing scale that their dominance can no longer be challenged. The newest forms of media are immensely capital-intensive. A new digital, satellite-based broadcasting platform might take years of losses before the capital cost is eventually repaid and the owners move into profitability. Only the very richest and most powerful international capitalists can afford such an investment.

New Zealand again offers an instructive example. Sky Television, a Murdoch-owned pay-for-view digital television broadcaster, spent seven years chalking up large losses as it invested in the programming required to sustain dozens of channels. It has now succeeded in signing up nearly 60 per cent of viewers and, with an advertising revenue to match, is generating substantial profits. These enable it to use its resources to outbid other broadcasters for the most popular programmes – something whose effectiveness it had already demonstrated, even when a loss-maker, by outbidding everyone else for the hugely popular broadcasting of Super and Test rugby.

The writing on the wall was then clear for the free-to-air broadcasters, and particularly for Television New Zealand (on whose board I served for six years), a publicly owned broadcaster with public service broadcasting obligations incorporated in a government-sponsored charter. A new government, led by avowed devotees of the 'free market', inevitably meant that the charter was dispensed with, and funding for the one remaining public service channel was withdrawn. With the abandonment of any commitment to even the last remnant of a public service broadcasting responsibility, there is now no compelling reason for resisting what seems to be the inevitable privatisation of Television New Zealand.

Now, with huge subscription and advertising revenue in the hands of Sky Television, it is game over. Sky Television is totally dominant, and viewers have had to accept that they must now pay, through both subscriptions and advertising, for much of the programming they want to watch.

This triumph for powerful media interests, at the expense of public service broadcasting, was ushered in by right-wing governments but had also been nodded through by governments of a supposedly more progressive disposition. No New Zealand government had the inclination, let alone the courage, to deny Rupert Murdoch the dominance he and his allies sought. There was no interest, for example, in passing anti-siphoning legislation, which has been widely used elsewhere to prevent dominant media interests from cornering the market in particularly popular programming such as sports coverage, so that they can drive viewers into their net.

To their credit, British governments have shown marginally more backbone, at least (and until recently) in the defence of the most prestigious of all public broadcasters, the BBC, on which News International, the Murdoch vehicle, has mounted a determined attack. Not content with a predictable commercial assault on the BBC's strength with audiences in the marketplace, Murdoch newspapers have done all they can to undermine the reputation and prestige of the BBC as a preliminary to using political influence to remove what they see as the BBC's public funding advantage.

It is not a surprise that the existence of public-service broadcasters in both the UK and New Zealand that are not directly obliged to bow to market forces has been seen as a challenge and threat by private-sector media moguls. The mere existence of successful and influential mass broadcasters that do not feel compelled to endorse market values at every turn is one of the few instances where the values of the global economy and marketplace can be challenged, if not directly at least by offering an alternative view and example. It is instructive, however, that both the BBC and TVNZ have shown a marked tendency to respond to commercial pressures by aping their commercial rivals to a considerable degree.

Consequently, no one should hold their breath if it is hoped that national rules might limit cross-media or foreign ownership, or limit 'siphoning', or provide staunch political and financial support for public broadcasters that are under ferocious attack. The global economy means that national governments will have little incentive to take such risks. Yet, if they are not taken, the commercial power of the private media seems likely to triumph and effectively to put an end to public service broadcasting except as, at best, a tiny minority interest – as is now the case in Australia.

Moreover, where once there was the possibility that the influence of a press baron might be offset by the newer media, such as radio and television, that hope has now been closed off. All around the globe, or at least that substantial part of it that can be fairly described as being within the global economy, the media barons – the Murdochs, Thompsons, Turners and so on – have created multi-outlet media empires. It is no longer enough to own and direct the output of the major organs of the press. Now, press ownership is almost invariably accompanied by controlling interests in broadcasting media of all other kinds. It will not be long before broadcasting, telecommunications and the internet converge, creating the possibility for even more capital-intensive, multinational, cross-media conglomerates wielding even more power to persuade and influence across the whole spectrum of people's lives.

The impotence of national governments and their inability or unwillingness to prevent cross-media ownership or the passing of local media ownership into the hands of multinational media corporations is particularly significant to the political debate. Just as the owners of national media have succeeded in dominating the political debate in a given country, so now – with the advent of the global economy and of global media in particular – the media barons can reinforce the dominance of neo-liberal economics by ensuring that the predominant view of what is happening is constantly favourable.

The process is not limited to one country. Rupert Murdoch's News Corporation, for example, has worldwide interests (in Central and Latin America, the UK, Australasia and Asia) in addition to its powerful position in the USA. Outside the major US-based media conglomerates, there are major media empires such as Germany's Bertelsmann that dominate news dissemination in all continents.

The power wielded by media moguls is not, of course, always as crass as trying to lecture readers, listeners and viewers on the merits of international capitalism. The political message is found in much less likely guises. People are constantly encouraged to make their judgements of others on the basis of their economic success. The 'rich and famous' are constantly eulogised; their lifestyles are celebrated; their exploits, irrespective of whether they would ordinarily be matters for congratulation or censure, are publicised on the basis that wealth alone means that other values do not count. Thus, even failures or criminals can find absolution in the media, simply by appearing and claiming the status of celebrities who can help to sell newspapers and advertising.

The businessman (or woman) as hero is held up as the epitome of success and what everyone should emulate. The message is consistent: wealth is the real – perhaps only – indicator of success and virtue; all other frailties are to be forgiven if wealth is achieved; material considerations are all that matter; the bottom line is what counts; everyone can achieve wealth; and we all benefit (the trickle-down theory) from the wealth of the few, who are benefactors to us all.

The impact of this constant barrage of propaganda is not only to skew the value systems of many societies but also to frustrate what might otherwise be a resumption of a significant political debate. The power of global economic forces to impose their ideology on the world is aided, reinforced and defended by the ability of global media to persuade people that neo-liberal economics is not only inevitable but is also natural, desirable, generally beneficial and to be admired. This propaganda is what the French call the 'pensée unique'. Journalist and political scientist Serge Halimi describes it as 'the ideological translation of the interests of global capital, of the priorities of financial markets and of those who invest in them. It is the dissemination through leading newspapers of the policies advocated by the international economic institutions which use and abuse the credit, data and expertise they are entrusted with.'[2]

As a consequence, the natural tendency to question current orthodoxy, and to see the pendulum of fashion in matters of economic policy and political doctrine swing over time, is much less likely to manifest itself. The media barons have at last become powerful enough to ensure that any debate that does take place is on their own terms and will produce outcomes that are acceptable to them.

Lifting the lid on malpractice

Over the last couple of years, we have seen these dangers manifest themselves in particularly striking form. The phone-tapping scandal in the UK, which has lifted the lid on the complete absence of any decent standards in the way in which news is gathered, has been matched by the complete indifference of leading media figures to the immorality and illegality of the methods they used, and by their arrogance in resolving to cover up the immense scale of the wrongdoing and in using their power to threaten those who have publicised their misdeeds.

It seems certain that further inquiries and prosecutions will bring more of these shocking events to light. No one can doubt that these revelations paint a frightening picture of what happens when media moguls believe themselves to be above the law. Yet the politicians who have belatedly woken up to their responsibilities are almost equally culpable. Nothing more clearly demonstrates the central thesis of this book – the hijacking of our democracy by a small cabal of powerful global financial interests – than the capitulation by democratic leaders to the supposedly overwhelming power of the media barons.

The inquiry headed by Lord Justice Leveson has revealed the degree to which political leaders of almost all persuasions believed themselves to be in thrall to the Rupert Murdochs of this world.[3] The close, not to say incestuous, relationship between News International executives and leading politicians, which provided the Murdoch empire with privileged access to ministers and the belief that Rupert Murdoch could make or break governments, was both a consequence and a constantly renewed cause of the political power he wielded. He was, according to the political journalist Lance Price, 'the twenty-fourth member of the Cabinet'.

The chief culprit in fostering this view seems to have been Tony Blair, who found it necessary to fly to Australia to seek Murdoch's approval when he became leader of the Labour Party. The general election victory of 1997 was widely seen, not only by New Labour but by the political class as a whole, as confirmation that Murdoch's endorsement was a sine qua non in the achievement of power. Blair gave further currency to this view when he took his relationship with Murdoch to new heights, and became a close personal friend, the godfather of Murdoch's child, and the cheerleader-in-chief at a News International celebration of success in California.

Lord Leveson did an excellent job in his report of analysing the deficiencies that had rightly caused such outrage, and he has recommended that there should be more distance between politicians and media bosses – and, perhaps, sotto voce, that politicians should have more self-respect and more regard for their responsibilities to their electorates than to prostrate themselves before powerful media figures. But the caution he showed in the remedies he suggested to ensure that excesses and abuses can be avoided in future, and the even greater caution demonstrated by David Cameron in indicating his response to these recommendations, suggest strongly that politicians have not yet found the courage to protect the public interest by facing down the media barons. We can expect further demonstrations of the power of the media to defy their critics.

The rottenness within

When David Cameron opined, following the riots in British cities in the summer of 2011, that parts of English society are 'broken' and declared a social 'fightback', he signally allowed the target of that fightback to remain unidentified. Punishing individual rioters was no doubt necessary and unavoidable, but that in itself did little to drill down into the real causes of social breakdown.

At this point, surely, step forward Rupert Murdoch and News International. Here, after all, are those who – by virtue of their power in the media – have arguably done more than any others to shape our society over recent decades.

We now have a fairly accurate idea of the values and principles they have brought to that task – the evidence provided by what we now know about their own disreputable business practices. We know that they have little regard for legality or honesty, that they feel contempt for those they report on, and that they will use their power to threaten or cajole when challenged.

They purport to hold up a mirror to society, to show people how they and others – their neighbours, their workmates, their families – actually behave. But the mirror has been distorted. They have, in an effort to shock and titillate so as to sell more of their product, pushed back the boundaries of what is regarded as acceptable. They show not what most people think or do but what those at margins of society get up to – and the more outrageous the better.

Underpinning this distortion of what is normal and responsible is the cult of celebrity. The constantly repeated and largely subliminal message is that, however despicable the behaviour, it is to be excused and even celebrated if the perpetrator is featured in the headlines. Celebrity cures all. Fame and money are all that matter.

The result is that young people in particular are left without a moral compass. Sexuality is a commodity and selling agent. Money is the greatest desideratum, however it is acquired. Those who deserve to be admired and emulated are those whose success is measured by how much they have been able to grab, even – and especially – when it is at the expense of others. In all of this, the personal mantra of the News International proprietors is faithfully reflected.

The Murdoch media have been major influences in creating a debased popular culture. The old social virtues of mutual support, helping one's neighbour, have been supplanted. Little wonder that young people, with little life experience and nothing much by way of role models to emulate or moral guidance to follow, have been especially susceptible to the message delivered to them unremittingly by the Murdoch media.

There are, of course, other contenders to shoulder the major responsibility for social breakdown. Among the leading candidates would have to be the development in a recessionary climate of an economy in which unskilled labour no longer has a part to play.

The young people who took their chance in the riots (manipulated no doubt by social media-savvy fomenters of trouble) saw no future for themselves because they knew they had been dismissed as worthless by the rest of society. They reasoned that grabbing what they could when the moment arrived was just the kind of behaviour that would be rewarded not just with material gain but with a brief and local celebrity. They are just a few of those who, in a multitude of ways, have suffered from the abdication of our leaders from any attempt to stand up to powerful people whose sole objective is to pursue their own interests.

Chapter 15

Widening Inequality and Social Problems

We have seen that the 'free market' allows those with dominant power in the marketplace to grab what they can, to keep it in defiance of any claims by wider society on the wealth that is concentrated in a few hands, and then to use that hugely reinforced advantage and much greater wealth to entrench and extend their power.

It is now widely accepted that inequality in both wealth and income – and, as a consequence, in power as well – has widened substantially in many western countries over recent decades. This trend has been most marked in the English-speaking democracies – countries such as the USA, the UK and New Zealand. This has been a particularly surprising development in a country such as New Zealand, which until recently was one of the most egalitarian countries in the world.

Nobel Prize-winning economist Joseph Stiglitz has highlighted, in a recently published book, *The Price of Inequality*,[1] the extent to which this trend has disfigured American society and handicapped American economic development. Stiglitz cites some remarkable figures to support his conclusions.

By 2007, he reports, the income of the top 0.1 per cent of households in the USA was 220 times greater than the average of the bottom 90 per cent, meaning that it took them just a day and a half to earn what it took a year for the bottom 90 per cent to receive, while the wealthiest 1 per cent also owned more than a third of American wealth. Between 2002 and 2007, 65 per cent of the increase in national income had gone to that same top 1 per cent. Worse, since the global financial crisis, the trend has intensified: 93 per cent of the increased national income in 2010 went to – yes – the top 1 per cent. The statistics look even more alarming as we dig into the detail. The six heirs to the Wal-Mart empire, for example, own wealth worth as much as is owned by the whole of the bottom 30 per cent.

While the American figures are the most extreme, they are reflected in the experience of other western countries as well. In the UK, Michael Meacher MP recently made a telling analysis of the annual *Sunday Times* Rich List for 2012.[2] He concluded that it offered some very important conclusions about the 'governance of Britain', finding that the wealth of the 1,000 richest people in Britain (just 0.003 per cent of the adult population), over the past three years, had increased by £155 billion. That increase alone would have allowed them to pay off the entire current UK budget deficit and still have about £30 billion left over.

These super-rich were mainly bankers, hedge fund managers and private equity operators – a group that had been largely responsible for the financial crash; yet while ordinary people had borne the burden of paying increased taxes (largely through increases in indirect taxation) in order to deal with the consequences of the crash, the super-rich had paid no increased tax specifically directed at them. The wealth of this super-rich group now totals £414 billion, about one-third of the UK's total GDP. If the increase in their wealth over the past fifteen years had been taxed at a 28 per cent rate on capital gains, about £88 billion would have been raised, enough to pay off 70 per cent of the entire deficit.

Salaries for senior managers in most of the western world have, of course, risen hugely over the last two or three decades, in line with the increased value apparently placed by the market on their services. In the USA, for example, 2011 saw the second year of double-digit pay rises, according to GMI Ratings' preliminary CEO pay survey,[3] continuing a strong recovery for American CEO pay following the global financial crisis; while not at the levels of 2010's 30–40 per cent increases, pay went up by more than 15 per cent in 2011. In addition, all kinds of bonuses, share options and other benefits are paid (but often not taxed) as part of the remuneration packages of executives. The top ten highest paid CEOs in 2011 earned about 77 per cent of their total realised compensation through stock option exercises and vested equity, while those who own and direct corporations, especially in the financial sector, have done even better.

These developments, coming as they do in the middle of a recession that has threatened the living standards of most people, are so startling that even *The Economist* has recognised the enormity of the swing in the balance of advantage. Zanny Minton Beddoes commented in a recent essay that a majority of the world's citizens now live in countries where the gap between the rich and the rest is significantly bigger than it was a generation ago.[4] The trend has been most extreme in the West. As Ms Minton Beddoes points out, in the

USA the portion of national income going to the richest 1 per cent of the population tripled from 8 per cent in the 1970s to 24 per cent in 2007 – an amazing statistic of which most people, not least in the USA, seem unaware.

In addition, as Gillian Tett pointed out,[5] that same 1 per cent also hold around 40 per cent of all wealth. She goes on to quote work by Professor James K. Galbraith,[6] which shows that, contrary to the constantly made assertion that increased inequality is the consequence of so-called 'real factors', such as the increased value of technology as compared to labour, the true explanation is that the huge growth in the financial sectors of western economies has made bankers rich, and – equally importantly – pumped up the value of assets such as stocks, bonds and real estate. As Galbraith notes, in respect of this new class of super-rich, 'The difference between the financial sector and other sources of income is a large source of changing inequalities.' This supports the point made by Joseph Stiglitz that the huge growth in wealth of the richest has not been earned in the ordinary sense but is rent income – that is, an income gained entirely by virtue of being already wealthy.

At the same time, the global financial crisis has been used as the chance, in many western countries, to reinforce the drive to reduce real wages and to further reduce the share of national income that goes to wage-earners. The share of wages in the UK's national income, for example, has been on a downward trend for three decades. Since the global financial crisis, however, that trend has intensified. In the two years 2010 and 2011, real wages fell on average by 7 per cent, a downward trend set to continue well into 2013 and beyond to at least 2016, if the Office for Budget Responsibility's forecast is accepted.[7] The suspicion must be that this is, at least in part, the consequence of a direct attempt by government to engineer, under the cover of the crisis, a further fall in the share of the national cake going to earnings.

The proportion of the British workforce in low-paid work has almost doubled over the last two decades and now stands at more than a fifth. This decline is the result of a four-year-long freeze (meaning a real cut after inflation) on public sector pay, the straitened finances of voluntary sector organisations and charities, so that many home care staff and those working with the homeless are facing substantial pay cuts, pay freezes in parts of the private sector including distribution and manufacturing, and the failure to maintain the real value of the minimum wage.

A similar and continuing picture is seen in other countries. In New Zealand, for example, a report from the Ministry of Social Development in 2012 showed that, after housing costs, real household disposable incomes fell across the board between 2010 and 2011.[8] At the median the drop was 4 per cent; for three of the lowest four deciles the fall was more than 7 per cent. By this measure, according to the report, 'from a longer-term perspective, in 2010 the incomes of the bottom 30 per cent of the population were on average only a little better in real terms than their counterparts almost thirty years ago in 1982'. By contrast, a household at the bottom of the top decile was 40 per cent better off in terms of real disposable income after housing costs than its counterpart thirty years ago.

These current trends reflect a long and unattractive history. In the Great Depression of the early 1930s, most developed economies followed the call made by the multimillionaire American treasury secretary Andrew Mellon, after the 1929 crash, to 'liquidate labour'. It is sad to see history repeating itself in this way, as the rich defend their interests and pile the burdens on to the poor. The tragedy is that, in most western economies, cutting pay simply squeezes even more of the lifeblood out of economies already suffering from a severe shortage of demand. Falling real wages over the last three years are the key explanation for economies struggling to escape from recession.

And this is not all. The benefits on which many unemployed are forced to rely are reduced, at least in terms of their real value. Their rights, either in work or out of work, are also reduced. The services on which they depend for the delivery of education, health care and housing attract fewer resources in comparative terms and are increasingly made available on a user-pays basis. The esteem they enjoy in their own eyes and those of others diminishes. And all this, in the case of the American worker in particular, in the aftermath of the global financial crisis which meant that for many such people their jobs, retirement incomes and homes had all been jeopardised by the monumental errors made by their supposed betters.

Cheating fellow citizens

Nor is the differential treatment of the rich and the poor in income terms the whole story; there are many other advantages delivered to the rich and powerful by the policies applied in most western countries over recent decades. In particular, tax rates on high income have been substantially reduced and taxes on capital have also been brought down, while in some countries, such as New Zealand, wealth is completely untaxed.

The tax burden has also been increasingly switched away from progressive taxes on income (so that high income-earners have been relieved of part of the burden) and towards regressive indirect taxation. A higher proportion of taxes on consumption necessarily impacts more severely on the less well-off, who spend a higher proportion of their incomes on goods that they need for day-to-day consumption, while a smaller proportion will go to capital goods, savings and investment, which is where the better-off tend to put their disposable income.

One of the starkest and most dramatic illustrations of the gulf that has developed between the small minority of super-rich and ordinary people was some research released in July 2012. James Henry, former chief economist at consultancy McKinsey and an expert on tax havens, detailed in a new report called *The Price of Offshore Revisited* his latest estimates of the amount of money squirrelled away in offshore tax havens by the super-rich.[9]

The total is truly staggering. Henry showed that at least US$21 trillion – perhaps up to US$32 trillion – has leaked tax-free into secretive jurisdictions such as Switzerland and the Cayman Islands. This sum is the equivalent or more of the total GDP of the USA and Japan combined. The detailed analysis in the report suggests that it would be enough to pay off third world debt many times over, or to finance the stimulus required worldwide to enable the global economy to recover from recession.

The figures are hugely significant in many different respects. First, they reveal the extent to which wealth has concentrated in a relatively few hands – on a scale undreamt of by most people. A tiny minority of super-rich people now control resources that are greater than the total national output of any single country, including the very richest. The sums involved also indicate how much ordinary taxpayers are short-changed by the scale of wealth that escapes taxation altogether – in itself, a stunning indication of the ability of the wealthy to manipulate the system to their advantage and to transfer the burden of paying taxes to ordinary people. It is truly the case that, as Leona Helmsley notoriously remarked at her trial for tax evasion in 1989, 'taxes are for the little people'.

The standard measures of inequality are shown by the report to radically underestimate the true gap between rich and poor.

According to Henry's calculations, nearly half of the assets lying in tax-haven bank accounts are owned by only 92,000 people, or 0.001 per cent of the world's population.

These revelations also provide some idea of the economic power that is controlled by a handful of people. These resources, whose size and even existence have been hidden from most people, allow the super-rich to use their economic clout on the grand scale to buy, dictate and influence the outcomes they want, and then to use the same resources to persuade ordinary voters that those outcomes serve their interests. Little wonder that the rich have succeeded, in the words of Thomas Frank in *Pity The Billionaire*,[10] in 'enlisting the powerless in a fan club for the super rich'.

Even when they declare their incomes, however, most of the world's super-rich pay tax at a lower rate than most in middle-income brackets or below. When the American Internal Revenue Service released data in 2012 from the 400 individual income tax returns reporting the highest adjusted gross income in 2009, the latest year available, they revealed that this group of super-rich earned on average $202 million in that year; but the most startling disclosure was that six of the 400 paid no federal income tax at all.

The IRS further reported that twenty-seven paid less than 10 per cent of their adjusted gross incomes and another eighty-nine paid between 10 and 15 per cent. So more than a quarter of those earning an average of over $200 million in 2009 paid less than 15 per cent of their adjusted gross income in taxes. None paid more than 35 per cent.

They did it by manipulating the tax system, through devices such as using paper capital losses from previous years to offset capital gains. And since the super-rich account for a disproportionate amount of dividend income, which averaged over $26 million for the top 400, they were able to take ample advantage of the fact that capital gains and dividends are both taxed at a maximum rate of 15 per cent, as opposed to the maximum rate on earned income of 35 per cent – a further example of how the super-rich have succeeded in creating a tax system that taxes them at a lower rate than most ordinary taxpayers.

The Institute for Policy Studies, a Washington DC think tank, concludes in a new report that Oracle's Larry Ellison, who recently bought Lanai, a Hawaiian island, as his private estate for US$500 million, took advantage of a 1993 loophole in tax law to designate $76 million of his income as 'performance-related pay', which allowed him to avoid paying any taxes on the money.[11]

Dozens of US CEOs have cashed in on this major tax incentive at an estimated cost to US taxpayers of $9.7 billion last year. Statistics provided by National Priorities Project suggest that that same amount of money could have paid for 142,625 elementary school teachers, or healthcare for 4.96 million low-income children. In 1980, the average American CEO was paid forty-two times as much as the average worker, when tax rates for the richest stood at 70 per cent. Today, that ratio has widened to 380 times, exacerbated in part, no doubt, by the fact that CEOs are able to reduce their tax burdens dramatically by a reduction in top tax rates in recent years.

In fact, some companies paid their individual CEOs more money than the entire companies paid in taxes. Aubrey McClendon, CEO of Oklahoma-based Chesapeake Energy, was paid $17.9 million in 2011, while his company paid just $13 million in taxes on sales of $11.64 billion. Chesapeake achieved this startlingly low tax liability by claiming a 'drilling-costs tax benefit' that allows generous income tax deferrals in case an oil well comes up dry. Yet this concession is now largely irrelevant since sophisticated technologies allow them to gauge accurately where to drill. The Institute for Policy Studies found that twenty-six of the hundred highest-paid American CEOs took home more in pay than their companies paid in federal income taxes. On average, each of these company bosses was paid $20.4 million in 2012.

Another device is deferred compensation. The way this works is simple: most taxpayers are expected to pay 35 per cent of their income in taxes the year they earn it. But CEOs do not have to pay the tax until they claim the cash, which can be earning interest in the meantime. Depending on how the money is invested, CEOs can engineer a substantial profit. Thus Michael Duke, CEO of Wal-mart, received $17,028,615 tax free in 2011, roughly 774 times more than one of his employees would have been allowed to do under normal tax rules.

Yet these sums shrink into insignificance compared with the money that hedge fund managers make. Raymond Dalio, for example, was paid an astronomical $3 billion in 2011, but paid just 15 per cent in taxes because the money was considered capital gains, as opposed to the average citizen, who would be required to pay 25 per cent (in income tax). The cost to the taxpayer in 2011 of this instance was $450 million.

Even in the small country of New Zealand, where salaries and incomes are much lower at the top end than in the USA, the Inland Revenue Department revealed in August 2012 that half the 250 people worth NZ$50 million had paid tax at a lower rate than those earning NZ$70,000 in the period 2009–11. Those who successfully avoid paying taxes at the rate enforced upon their poorer fellow citizens are often then acclaimed for acts of charitable giving, and rewarded accordingly with gratitude, respect and honours.

The tax advantages enjoyed by the rich are not just a matter of low rates and ease of avoidance; they also reflect the structure of taxation in most advanced western countries. Remarkably little attention is paid to the fact that property – the form in which the wealthiest often accumulate their wealth – is largely immune from taxation. As George Monbiot points out in *The Guardian* of 21 January 2013,[12] while British politicians have competed with each other in boasting about who has produced the lowest corporation taxes, and have united in rejecting with minimal consideration the possibility of a 'Tobin' tax on financial transactions, the real scandal is the fact that the owners of property worth millions of pounds will pay a property-based tax, such as the council tax, at minimal rates, and will escape any tax at all on the development value of the land they own.

Monbiot quotes that well-known radical Winston Churchill, whose 1909 exposition of the case for a tax on the development value of land retains all its force today. Churchill said:

> Roads are made, streets are made, services are improved, electric light turns night into day, water is brought from reservoirs a hundred miles off in the mountains – and all the while the landlord sits still. Every one of those improvements is effected by the labour and cost of other people and the taxpayers. To not one of those improvements does the land monopolist, as a land monopolist, contribute, and yet by every one of them the value of his land is enhanced. He renders no service to the community, he contributes nothing to the general welfare, he contributes nothing to the process from which his own enrichment is derived … the unearned increment on the land is reaped by the land monopolist in exact proportion, not to the service, but to the disservice done.[13]

Similar points were made, I recall, when Harold Wilson's Labour government introduced the Community Land Bill in 1975; I had the privilege of serving on the standing committee during its committee stage. The 1979 election, and the arrival of Margaret Thatcher in 10 Downing Street, put an end to the Community Land Scheme, and to the attempt to rationalise the taxation of land and to retain for the public benefit some of the development value created by the community.

A further startling instance of how thoroughly the taxation system has been suborned by those whose liability is or should be greatest has only recently come to light. As Polly Toynbee reported in February 2013,[14] the House of Commons Select Committee on the Treasury took evidence from the major accountancy firms as to their involvement in advising the British government on tax arrangements that should be put in place, and which applied to firms looking to the selfsame accountancy firms for tax advice.

The case that particularly attracted the select committee's attention was that of the Patent Box. This is a scheme that offers tax relief on patents, designed to encourage companies to innovate, invest in R&D and entice foreign companies to relocate to the UK. The relief is available on any product, provided that some part of that product – perhaps a very small part – contains a patent; the relief is retrospective, and therefore covers old patents as well as new ones. The Treasury estimates that this one scheme for tax relief will cost £1.1 billion per year in lost corporation tax, roughly the annual cost of benefit fraud in the UK – yet it is benefit fraud that hogs the headlines week in, week out.

The policy was framed by Jonathan Bridges, senior KPMG corporate tax adviser, who was taken on as lead policy adviser to the government. Once he had returned to his proper job, KPMG promptly advertised his services: 'The Patent Box: What's In It For You?' and quite blatantly proclaimed, 'While on secondment to HMT, Jonathan Bridges also acted as lead policy adviser on tax and innovation, including the Patent Box.'

Paradoxically, the hugely increased advantage in both wealth and income enjoyed by the super-rich, and the low rates of tax that they succeed in engineering for themselves, seriously undermine the argument traditionally advanced against raising taxes for the rich. It is usually argued that higher taxes for those at the top end of the scale would be little more than at best a gesture and at worst an expression of envy and class warfare, since they would raise relatively little by way of additional tax revenue. But that argument no longer holds water: such is the proportion of national wealth and low rate of tax now enjoyed by a tiny minority that an additional (and reasonably small) tax increase would produce substantial revenue. Joseph Stiglitz points out that in the USA a tax increase of 10 per cent on the income of the top 1 per cent would produce 2 per cent of the American GDP.[15]

No one disputes these trends or their consequence – that inequality as measured by the usual indices (such as Gini coefficients) has widened sharply in western countries over recent decades. In New Zealand, a three decade-long trend towards greater inequality, as a consequence of neo-liberal policies, culminated in 2011 with inequality reaching its highest level ever. The Household Incomes Report, produced by the Ministry of Social Development in 2012, measures total after-tax incomes and revealed a fall in average incomes for the first time since the early 1990s, with the gap between rich and poor widening substantially in 2011 to a record level. Middle- and lower-paid workers saw their incomes fall sharply, while the rich saw their earnings increase. Incomes for the richest New Zealanders, the top 10 per cent, rose the most sharply.

The report shows that while the recession exacerbated these trends, they had been a feature of New Zealand income distribution for decades. Over the past thirty years, real incomes grew four times faster at the high end than at the low end of the distribution. Not surprisingly, the Gini coefficient for New Zealand had risen sharply by 2011 to its highest level in thirty years.

Does widening inequality matter?

Given the plethora of evidence that inequality in many western countries has widened substantially, and is the direct and intended result of policy deliberately pursued, the only point at issue is whether we should be worried about this or not. The first reason for concern is that the inequality we find in today's society is qualitatively different from the power of privileged minorities in past times. In a feudal or hierarchical society, the disposition of power and wealth was part of the established order; the relative position of the powerful and the powerless was ordained by social rules. The degree of inequality was more or less static and was mitigated by responsibilities recognised by the privileged to the less privileged, in accordance with the doctrine of noblesse oblige.

Today, however, inequality is, as we have seen, largely a function of the 'free market'. As long as the outcomes are sanctioned by the market, there is thought to be no limit to the share that some are entitled to take at the expense of others. Growing inequality has, therefore, a momentum all of its own; we find that even in hard times the rich and powerful continue to make gains while the rest languish. It operates on a ratchet, impossible to turn back, constantly clicking forward.

This is not a function of superior wisdom or skill; as the global financial crisis demonstrates, these increases in income and wealth have occurred despite, rather than because of, superior performances by the very rich. It is rather a function of the power to manipulate the market which wealth bestows on its holders. It is increasingly accepted that the pursuit of individual advantage trumps obligations to others and the upholding of what society holds in common.

Wealth, of course, entrenches and grows itself. It is now well established statistically that the best chance of being seriously wealthy is to be born into a seriously wealthy family. Even in the supposed land of opportunity – indeed, especially in the USA – social mobility has largely ground to a halt. Across the western world, wealthy parents buy their children the best education, the most useful contacts, the most lucrative opportunities.

In the USA, Robert Putnam, the pioneering social scientist, has revealed that class is now the most important determinant of outcomes in American life; these differences can be observed very early on in the children of different classes.[16] Well-off families now spend eleven times more than the working-class on what Putnam calls children's 'enrichment activities', which are so important for psychological well-being and character building. It is not just educational advantage, in other words, that can be bought; life chances of all kinds, including social exclusivity, are scooped by the well-off.

As a result, the arteries of American society are hardening and social mobility is in decline. The poorest third of Americans have become 'cynical and even paranoid', writes Putnam, because the very institutions that might be expected to alleviate their plight – family, school, voluntary organisations and church – have become dysfunctional. The rich, on the other hand, move into ever stronger and sealed ghettoes of their own, and become ever more ignorant of the world around them.

As society becomes more unequal, the growing inequality intensifies and feeds upon itself. On the part of the wealthy there is less understanding of the plight of the poor and disadvantaged, and there is less willingness to accommodate their interests and meet their needs. If a necessary part of the justification for the inequality is that the wealthy deserve their advantage because it is a proper reward for superior virtue, then it must follow that the poor are undeserving, and should not be mollycoddled but made to see the error of their ways. The myth of the 'feckless' or 'undeserving' poor is sedulously fostered and believed.

From the viewpoint of the disadvantaged, things look a little different. The good fortune enjoyed by the rich and powerful seems virtually inexplicable in rational terms. It can only be explained by the vagaries of outrageous fortune; Providence must somehow have smiled on the fortunate. What is needed is to win the lottery – the winning tickets must be available somehow and somewhere.

Therefore, we see as an accompaniment to widening inequality a growing emphasis on discovering the short cuts. Gambling becomes widespread – duties on gambling collected in the UK, for example, increased by 22 per cent in the five years between 1993–4 and 1998–9. Crime is seen as a viable option. Young women who sense that they have restricted life chances opt for early pregnancy. Discontents of all kinds manifest themselves. Respect for kinds of achievement other than the purely material diminishes. Envy is commonly seen and felt.

The free market in its current extreme form has had the effect of weakening social cohesion and in particular the family. Paradoxically, the family is often held up by the proponents of 'free-market' reforms as the epitome of what is valuable in society. The rate of family breakdown, of single-parent families and of divorce has, though, grown sharply in those countries, such as the USA and the UK, where the global economy is most firmly entrenched, and that has in turn contributed to the growth of an underclass in those same countries. That underclass and its predictably antisocial attitudes become a further target for those who see its emergence as a consequence of welfarism rather than an inevitable reflection of widening poverty and social dislocation.

The response by the wealthy to these perceptions and developments reinforces the divide in society. They opt to live behind locked gates – John Gray records that 28 million or 10 per cent of all Americans live in gated proprietary communities.[17] They demand tougher penalties for crime and more jails are built – 5 million Americans are in prison at any one time, and even New Zealand has found itself constrained – at a time when public spending is being cut – to build more prisons in a hurry, so as to accommodate a rapidly rising prison population.

Private security firms, offering services that only the wealthy can afford, prosper. Less is spent on social security. 'Welfare dependency' is attacked politically, the attack seemingly justified by the growing cost of social security benefits as poverty becomes endemic. The wealthy insist on keeping more of their money and spending less on public services. The peccadilloes of the wealthy are excused, even celebrated, while the frailties of the poor are condemned.

The governments that might most obviously be expected to protect the weak and disadvantaged against these consequences not only fail to do so but join in on the other side. Those who have presided over the increased inequality, intensified comparative disadvantage and reduced life chances suffered by the weakest in society, and who have encouraged and celebrated the debasement of popular culture in the interests of maximising the profits of the private owners of the media, then target the lack of 'respect' shown by the victims of these trends towards a society that seems to have abandoned them. Governments that were truly and effectively concerned about the lack of respect shown by some towards society as a whole might themselves reflect on the impact, as a social phenomenon, of greater inequality on the sense of belonging.

There is often a wilful refusal to distinguish responses to broad social trends from responses to individual acts. Society may well be justified in punishing (one hopes in a measured way) individual acts that are damaging to it. But if those individual acts follow a well-established pattern that specific responses seem unable to change, then we must conclude that this is a social phenomenon and treat it as such. We are then surely required to address the broader phenomenon and seek explanations beyond the simple wickedness or thoughtlessness of individuals. The political failure to counteract these elements or even to take them seriously is evidence of a significant change in political perceptions, sensitivity and responsiveness, and is again a consequence of the global economy's ability to shape and constrain the political debate.

One obvious indicator of these kinds of developments is the differing treatment accorded to different kinds of people when they lose their employment. When ordinary people lose their jobs (which, at a time of recession and with the increasing likelihood of acquisition by overseas owners, merger and takeover, is a much more frequent and likely occurrence) and are consequently unemployed for a period, the pressure is on to make sure that they are forced back into the workforce as soon as possible. The value of unemployment benefit is carefully monitored to ensure that the unemployed are not too comfortable, and that even low wage rates are more advantageous than the benefit. Those who stay on the benefit for any length of time are 'encouraged' to return to employment, even if it means accepting lower pay and less attractive work. As we have seen, this is an intrinsic aspect of the belief that labour is a commodity like any other, and that the 'stickiness' of wages means that the costs of labour are higher than the market would normally allow.

Top executives, on the other hand, enjoy a rather different experience if it is decided to dispense with their services. Many will have negotiated contracts that provide for substantial golden handshakes, irrespective of the reasons for the termination of those contracts. Thus, even those whose performance has been abysmal and who are in effect dismissed for incompetence will walk away with generous compensation for the loss of their job. Nor does their lack of success, and in some cases proven incompetence, appear to disqualify them from rebounding into another highly paid job. And that is to say nothing of the share options and the performance bonuses with which they will have been rewarded before their services were no longer needed, and which will no doubt ease their temporary loss of income as they wait for their next highly paid job.

This generous treatment of top executives extends to those who sit in the boardrooms of major companies. This, again, is no accident. The chief executives and senior managers of one international company are all too likely to be the directors of another. Salaries for senior executives are determined and approved by directors who are well aware that there is a common interest in ensuring that top salaries continue to rise, and that the quid pro quo is that directors' fees should also reflect the 'reality' of the international marketplace. This international and interlocking oligarchy of directors and executives is able to set its own rewards and to protect its members from failure. It is no accident that top salaries and fees have risen much faster than other forms of pay. It is one of the miracles of the global economy that, while it requires wages to fall so as to keep costs down, it also means that top incomes must rise so that economies are not left behind in the competition for 'talent'.

The notion that the rich, even in hard times, should be generously treated, so that their well-being improves even while the less fortunate lose ground, has been given an extended trial over recent decades. The theory is that the increased wealth will 'trickle down' and that it will therefore – over a period – benefit everyone. The evidence, however, offers no support for this comforting view.

The increased resources of the rich – whether as individuals or as corporations – stay firmly in the hands of those who control them, doing little to benefit the economy as a whole. The big corporations who were bailed out by the taxpayer after the global financial crisis used the billions they were given to rebuild their balance sheets and to go on paying themselves huge bonuses.

'Trickle down' should surely be rejected for what it is – a piece of special pleading by those who already have much more than their fair share. It would make more sense to pursue an economic policy based on 'bubble up' – an approach that would put more spending power in the hands of the less well-off, in the confident assurance that they would spend it immediately on real goods and services, providing a direct stimulus to economic activity and wealth creation for all of us, and a hopeful way out of a recession that will otherwise be around for a long time to come.

But the price we pay for the ignorance of the rich concerning what it means to be poor may extend well beyond social factors. It may be that we, including the rich, suffer not just in terms of a fractured society but in economic terms as well. A quest for greater equality (in other words, less damaging inequality) is often seen, even by its proponents, as somehow at odds with economic efficiency. Yet nothing is further from the truth.

There is nothing efficient about an economy that amasses great wealth in just a few hands. The decisions the super-rich take as to how they spend their money are often irresponsible, and at best capricious. The most common use of wealth is not to create new productive capacity and new jobs but simply to earn what Stiglitz calls a 'rent income'. Instead of spreading purchasing power across the whole of society, in other words, where it can flow into and irrigate every diverse part of the economy, the concentration of wealth in effect compresses it so that it can do little good.

In any case, what is economically efficient about keeping large numbers out of work, as western countries are currently doing, so that their productive contribution is lost? What is economically efficient about cutting the real incomes of the low-paid so that their purchasing power is not available to stimulate the economy? What is economically efficient about cutting benefits so that the health and education of large numbers in western workforces suffer?

And what chance do we have of achieving an efficient and productive economy if competence and merit are overlooked, while privilege determines who occupy positions of power and accordingly take the decisions that matter? How can it be efficient when the people who run our affairs have little idea of how the economy and society really work?

In a society where the interactions of a socially exclusive and privileged minority create a sort of parallel universe in which the real decisions are taken, democratic instructions and processes are merely a form of window-dressing, permitted so as to give the appearance of being consulted but in reality being sidelined and bypassed. Growing inequality comes, in other words, at a price, and that price is political and social as well as economic, and is paid in the daily lives of many millions of our fellow citizens in western countries.

There is a tendency, when the problems arising by virtue of increased inequality manifest themselves, to treat them as unrelated and therefore susceptible to specific counter-action. Governments tend to address each of these problems, one by one. But that misses the real point. There is an underlying factor that unites all of these issues, and that is the growing inequality that has disfigured our society in recent decades.

Sick societies

To make this link between inequality and the problems confronting western societies today is more than mere speculation. We now have some authoritative evidence that inequality is the common factor that accompanies social problems in many western countries. In a groundbreaking piece of research, two British epidemiologists, Richard Wilkinson and Kate Pickett, in a study called *The Spirit Level*,[18] have established that in countries where inequality has increased most sharply – the USA and the UK, for example – there is also the most damaging rise in social problems such as crime, drugs, early pregnancy and gambling, and – even more significantly – the most significant impairment of the physical and mental health of the population. It is obvious that these are the same countries whose failing financial systems precipitated the global recession.

In countries where equality is much more evident – such as Japan and the Scandinavian countries – the record on social ills is much better. The researchers are able to show that the statistical correlation between inequality and social dysfunction is too sustained, over time and place, to be accidental.

Wilkinson and Pickett based their research on World Bank data that identified for them the richest fifty counties. They then excluded those for which there was not a complete set of data and those with a population of less than 3 million people. They were left with twenty-three countries as the basis for their research.

They found that a relationship between social and health ills on the one hand and income inequality on the other was a feature across these countries. This relationship was reinforced when data from the various states of the USA were compared and the same relationship between increasing income disparity and increasing health and social ills was found. Moreover, in any given country, when changes in income disparity occurred, so social and health indices changed too. The research also shows that when we look at levels of trust in particular societies they are significantly worse in more unequal societies.

Wilkinson and Pickett found that the steeper the income-inequality ladder the harder it is to climb, and the slower and more difficult social mobility becomes. At the same time, greater equality improves the quality of life for everyone, and not just the poor; even the wealthy will enjoy life more in an integrated and whole society. People across the board will live longer and will be less likely to suffer violence or have a problem with obesity; their children will have a better chance of doing well at school, and will be less likely to use drugs or become teenage parents.

Our best chance, in other words, of giving children a better chance at school, or of keeping them out of jail, is to reduce income inequality. Our best chance of improving national economic performance is to focus on improving the education and health of the whole population so that everyone can make a full contribution. Conversely, to allow or encourage the income gap to widen is seriously to prejudice the chances of dealing successfully with current problems, and to risk making future problems worse. Why is this apparently clear-cut message, which accords with common sense and the evidence of our own eyes, not accepted and acted upon?

The rich – a failure of imagination and a blind spot

The rich, like most people, are more than capable of seeing only what they want to see and ignoring what they wish not to see. The advantage they have is that their wealth allows them to indulge these idiosyncrasies to a much greater degree than the rest of us.

In a fifty-year involvement in politics, I have often found that friendship is perfectly possible with people who hold very different political views from my own. Over a twenty-year period as a member of the House of Commons, I often found that some of the more stimulating and amusing companions came from the ranks of those whose political views I abominated.

I have often puzzled over the fact that people who are so agreeable in personal terms can hold views about society and social issues that are so unattractive. People who are kind to animals, generous to their friends, supportive of family members who need help, exhibit a breathtaking and at times cruel lack of generosity, compassion and understanding when it comes to those who are a little more distant from them in social or cultural or ethnic terms.

My explanation of this apparent paradox is that people who hold right-wing views (excluding those who are just plain nasty) often suffer from a failure of imagination. Their impulses are fine and generous when they relate to people who are recognisable and close to them, but they are unable to project those commendable responses to a wider range because they are simply unable to understand that society is made up of people who are just as dear to others as their own friends and family are to them.

The start, or default, position for many people, in other words, is that looking after themselves and their immediate families is the first priority. It requires real effort to persuade them that they can afford what might be seen as the luxury of thinking of others, or of wider social issues. People are often reluctant to lift their eyes from the immediate and close at hand, and to understand that taking the wider view can lead to a better life and a stronger society. But even when that effort is made, the prospect of hard times is often enough to send people hastening back to base.

When crisis threatens, the hatches are battened down and the wagons are circled to face the enemy. Any thought of social concern is abandoned; self-preservation is the first consideration. That is, I think, the explanation of the otherwise inexplicable fact that in the midst of recession, when it would seem even more important than usual that people should recognise common cause and support each other, the response is in the opposite direction, and many become more fearful of other similarly disadvantaged people, more focused on self-protection and self-preservation, and less generous towards the claims of others.

A case in point was the debate over Barack Obama's health care bill put before Congress in 2011. For many observers, it was almost beyond belief that people who would surely be regarded as pillars of their local community and as exhibiting all sorts of civic virtues could possibly have held views that were so downright vicious and hostile to those who are among the most deprived in their country, and the most in need of sympathy and help.

Some things never change. The rich have always claimed that their good fortune is a recognition of and reward for their superior virtue – with the inevitable corollary that the poor have no one to blame but themselves.

The myth of the undeserving poor has a long and discreditable history. It has underpinned social policy over long periods, from the workhouses of early industrial England to the present day. The frequently told story that poverty is a lifestyle choice commands more attention in the media than other (perhaps more credible) accounts of how and why inequality in our society has widened. An enhanced access to the media is, after all, an important aspect of privilege.

It is not that those telling the story deliberately invent it. They are no doubt quite genuine in believing it to be true. The capacity to protect oneself from an unwelcome reality is, after all, one of the privileges that the rich enjoy.

This is because an inevitable feature of an unequal society is that the privileged, without even trying, insulate themselves from the less fortunate – and the wider the gap, the more substantial the insulation. They use their wealth to live in a separate part of town, to send their children to exclusive schools, to pursue expensive leisure interests and travel to different destinations – in short, they live quite different and separate lives.

Exclusivity then becomes an end in itself. The rich feel that belonging to an elite, distinct from the common herd, is a valuable and legitimate element in the enjoyment of their wealth. Their ignorance of the lives of the poor becomes a badge of status. It is then all too easy to believe what one chooses about those whom one rarely comes across in the flesh. It is on this flimsy basis that common sense flies out the window, that unthinking judgements are made, and that issues of social justice are disregarded.

Chapter 16

Misreading the Non-Western World

It is not just in the economic and social arenas that western values and attitudes have come under pressure. The conclusion of Fukuyama's work was that, with the fall of communism, the major challenge to western liberal values had ended. So confident were western leaders of the attractions of western democracy and the market economy that serious errors of judgement were made. Those errors were often based on an almost complete ignorance of how people in other parts of the world saw themselves and their place in the world. The ignorance was born of an arrogant assumption that no knowledge was needed, since it was obvious that everyone, given the chance, would opt for western values and the western way of life in preference to their own supposedly miserable existences.

The invasion of Iraq, for example, was clearly predicated on the belief that the only reason that Iraqis had not long ago adopted a western outlook was that they had been prevented from doing so by a dictatorial regime. The removal of Saddam Hussein, it was thought, was all that was needed to produce an enthusiastic adoption by Iraqis of western culture and modes of government.

So great was the confidence that people around the world would willingly forgo their own cultures and histories (whose very existence and significance were given no value by western opinion) in favour of becoming Californians that it was fully expected that the American invaders of Iraq would be welcomed with flowers and garlands. There was virtually no understanding at that point of the great influence of Islam and its importance as a religious and ethical doctrine for a very large part of the world's population, or of the extent to which Christian countries were seen by Muslim opinion as demonstrating by virtue of the invasion a hostility to Islam that dated all the way back to the Crusades.

This lack of understanding meant that the attack on America in 2001 by Al-Qaeda, shocking as it was, was interpreted by some western leaders as a statement made by Muslim opinion in general of a broad hostility towards the West that had to be combated by 'a war against terror'. Terrorism was equated with religious views that were held by a wide and increasingly important part of world opinion. There was little recognition of the contextual factor of a worldwide resurgence of Islam as a radical political as well as religious force.

The motives of a Tony Blair, for example, appeared to be an acceptance of the view taken by the hawks in Washington – the Richard Perles, the Donald Rumsfelds, the Dick Cheneys – that 'we have the power, let's use it', combined with a rather demeaning wish in his case to tag along with the American superpower. Others have suggested that he was a bit player in the American realpolitik that saw the opportunity to guarantee oil supplies into the future. But, according to the man himself, he felt an almost moral or religious compulsion to oppose and root out evil – and he may therefore have unwittingly epitomised the arrogance, ignorance and simple lack of understanding implicit in western attitudes to parts of the world other than their own.

This failure meant that western leaders proceeded quite unnecessarily to alienate Muslim opinion around the world, ensuring that the West was increasingly seen as the self-professed enemy of Islam. No sooner had the communist threat subsided, in other words, than western leaders succeeded brilliantly in creating another sworn and worldwide enemy, and managed in the process to divide the world dangerously along religious as well as ideological lines.

The invasion of Iraq undermined the standing of the West in the eyes of much non-western opinion in a wide variety of ways. The attack was seen as confirmation of the West's readiness to use force whenever it suited its interests, of its willingness to ignore the United Nations and to undermine international law (despite constant protestations of their commitment to it), of its lack of sympathy for or understanding of the aspirations of populations who were just beginning to identify themselves as separate entities and to seek self-government and democracy.

A striking example of the impact of the Iraq invasion on world opinion, and of the damage it has done to the standing of the West in global terms, was the article written for *The Observer* on 2 September 2012 by Nobel Peace Prize-winner Archbishop Desmond Tutu, in which he called for George W. Bush and Tony Blair to be indicted for war crimes in the International Criminal Court. He went further; he argued that to do otherwise, when leaders elsewhere – in Africa, for example, and the Balkans – had been brought to justice and punished severely, would demonstrate unacceptably double standards on the part of western leaders.

Not only, therefore, has the West found itself on the back foot in terms of its relationship with the Muslim world; its crass failures have also reduced its standing in the eyes of many non-committed nations. The moral, economic and political leadership it assumed after the victory in the Second World War has been eroded and dissipated. Other countries, other values, are increasingly seen as offering alternative poles of attraction.

The claims by western leaders to represent values and principles – of the rule of law, democracy and self-determination – that were ethically superior to those of other nations have sounded increasingly hollow, in other words, in the light of what the West has actually done with the superior economic and military power that was its inheritance.

The mistakes made as we turned into the twenty-first century after all came hard on the heels of a sorry record in the decades following the Second World War of supporting disreputable dictatorships in South America, Africa, Asia and the Middle East, of frustrating the aspirations of those who were seeking more control over their own lives, of putting the interests of powerful capitalists above those of the inhabitants of some of the poorest countries on earth, of destroying the environments in which those populations lived, and of using military force to ensure control of the resources needed by western economies.

In country after country across the globe, western democracies which trumpeted their commitment to the democracy they claimed to practice instead betrayed those principles by giving priority to the commercial interests of powerful western-owned companies, which often made common cause with dictatorial domestic regimes. In vain did nascent democratic movements in non-western countries look to the West for help and support; western leaders simply averted their gaze and held their noses while profitable deals were struck with bloodstained tyrants. Little wonder that a jaundiced view was taken of western sincerity by those countries that did eventually succeed in throwing off dictatorships and establishing some semblance of democratic self-government. And it is still the case that many countries and peoples which have in their different ways sought self-determination have found the West to be an obstacle rather than an ally – not least the Palestinians, who find that the unconditional support offered to what is seen as a western-created entity in Israel requires that the claim to a Palestinian homeland is constantly denied.

Even in those countries, particularly in the Middle East, which have recently struggled – occasionally with success – to overthrow dictatorial regimes, the struggle for democracy only belatedly attracted the support of western countries. In Libya, for example, Gaddafi was for a long time feted by western leaders; the dictator might perhaps have been excused some degree of surprise at finding himself abandoned by his friends and supporters, particularly in the British government, so late in the day.

And, as we have seen, one of the techniques often, and still, employed by western interests is what Canadian social activist Naomi Klein calls 'disaster capitalism' – the exploitation of the opportunity provided by disasters, whether man-made or natural, of wiring in 'free-market' ways of doing things, as economist Milton Friedman and his Chicago colleagues did when they took advantage of General Pinochet's military coup in Chile in 1973. By such means, a radical programme of deregulation, privatisation and market fundamentalism was forced through, and similar changes were subsequently engineered by western interests in Argentina, Bolivia and Uruguay, then Poland and Russia, following their periods of financial or political turmoil. Economies were remade to suit western interests and to reflect the primacy of neo-liberal ideology.

What credence, in the light of this record, could be given to the stance of moral superiority adopted by western leaders, a stance whose undermining has been greatly intensified by the increasingly concentrated hands into which the leadership of the West has now been allowed to pass? If, having circumvented efforts at democratic restraint, the increasingly small group of unrepresentative western leaders and power brokers are prepared to ride roughshod over the interests of their own fellow citizens, what chance is there that they will pay any attention to the interests of populations of which they have no knowledge and to whom they attach no value?

These important worldwide perceptions have been reinforced by other developments. The more or less complete demise of colonialism has in many cases left behind a legacy of exploitation, repression and underdevelopment in the former colonies, which persists in real feelings of resentment on the part of newly independent peoples against their former colonial masters.

The attempts now being made by western countries to protect the global environment against global warming, the exhaustion of natural resources and the pollution of air and water are viewed with considerable scepticism in countries that are making strenuous efforts to follow a path already trodden by the West. The perception is that western countries – having exploited and in some cases virtually exhausted the world's finite resources – are now intent on pulling up the ladder behind them, and are attempting to frustrate the rise of potential rivals in the developing world by barring the path to development for them.

It is, moreover, an astonishing achievement on the part of western leaders that they have brought about a sharpening of global religious differences at the same time as the religious identity and commitment of western countries has reached a low ebb. The loss of faith and religious belief in many Christian countries (by contrast with the zeal and religious certainty shown in Muslim countries), the tribulations endured by some of the most important Christian churches in matters such as the sexual abuse of children, and the adoption of extreme interpretations of Christianity by minorities in western countries (in some cases specifically to point up differences between that religion and others) have led to feelings of both resentment on the one hand and religious superiority on the other on the part of adherents of other religions. Indeed, that the Christian banner is now often carried, in the case of the USA at least, by an extreme group whose members preach hatred, even of their own government, defy science, distrust education and condemn non-believers, so that they constitute a sort of western Taliban, can only have reduced the standing of the West in the eyes of many.

The well-publicised rise of social problems such as drugs, crime, gambling and prostitution in the West – to say nothing of the increasingly frequent instances of mass shootings by deranged or deluded individual gunmen – have also undermined any claims that western countries are happier and more successful than others. These doubts have been reinforced by the atomisation of community, and ultimately even of the family as a social unit, which have been features of western societies over recent times. Even in New Zealand, where early settlers (both Maori and pakeha) produced a successful synthesis of individual effort and community support to produce both an amazing economic achievement and a bicultural accord between two races, the values that now prevail are those of individual self-aggrandisement.

While there remain many aspects of western popular culture, especially in music, film and sport, that are seen as world-leading, there are others that are less well regarded. The irresponsibility of western media, the seeming loss of any moral compass, the adulation of those 'celebrities' who command attention despite (or possibly as a consequence of) defying decent moral standards, are all seen as evidence of a malaise that increasingly afflicts western civilisation.

The consequence of all this is that many of the world's ills are increasingly laid at the West's door. The failure to use the great resources available to those who control the global economy to lift the poorest people in the world out of poverty, despite constant protestations that real efforts are about to be made, is one example of the counts brought against western leaders. The hard bargains driven in trade negotiations with less-developed countries and the ruthlessness of the contracts signed by western multinationals, particularly in respect of the natural resources of third world countries, are others. Again, the self-interest and narrow perspective of those who now direct and control our affairs and accordingly drive these issues have done the West no favours and made the West few friends. Little wonder that Fukuyama's optimism now seems hopelessly misplaced.

Chapter 17

The Anglo-American Model

We have looked in detail at the way in which handing control over to market forces has delivered overwhelming power into a few hands and thereby created less efficient economies, less healthy and integrated societies, lower ethical standards of behaviour and a dangerously imperfect understanding of how economies, societies and the world as a whole actually work.

These changes have been a long time coming. As long ago as 1933, John Maynard Keynes expressed his concern at how the modern market-based system was developing. His language is old-fashioned but his concerns have an all too modern ring. In explaining his (and others') abandonment of a complete faith in the infallibility of the market in favour of a much greater scepticism, he wrote:

> There is one more explanation, I think, of the re-orientation of our minds. We have carried to extravagant lengths the criterion of what one can call for short 'the financial results', as a test of the advisability of any course of action sponsored by private or by collective action. The whole conduct of life was made into a sort of parody of an accountant's nightmare. Instead of using our vastly increased material and technical resources to build a wonder city, we built slums; and we thought it right and advisable to build slums because slums, on the test of private enterprise, 'paid', whereas the wonder city would, we thought, have been an act of foolish extravagance, which would, in the imbecile idiom of the financial fashion, have 'mortgaged the future' – though how the construction today of great and glorious works can impoverish the future, no man can see until his mind is beset by false analogies from an irrelevant accountancy.
>
> Even today I spend my time – half vainly, but also, I must admit, half successfully – in trying to persuade my countrymen that the nation as a whole will assuredly be richer if unemployed men and machines are used to build much needed houses than if they are

supported in idleness. For our minds are still so beclouded by bogus calculations that they distrust conclusions which should be obvious, out of a reliance on a system of financial accounting which casts doubt on whether such an operation will 'pay'. We have to remain poor because it does not 'pay' to be rich. We have to live in hovels, not because we cannot build palaces but because we cannot 'afford' them.

The same rule of self-destructive financial calculation governs every walk of life. We destroy the beauty of the countryside because the unappropriated splendours of nature have no economic value. We are capable of shutting off the sun and the stars because they do not pay a dividend. London is one of the richest cities in the history of civilisation, but it cannot 'afford' the highest standards of achievement of which its own living citizens are capable, because they do not 'pay'.

We have until recently conceived it a moral duty to ruin the tillers of the soil and destroy the age-long human traditions attendant on husbandry, if we could get a loaf of bread thereby a tenth of a penny cheaper.[1]

The attitudes that Keynes criticised have manifested themselves to a hugely greater degree today than those he recognised in 1933. Those attitudes have been a peculiarly powerful feature of a form of capitalism that is best described as 'Anglo-American', because it is found in its most extreme form in the leading English-speaking economies of the western world.

Although 'the West' is a commonly used term, and is used in its usual sense in this book, it is not to be regarded as a single entity. There are important parts of what might be regarded as the western world which have largely managed to avoid the excesses which have disfigured western civilisation over recent decades. Parts of Northern Europe, and Scandinavia in particular, have succeeded in maintaining many of the values of western liberalism; France and Germany are examples of major western economies which have managed to avoid, by preserving a sense of cultural identity and an awareness of where we have come from, at least some of the excesses criticised in this work; and there are other parts of Europe and of the wider western economy which have stopped short of embracing the wilder reaches of neo-liberalism.

While the Eurozone economy is a prime example of economic mismanagement, the social policies applied domestically by a Germany or a France have succeeded at least partially in maintaining relatively cohesive societies in which the willingness to accept a wider responsibility for the disadvantaged, the sick and the elderly has produced a gentler, kinder and more united ethos than is to be found in the harsher climes of the USA. It is, as we have seen, the societies that have exhibited the most extreme decline into inequality that have experienced the most damaging social problems and the most fractured and divided societies.

Even in purely economic terms, there have been instances of western countries escaping the thrall of neo-liberal recipes for liberating themselves from collapse and recession. When, for example, Iceland's economy hit the buffers in the autumn of 2008, most thought that the future looked grim, and that there was no way that a major meltdown could be avoided. In the immediate aftermath, of course, that pessimism seemed entirely justified. An unstable banking sector collapsed in a week; the exchange rate plunged 40 per cent against the euro, inflation and interest rates jumped to 18 per cent, the standard of living fell sharply and unemployment rose from near zero to nearly 10 per cent.

It seemed inevitable that Iceland would default on its obligations. But, as Iceland's former finance minister, Steingrímur Sigfússon explained, measures were taken to reduce the fiscal deficit by cutting expenditure and increasing revenues by raising taxes.[2] The Icelandic government pursued these objectives, however, while at the same time paying attention to issues of social and economic inclusion. Those on higher incomes contributed more in absolute terms through the adoption of a progressive system of taxation, while those on lower incomes were sheltered. Welfare services were cut less than other areas of public spending. The result was a more equitable net income distribution. Purchasing power among lower-income groups was better maintained than among those with higher incomes, enabling them to continue as active participants in the economy.

The depreciation of the krona contributed to the rapid adjustment of Iceland's economy, not least by creating highly favourable conditions for exports. The key areas of the economy – tourism, low carbon energy, the creative sector, high-tech and knowledge industries – found themselves enjoying newly competitive conditions. The result was that Iceland's 2011 growth rate was 3.1 per cent and will be similar in 2012, driven increasingly by business investment.

The Iceland government decided against a full-scale bail-out of Iceland's failed banks. Only the strong institutions survived; the others were allowed to go to the wall. The decision was taken to give priority to depositors over other claims against failed banks. As a result, depositors claims will be covered in full, which contributed greatly to the restoration of consumer confidence.

While the Icelandic example shows that 'free-market' orthodoxy can be avoided, and that the prize for doing so is that economic recovery is achieved more easily and with greater social cohesion, it is, sadly, in the major English-speaking democracies, where 'free-market' capitalism has taken its most extreme form, that the downside has been most marked. In this study, we have drawn examples most often from the UK and the USA, from Australia and New Zealand, because it is in these countries that we have seen most consistently and damagingly the beliefs that the value of everything is best, indeed only, to be measured in monetary terms as determined by market operations, and that the primacy of the market means that there is not and should not be any role for government.

It is perhaps in the USA that we have seen these doctrines at their most extreme. That is not to say that there are not many Americans who would contest such views, but the evidence is overwhelming that the last two or three decades have seen a wholesale shift of the political spectrum to the right. This is most apparent in the modern Republican Party, where policies that would until recently have been dismissed as from the realm of the crackpot or the extremist have now been adopted as mainstream.

As Eduardo Porter pointed out, today's Republicans would characterise the policies of a Richard Nixon as hopelessly and unacceptably left-wing.[3] He reminds us that the Nixon administration not only supported the Clean Air Act and affirmative action, but also established public bodies such as the Environmental Protection Agency, with the remit to ensure that business was obliged to take environmental considerations into account, and the Occupational Safety and Health Administration, to police working conditions. He quotes Herbert Stein, chief economic adviser during the administrations of Nixon and Gerald Ford, as remarking that 'probably more new regulation was imposed on the economy during the Nixon administration than in any other presidency since the New Deal'.

Porter recalls also that Richard Nixon raised Social Security benefits, introduced a minimum tax on the wealthy and championed a guaranteed minimum income for the poor. He even proposed a health reform that would require employers to buy health insurance for their employees and subsidise those who could not afford it.

Policy initiatives such as these would never get to first base in today's Republican party. Nixon, like most mainstream Republicans of that time, accepted that there was an important role for government. While polls show that Americans believe that their political ideology has changed little since that time, this is to overlook how far the meaning of terms such as 'conservative' and 'liberal' have changed (the latter is now a term of abuse in many circles); and that change is testimony to the success achieved by extreme right-wingers in moving the whole spectrum to the right.

Porter drew attention to the rightward drift in economic thinking revealed by surveys asking about specific issues. In surveys twenty-five years ago, 71 per cent of Americans believed it was the government's job to take care of those who couldn't care for themselves. That percentage has now fallen to 59 per cent, and the decline is mainly to be found among Republicans – a shift whose force and direction is illustrated by the shrillness and fundamentalist nature of the debate that took place about Obamacare.

We can see these attitudes at work in much of what has underpinned the progress (if that is the right word) of these Anglo-American democracies over the last three decades. We see them not least in the day-to-day operations of Anglo-American businesses. Those operations are characterised by a single-minded drive for profitability in the short term and a determination to ignore or override any considerations which cannot be pressed into service in pursuit of that goal. The interests of shareholders are thought to prevail over all others – those of employees, business colleagues, customers, as well as of citizens in general.

The result is, as Cornell University Law Professor Lynn Stout has asserted, that shareholder value thinking encourages a myopic focus on short-term earnings, discourages investment and innovation, harms the interests of employees, customers, and communities, and prompts reckless, sociopathic and irresponsible behaviours. In other words, even in terms of the most narrowly defined of economic goals, the attitudes demonstrated by the Anglo-American form of capitalism have produced much less than optimal outcomes.[4]

A good example of those 'sociopathic and irresponsible' behaviours identified by Professor Stout is the determination to treat labour as just another commodity, rather than as the contribution of time, effort and skill made by the majority to the general welfare, as the determinant of their life chances and as their membership subscription to the benefits arising from living in society. It is this blinkered approach that explains to a large degree the failure – indeed refusal – on the part of most western governments and business leaders, in the aftermath of the recession induced by the global financial crisis, to treat high levels of unemployment as deserving of any special effort to reverse them.

Unemployment remains, of course, a centrally important factor in the economic and social ills besetting western economies and societies. Yet very few governments have bothered to place the issue high on their agenda. The reason is that most of those running big businesses and advising governments have tacitly accepted the argument, peddled by extreme 'free marketeers', that there is no such thing as involuntary unemployment. The jobless are without work, it is said, because they choose to be.

Yet the real reasons for continuing high unemployment are the errors that have been made in the way our economies are run. The correction of these errors is very much within the control of governments; people are out of work because that is what suits the interests of major employers, and is what 'free-market' theory dictates.

That theory takes a very simple view, as we have seen, of how markets work. If the supply of a particular commodity exceeds the demand, the price will fall. So far so good; that analysis is true of, say, sugar or coffee, and of commodities in general. Where the 'free-market' ideologues part company with common sense, however, is in insisting that labour is just such a commodity.

Unemployment happens, they say, because the supply of labour exceeds demand. This should mean that if the market is allowed to operate as it should the price of labour will fall – in other words, wages should come down. The remedy is therefore in the hands of the unemployed themselves; they can correct the situation by accepting lower wages.

There are several points to make about this. In taking this simple view, the theorists are looking at only one side of the equation; by concentrating only on the supposed excess supply of labour, they take a completely static view of the demand for labour and of how a market economy really works.

The demand for labour is not, as the theory suggests, fixed for all circumstances; it could easily be raised. A more buoyant economy would mean that employers were keen to take on more people, but that could only happen with a change in policy – and that is negated by the insistence that, as the theory requires, wages must be cut. If the priority of economic policy is to cut incomes and therefore spending, there is no hope of increasing demand in general and demand for labour in particular; cuts will inevitably mean that demand falls rather than rises.

It is not just the theory that is deficient. After four years of recession-induced and high unemployment in most western countries, we can say with some confidence that the policy has failed in practical as well as theoretical terms. Unemployment remains stubbornly high. Economic activity has stalled, if not nosedived. But governments are not deterred. They dare not say so publicly, but they use economists' jargon to explain why unemployment remains high. Labour costs are 'sticky' – that is, they have not fallen in order to clear the market, as the theory says should happen. The best way to cure unemployment, therefore, is that the government should help the market along by 'unsticking' labour costs to force them down.

This explains so many of the features of policy in so many western countries. It is why workers' rights at work have been weakened. It is why benefits are removed, so that in New Zealand, for example, even solo mothers with young children are forced back into the labour market, whether or not there are jobs. It is why the level of benefits is cut and minimum wage levels are held down while top salaries zoom upwards. It is why beneficiaries are demonised and singled out for special treatment – forced, in New Zealand, to undergo drug-testing as a condition of receiving benefits. It is why the partners of those convicted of benefit fraud can, as a virtually automatic consequence, also be convicted and sent to jail, on the grounds that they too might well have benefited from the fraud.

It is why governments lend covert support to big employers as they cut the real wages paid to already low-paid employees. It is why 'out-sourcing' is so popular with many governments and large employers, since the firms that provide casual labour pay lower wages than are paid to unionised labour and provide lower or non-existent conditions of health and safety at work. It is why, in other words, unemployment is so low on the list of priorities of so many governments across the western world.

And the sad truth is that, even if the strategy succeeded in its immediate goal, it would still be bad news in economic terms. Lower wages would just mean less purchasing power, and that would mean more sluggish economies, lower demand, less money for investment – and it would mean labour markets chasing their own tails downwards so as to make the problems worse.

All this, despite the fact that, if we really want to price our workers back into work, as we should, there is a much more obvious, more effective and fairer way than heaping the burden on to the poorest in our society. A lower exchange rate, as we have seen, would immediately cut costs across the board and ensure that everyone made a proper contribution to stimulating economic activity. But that would be to contradict the theory that says that it is wages that are too high and must accordingly be forced down – the conclusion inevitably to be drawn once it is accepted that labour is just a production cost and that the bottom line is all that matters.

At the other end of the income scale, there is a further instructive – and destructive – feature of Anglo-American capitalism that warrants attention. That feature is the huge bonuses – contributing to even bigger remuneration packages – notoriously paid out to the executives of many leading companies, and particularly banks. Nothing more strongly suggests that the lessons that seemed such a clear legacy of the global financial meltdown just a short time ago have been quickly and conveniently forgotten.

Even the justifications offered are redolent of a distinctly pre-recession complacency. 'If we are to attract the talent we need,' we are solemnly assured, 'we have to pay salaries to match those paid in the rest of the world.'

The supposed need to pay a top executive 100 times or more the income of his skilled employees is a self-serving nonsense produced by a small charmed circle who claim the right to set their own (and their mates') pay rates. But the bonus culture which seems to have emerged unscathed from the recession is objectionable, not just because it produces scandalous inequities in terms of total remuneration but also because it is seriously deficient as a means of producing better economic performance; indeed, it promotes attitudes that are the very antithesis of those we need. The theory is that if executives have 'skin in the game' (or any of the other macho phrases used to justify the practice) they will try harder and produce a better performance. In reality, bonus schemes encourage the very deficiencies which have bedevilled our economic performance over a long period.

First, they engender a focus on the short term at the expense of the longer-term health of the enterprise. Most criteria for determining whether and what sized bonus should be paid necessarily assess that performance over a single financial year. That, therefore, becomes the time frame that matters most to many senior managers. It is precisely that short-termism that is a well-recognised affliction of Anglo-American economies; it leads to cost-cutting and profit-taking over a short period as alternatives to what we really need – investment, building new capacity, productivity improvements and strategic perspectives.

Second, bonus schemes often distort performance, diverting attention from the issues that should really be addressed in favour of those that happen to be relevant to the bonus. It is inevitable that there is a bias towards factors that can easily be measured or quantified, but such factors are often of little importance to a true assessment of the value of performance. And because many of the factors that determine a company's performance are beyond the capacity of an individual executive to influence – macroeconomic conditions are the most obvious example – those factors either have to be ignored, or applied even though they have no relevance and it is clearly irrational to do so.

The result is that boards usually either make a broad judgement about what constitutes good performance in given circumstances, thereby destroying the fiction that performance evaluation is based on measurable and accurate data, or they substitute for their own judgement a set of criteria which at least have the merit of being measurable, even if they are seriously irrelevant. In any event, the danger is that the executive focuses on the bonus criteria, even if they are barely relevant to any sensible judgement of good performance.

The issue of whether or not a bonus is paid, and how much, can also be destructive of a good relationship between governance and management. Some boards will foolishly purport to be able to measure performance to the last percentage point. But an executive who has done well may well feel cheated if the board says that only 75 per cent of a bonus is to be paid. And if the bonus scheme extends to a larger group of executives, the issue of who gets what percentage of bonuses (bearing in mind that such information rarely stays confidential) can engender feelings of resentment and unfairness – hardly conducive to good human resource management.

The better practice, to be found in better-run economies than the Anglo-American, is that executives should be paid a proper rate for the job on the assumption that they will deliver a satisfactory performance. A less than satisfactory performance should then be dealt with as a performance issue. An exceptional performance – above and beyond the call of duty – should be rewarded with a genuine, but one-off, bonus.

A further suggestion is made in the report on short-termism recently made by Professor John Kay.[5] He proposes, on the basis that short-term bonuses are undesirable and encourage short-termism, that any bonuses should be paid in shares and the required holding period should extend beyond the executive's tenure with the company – in other words, chasing short-term targets at the cost of a company's long-term strength should be discouraged.

Proposals such as these would require many employment contracts to be renegotiated, not necessarily with a view to bringing total remuneration down but with the aim of removing many of the deleterious effects of the current practice, and producing more transparent and defensible arrangements. It is unlikely, however, to commend itself to those who like to think that the market works best when it is 'red in tooth and claw'.

The insistence in Anglo-American economies that only those items that have a market price have any value is not just a matter of attitude and judgement; it produces a number of hard practical consequences as well. One example is the deficiency in the way in which we keep the accounts, both of individual businesses and of national economies.

The deficiencies of the accounting systems we currently use have contributed to major meltdowns in the private sector of the economy over recent years; Enron was just one, perhaps unusually notorious, example. But national income accounts are full of similar holes. Official calculations of GDP, for example, ignore unpaid work, count spending on education as a form of consumption rather than investment, and treat the depletion of natural resources, pollution and global climate change as irrelevant to the economic scorecard. And these mistakes and omissions contribute significantly to flawed decisions that have a real impact on the way we measure, and therefore direct, economic activity.

A clear example of the risks we take in this regard, to which Professor Nancy Folbre of the University of Massachusetts has drawn attention, is the insistence on the part of the American coal industry that environmental regulation of that industry destroys jobs and weakens recovery from the recession.[6] The industry has made considerable efforts over many years to avoid explicit economic accounting for environmental damage. They have mounted fierce political opposition to the measurement of the coal industry's effects on resource depletion and air pollution.

But in an article published in 2011 in the *American Economic Review*, economists Nicholas Muller, Robert Mendelsohn and William Nordhaus advanced considerable evidence that air pollution damage from coal-fired electricity generation, measured primarily in terms of health effects, such as premature mortality, exceeded the value added of the industry in 2002.[7] As Paul Krugman has pointed out, the study illustrates the huge gap between market prices and social costs.[8]

They also established an analytical framework for measuring the gross external damage caused by a given activity, which should then be subtracted from measures of value added to arrive at a measure of net value added. In principle, this analysis could be extended to other forms of damage to human and social capital. This would make it possible to report for any given economy the total gross external damage as well as GDP.

It would take a revolution in the way we think about the economy before people became accustomed to recognising that spending on education and environmental regulation increases economic growth. Most people will continue to be conditioned to think of the economy in terms of the market economy, goods and services that are bought and sold, and there will continue to be resistance from powerful interests to any changes that threaten the short-run profitability of major industries.

It is not just the boards and top executives of our largest companies who have an unusual view of how their enterprises work best in an Anglo-American type of economy. Governments, too, can often make decisions on the basis of complete misunderstandings of how economies work and, in particular, of how government can impact on the economy.

Politicians sometimes, as Hillary Clinton once put it, 'mis-speak', and in doing so can often reveal more than they intend. A case in point was a surprising statement by the New Zealand Prime Minister John Key, in a television interview on 13 February 2012 in which he said that 'any tax sucks money out of the economy. There's a limited amount of money in the economy. So when you put up a new tax, or you tax people more, then it sucks that money out.'[9]

Mr Key, who enjoys a reputation as someone who knows about economics, would presumably admit, on reflection, that no one claiming to understand the economy would stand by that statement. But like so many 'mis-speakings', it provides an insight into how the speaker really thinks.

Let us put to one side the dubious assertion that 'there's a limited amount of money in the economy'; the money supply is never a fixed amount and varies greatly according to its price (the whole basis of using interest rates to control inflation), and varies even more according to the banks' lending, which as it goes down (or more usually up) is responsible for creating by far the greater part of the money in an economy. The really interesting part, though, of Mr Key's brief foray into economic theory is his apparent belief that money raised through taxation, and then spent on public purposes of various kinds, is somehow no longer part of, or of any value to, the economy.

If it is 'sucked out' of the economy, where does he think it goes to – into the stratosphere? And are all those schools and hospitals, all those police and servicemen, all those roads and railways, all those elements that are critical to our living standards and that are paid for out of taxation, of no economic value? If that is the case, then perhaps the emphasis that he, and many other governments across the western – and particularly Anglo-American – world, have placed on cutting public spending becomes easier to comprehend, if not to support.

But there are wider issues still. The notion that the only economy that matters is the private sector, and that government is always a drag on that economy rather than a partner and supporter, is peculiar to that form of Anglo-American capitalism that is now struggling with its demonstrable failures. In the USA and the UK, and in other English-speaking economies as well (for example, New Zealand), it is an article of faith that the best thing the government can do for business is to 'get off our backs', whereas, as we have seen, the most successful economies succeed in harnessing the power of government to support the general interest and the development of the economy as a whole.

Chapter 18

Conclusion:
What Can Be Done?

We are now in a position to attempt a comprehensive answer to the questions identified in the introduction to this book. We asked why the apparent triumph of the West, of western economic management, of western values, of western civilisation as a whole, had proved to be so short-lived? Why is the West now on the back foot in so many ways, suffering a manifest loss of confidence, and facing challenges from all quarters on matters economic, social, political and cultural?

The answer that seems inescapable is that the West has lost its way because we have been betrayed by those whom we have allowed to guide our fortunes. Rather than seeing themselves as standard-bearers for a humane, liberal and inclusive civilisation, our leaders have preferred instead to maximise ruthlessly, irresponsibly and selfishly the power that economic dominance has brought to them. Their goal has been self-aggrandisement, and the greater the success they have had in that, the less they have had to concern themselves with anything else, and the more they have abandoned the values that western civilisation had thought to be its greatest glory.

So we find that the West's economic leadership is seriously under threat because the managers of western economies have made fundamental mistakes. They have believed that the market, if allowed to operate in an unfettered way, will automatically deliver optimal outcomes, and their confidence in this thesis has been fortified by the alluring certainty that it will deliver to those who are dominant in the marketplace the self-interested and differential advantages they seek. The tragedy is that, while their differential advantages have grown, the economic fortunes of the rest of us – and of the West as a whole – have foundered.

We have seen that the social cohesion, the concern for others, the diffusion of power, the tolerance, the compassion, the drive for social justice, the freedom enjoyed more or less equally by all citizens that have characterised western societies at their best and have allowed western leaders to claim (with at least a semblance of justification) a kind of moral leadership, have been gravely undermined by the growing worldwide perception that western societies are sick or broken, that they have been undermined by division, violence, social ills and a loss of confidence in themselves and trust in each other.

We have seen as well that, as a consequence of these changes, the western way of government – through principles such as the rule of law – and of managing the relations between citizens and authority have been increasingly seen as flawed and as not necessarily offering a blueprint for successful civil society. Western claims that we have achieved a superior way of guaranteeing equal rights to all our citizens, and western criticisms of the supposed flaws revealed by other political systems – especially in matters of human rights – are increasingly dismissed as having no foundation.

We have seen that, in international terms, the West has thrown away any claim it may have had to leadership, and has alienated a large sector of world opinion through the ignorance and arrogance of western leaders, and their insensitivity and lack of understanding of how others see themselves and the world. The religious and moral certainties enjoyed by other cultures, whether justified or not, are compared favourably to what is seen as the loss of any moral compass in western societies.

The values that are now advanced as representative of western civilisation are not those of our great humane and liberal tradition; they are instead those of 'dog eat dog', 'devil take the hindmost', 'look after number one', 'winner takes all' and any other of those phrases that have been traditionally used to describe with contempt and distaste the sentiments of selfishness, aggression and greed, but which are now seen as the guiding lights for those who seek wealth, power and fame. Little wonder that the rest of the world is now inclined to dismiss those values as not worthy of emulation.

While these explanations about what has happened seem clear, there remains a puzzle; how did this happen and why? It is, after all, understandably – if regrettably – always the case that powerful people, given the chance, will grab what they can, and then use that advantage to entrench their power and protect it against attack, and then extend and intensify their advantage still further. But why did the rest of us allow that to happen? Wasn't that supposed to be the role of democracy, to ensure that the political power of elected governments, representing all the people and not just a small minority, would provide a guarantee that the principles of inclusivity, social cohesion and equal rights would be maintained?

We have explored some of the reasons why this has happened. We have seen that powerful people found a way to bypass elected governments, and have unhesitatingly used their power and wealth to skew the democratic process. As a result, the confidence that our forefathers felt in the power of democracy to produce a fair and inclusive society has been undermined. We are left with the shell, the illusion, of democracy, but with the reality that we are now largely powerless to defend ourselves against the dominance of a small, selfish and unrepresentative cabal.

What, then, is to be done? Is it possible to reclaim what is in danger of being lost? Or is the damage that has been done irreversible? Is it too late?

The way back will be difficult but it is not impossible. The values that we are in danger of losing have not disappeared; they are still present in the hearts and minds of most citizens. Most people in western societies will affirm, if asked, their continued belief in the values of fairness, compassion, tolerance, concern for others. But those values have become submerged under the tidal wave of 'free-market' propaganda; if we are to save the best features of western civilisation, we need to find effective ways of bringing them back to life.

What we need to recognise is that most of our fellow citizens do not think about politics or economics in any systematic way. It is only a small minority, whatever their position on the spectrum of political views, that has developed a fully coherent set of beliefs and principles. The majority are perfectly capable of holding in their minds quite contradictory notions and allegiances, and of nodding in agreement to any one of the propositions offered from any part of the political spectrum. What matters, what determines the way they will think on any particular issue is which of those contradictory values is closest to the surface, or in other words has the greatest salience, at any particular time.

Those who have hijacked our democracy have discovered the means by which they can raise the salience in the popular mind of values that suit their interests. They have become expert at 'tweaking' particular issues – outrage at social security 'scroungers', perhaps, or concern about the supposed threat to jobs or housing posed by immigrants, or fear of an allegedly threatened tax increase. They have learned to practise what the Australians have called 'dog whistle' politics – the technique by which politicians make statements, formulate policies or take actions which convey a subliminal message that sentiments and emotions which they dare not encourage openly and which voters would be ashamed to admit to should nevertheless decide voting intentions.

As we have seen, the control exercised by the powerful through their ownership of most media outlets gives them a great advantage in such efforts. But they are also able to exploit a natural human tendency which means that the values of self-interest and self-preservation, at least in the heat of any particular moment, will often take precedence over more socially aware and responsible attitudes. Most people will quite naturally give a high priority to looking after the interests of their nearest and dearest; it is this that explains the fact that, as we have seen, those who are dismissive of the rights of others will nevertheless show compassion and generosity to their own friends and family.

This order of priorities is, if you like, the default or primitive position. It is only as people are able, through better education, a wider range of experience and perhaps improved material conditions, to lift their eyes to wider horizons that they begin to realise that the people whose interests they have hitherto ignored or dismissed, on the grounds that they are remote and different, are in fact the same in their fundamental humanity as those whose claims are more easily accepted, because they are close at hand.

It is only then that they are able to understand the compelling argument that the whole can be greater than the sum of its parts, that society can be better and stronger if all its members are able to rely on the same degree of help and support as we are ready to offer to our own closest family and friends, that we can all be better off and happier if we live in such a healthy and integrated society. It is only then that we recognise our common humanity, and the qualities and experiences that we share with all our fellow citizens.

As we confront the various issues and challenges that are the stuff of politics – the necessary compromising of conflicting interests and the proper allocation of scarce resources, power and freedom – we will find that each of those issues and challenges can be defined and described according to competing narratives. The battle for political support and the disposition of political power will depend on which of these narratives is the most persuasive.

This, then, is the task that faces us if we wish to re-establish the values that have built our civilisation. The narrative that we offer to define and describe the issues that must be resolved must persuade people that the best guide to a proper resolution of those issues is the reaffirmation of the values that have served us so well for so long.

We must show that the values of fair treatment for all, of equal freedom for each individual and not just a few, of concern for the disadvantaged, of self-determination, self-government and political democracy, of a strong and whole society able to support, encourage and reward individual achievement will help us to the best outcomes on most of the issues we face. By defining our attitudes in terms of those values, and by making it clear through identifying them consistently that they remain our touchstone, we can powerfully raise their salience and counteract the advantage enjoyed by virtue of their economic dominance by those who would deny them.

Let me take a couple of examples of how this should be done. Growing inequality is acknowledged to be a leading characteristic of modern western societies. Many people will accept that this development is an affront to principles of fairness and equity, principles that they continue to hold and support, and that it produces social consequences which undermine and debilitate our society. But those who benefit from inequality (at least in the short term and in the narrowly focused perspective they choose to adopt) work hard to use their power and influence to establish a rival narrative that suits their purpose.

According to this narrative, inequality is unfortunate, but it reflects the failings of those who lose ground rather than the greed of those whose wealth grows. They ask whether it is fair to deprive the rich of the rewards to which they are entitled; they argue that to do so would be to threaten the loss of the mainspring of economic growth so that everyone would suffer from penalising the rich. They say that growing inequality may be the price we have to pay for continued economic advancement.

The response that should be made to this is a consistent reminder that social justice and a fair distribution of income and wealth have always been, until recently, the hallmarks of a well-functioning society and a fully effective democracy. They are the foundations on which the success of western societies has been built. Basic concepts of fairness and inclusivity are grossly offended if society is to be so brutally divided into a minority who have many times more wealth and goods than most people could reasonably want or deserve, and a majority who lose not only the ability to get full enjoyment from living in a modern society but are also denied the freedom that comes from exercising the power to choose and the self-esteem that comes from being full contributing members of that society.

We should, in other words, constantly link the growing incidence of inequality and the increasing evidence of its deleterious effects to the criteria that we know are still regarded as important by most people. But we should go further. We should point out on every possible occasion that inequality cannot be justified on the grounds that it promotes economic efficiency and prosperity, when the record shows that as we have become more unequal so we have become comparatively less efficient and productive. Inequality, in other words, is to be regretted and condemned in terms of both rival narratives.

Similarly, let us take, as the power and reach of international investors have grown, the issue of increased foreign ownership and control of each of our own domestic economies. Most people will intuitively react adversely to these developments, on the grounds that they mean a loss of the power of self-government and a susceptibility to decisions taken by those with little knowledge or concern about the lives of the people they are affecting.

But the narrative peddled by those who stand to gain – the investors who see the prospect of fat profits by cherry-picking the assets of other countries – is that foreign 'investment' is a net gain to the domestic economy, that it stimulates increased activity and introduces new ideas, that it widens and deepens capital markets in the host country, and that the proceeds of a sale can offer governments a short cut to a reduced need to borrow. They dismiss any criticism as xenophobic.

The response that should be made is to remind people that their instincts are right, that decisions taken close to home are likely to be more respectful of local needs and interests, that foreign 'investment' usually means the loss of productive assets and the diversion of income streams into foreign hands and across the foreign exchanges, and that an economy that is substantially in foreign ownership will be smaller, weaker and less responsive to the people of the country than should be the case.

Again, then, we should not just fight the issue on our own grounds; we should also carry the fight to those who peddle the supposed advantages of foreign ownership by highlighting the economic downsides, and pointing to the dismal economic record of countries that have sold their powers of decision to foreign owners.

On all such issues, we should tirelessly reject the supposed need to choose between economic efficiency and a healthy and just society; it is the insistence that this choice must be made that is one of the strongest weapons deployed by those who have claimed the power to lead us. We should assert instead that a whole and healthy society is not a misplaced diversion or byway but is the route by which a successful economy is to be achieved, and that it is to be justified by economic as well as social criteria.

On all of these questions, in other words, we must make a consistent analysis of each individual issue as it arises and link it back to the core values that we know people still hold but which they may have lost confidence in proclaiming. It is that loss of confidence that must be counteracted so that the defeatism that has afflicted so much liberal opinion no longer prevails. All too often, we have given up the fight and accordingly have had no competing narrative, no alternative analysis of where individual and social interests truly lie, to offer a confused public opinion.

It is in the end that surrender to what are apparently acknowledged to be superior forces and a more persuasive description of how society should operate that has characterised western societies over recent decades. The spirit that animated the long and successful campaign for democracy seems to have weakened, and become instead an apathetic acceptance that even democracy can no longer be relied on to withstand the economic power of those who now rule the global economy. There is resentment, confusion, occasional outrage, but no consistent or persuasive analysis of what has gone wrong or of what can be done about it.

It is at this stage that we should perhaps remind ourselves of an important point made by Francis Fukuyama. We may be able to say, with the benefit of hindsight, that he got some things wrong, but he reminds us that in pre-democratic times, and even today, autocratic regimes survive for as long as they do because they enjoy a certain legitimacy. Even when freedom is curtailed, and people's lives are adversely affected by the overwhelming power of a despot or an oligarchy, the most likely response of many will be an acceptance of the status quo.

A dictator or tyrant is, Fukuyama points out, just one person in the face of many. The dominance of that one person can be maintained only because there is a power structure that supports and protects him. That structure can be one that uses physical force or repression, or it can take the form of the imposition of an ideology or set of religious beliefs that appears to validate the tyrant's claim to supreme authority. But, for whatever reason, autocracies survive because powerful elements in society are happy that it is so, and the remainder of society is prepared to live with and accept that outcome.

Sooner or later, history shows, that acceptance may and almost certainly will come into question. It is only then that an assertion of the popular will might bring about a regime change and that, if we are lucky, some form of democracy will emerge. Fukuyama's mistake was to believe that once this had happened there was no turning back. The great benefits of political democracy and economic development based on the free market would, he believed, ensure that the popular will would guarantee that there would be no return to autocracy or oligarchy – and, even more significantly, there would be no return to passivity or acceptance in the face of overwhelming power being exercised by a minority over the majority.

It is fair to say that Fukuyama was not entirely blind to the possibility that some elements in a democratic society, a society in which power and wealth were widely distributed, might nevertheless seek to establish an advantage over their fellow citizens. Human nature, he suggests, will conspire to preserve a substantial degree of what he calls 'megalothymia' – a neologism of Greek origins that means the impulse to establish oneself as recognised as being superior to others.

He foresees that this impulse will remain a feature even in a 'post-historical' democratic society, and he goes so far as to warn that a democracy's health and stability will depend on the quality and number of outlets for it. He identifies entrepreneurship, political leadership, sporting achievement, scientific advances and social standing as examples of the areas where that impulse is most likely to be manifested. He concludes, with heroic optimism, that these strivings by particular individuals are more likely to benefit society rather than undermine its post-historical, that is its permanently democratic, nature.

In this, we can now see, he was mistaken. What he failed to foresee was that the 'free market' was not, as he thought, the guarantor of political democracy but was a powerful and dangerous challenger to it. The challenge has come from within, from those who have discovered how to use the free market to their own advantage, so that the majority are persuaded to accept its dictates even when they threaten the very freedoms that the 'free market' is supposed to protect.

Democracy has been disabled, in other words, because its supposed comrade-in-arms, the 'free market' – which it has propagated and nurtured – has turned out to be a cuckoo in the nest. It has grown so big and powerful that it is now as great a threat to a functioning and effective democracy as would be the seizure of power by a dictator or oligarchy. Indeed, it is in many ways even more dangerous because it operates under the guise of the expression in economic terms of the same values that democracy claims to guarantee in political and social terms, and therefore avoids any appearance of denying the basic principles of democracy.

If our democracy operated in such a way as to allow the politically active and successful to gain ever more votes and voting power, and if those additional votes were gained at the expense of the majority of others who were increasingly denied a democratic voice, we would immediately see that something was going wrong and act to stop it. But the loss of power as a consequence of the operation of the 'free market', so that economic power concentrates in increasingly few hands, passes not only without comment or expressions of concern but is actually welcomed and celebrated, even by those whose lives are unnecessarily constrained and diminished as a consequence.

This to be explained by another phenomenon which distinguishes the current loss of freedom and undermining of democracy from other autocratic regimes. In the past, and on other occasions, the barrier to the achievement of democracy or the threat to an existing democracy has come from an identifiable and discrete force – perhaps a powerful individual who behaves as a dictator or a cabal, for example a group of army officers, who seize power by force, or a doctrine, religious or political, which is accepted by some and is the basis of denying freedoms to others. No one has had any difficulty in identifying who holds power, or who or what has to be challenged and overthrown, if democracy is to be achieved or restored.

With the successful resistance to fascism and communism, and with the achievement of the universal franchise and the rule of law in western countries, people have relaxed, confident in the belief that any new threats of that nature would be quickly recognised if and when they emerged. What they were not prepared for was a threat to democracy that came from those who claimed to be its most successful exponents.

Those challengers did not identify themselves, and probably did not see themselves, as direct threats to democracy. They belonged to no organisation, were members of no organised conspiracy, planned no *coups d'état*. They espoused no overtly doctrinaire ideology and made no explicit threats to rights and freedoms. They posed as the bringers of good news, the generators of jobs and prosperity, the guides to the sunlit uplands, the champions of freedom and enterprise.

They made their grab for power by small incremental steps, each of which was justified as being needed if the drive towards even greater success was to be maintained. The process by which they concentrated power in their own hands, siphoned off the greater proportion of new wealth for themselves, used that wealth to create an even greater imbalance, subverted governments, and accordingly limited the control most people had over their own lives was so gradual that it was scarcely noticed; and because it was driven by the most successful, the most celebrated, the most admired, the most emulated, it was almost never recognised as posing any threat.

There is another factor at work as well. The current and recent generations who have seen their democracy undermined and eroded and have failed to react or protest are no different from those other quiescent and apathetic people throughout history who, as Fukuyama points out, have accepted and tolerated other forms of autocracy. We are, however, more culpable because – unlike those earlier generations – we have tasted freedom; we know what it is that we have lost; yet still we are too comfortable, too narrowly focused on the pursuit of our own immediate self-interest, to bestir ourselves when the power to control our own lives is taken from us. It is that lack of vision and understanding, that lack of concern, that has made us vulnerable to the emergence of a new and dangerous threat to freedom from within.

Fukuyama was therefore quite wrong to believe that history, in the sense of a progress towards an ideal democracy, had come to an end. The advent of democracy is not after all a landing point, the final culmination of a process that produces the ideal state; it is merely an event, something of limited duration which, if it is to have any continued existence and influence, must be continually renewed and maintained.

The lesson, as we should always have known, is that, as Jefferson and others are reputed to have observed, 'the price of freedom is eternal vigilance'. Those of our forebears who fought for democracy understood the value of what they were fighting for; they did not form part of that majority who were prepared to live under the yoke. We can see now that they were exceptional people who were not simply the accidental handmaidens, the ushers-in, of an inexorable historical process. They were activists; they made it happen and changed the course of history. Without them, we would still be languishing under repressive and undemocratic regimes, too lazy or apathetic to do much about it. They were the achievers, the individuals whose talents and commitment raised them above the common throng – great and heroic figures who would have deserved every accolade that an Ayn Rand could have bestowed upon them, except that their achievements were made not for the self-regarding reasons that she extolled but for the common good.

We all owe those heroes of democracy, operating in theatres great and small, many of them unknown, those who refused to accept their lot but who fought for justice for themselves and others, a huge debt. Regrettably, we have not only made little attempt to recognise or repay that debt; we have also allowed their achievements on our behalf to be devalued and forgotten.

The lesson is that if we want to make a reality of our democracy we must fight for it. That battle will never be finally won, but nor need it be conceded as hopeless. There are never any final victories in human affairs. We are, as I hope I have shown, in real danger of giving up that fight, because we have been persuaded that resistance is hopeless and that, as in the case of the rabbits of Cowslip's Warren, life in servitude for most of us is at least reasonably comfortable and perhaps preferable to the effort and struggle needed to regain control of our lives. If we want to reverse that sad state of affairs, we need to reignite the spirit of our forefathers.

Oddly, the closest parallel that we can find in modern times to the kind of effort that is now required is the Cultural Revolution introduced by Mao Tse-tung in China in the 1960s and 1970s. Mao recognised that the revolution he had helped to bring about was, by virtue of the overwhelming dominance of the Communist Party as a political force and the stultifying effect of economic centralism on economic development, in danger of bringing about a kind of sclerosis. In this, he was certainly right; his mistake – in trying to rectify this by encouraging a kind of permanent revolution – was in introducing a remedy that was just as bad as the illness.

The lesson we should nevertheless learn from that failed and flawed experiment is that our democracy is itself, even when it seems to be at its strongest, suffering a similar sclerosis as its arteries block and thicken. It is in real danger, and always will be, of relapsing into the familiar state of most societies, where those who are more powerful use their power to entrench it and increase it to the disadvantage of others. Even when great and successful efforts are made – as they were in the relatively recent history of western countries – to reverse the growing imbalance in power that afflicts most societies, the advances made are inevitably threatened by the reassertion of the natural tendency to concentrate power in a few hands.

What is now needed, in other words, is a renewed and, this time, continuing and never-ending battle for democracy – a battle that we should now recognise will never be finally or entirely won but must be continually fought. It is fighting the battle that matters, so that not too much ground is conceded and the odds do not mount too sharply against the reassertion of democratic values. That requires us constantly to analyse what is happening to our society, a society that today is naturally in a process of ever more rapid change, so that we can identify the emerging threats to democracy at the earliest moment and counteract them effectively. We cannot battle successfully if we do not understand the forces ranged against us.

This book is a small attempt to identify and analyse those forces and the threats they represent before it is too late, so that the champions of a reasserted democracy are properly equipped to take up the struggle. The battle that was largely won, not only against communism and fascism and repressive regimes around the world but against injustice and inequality in the West, now has to be fought again – and will continue to be fought by future generations. It is our task and duty to ensure that the odds they face are not too great.

Notes

Introduction

1. Francis Fukuyama, 'The end of history', *The National Interest* (1989).
2. Francis Fukuyama, *The End of History and the Last Man* (Free Press, 1992).
3. Anthony Crosland, *The Future of Socialism* (Jonathan Cape, 1956).
4. See http://webarchive.nationalarchives.gov.uk/+/http:/www.hm-treasury.gov.uk/newsroom_and_speeches/press/2005/press_57_05.cfm.

1 The Triumph of the 'Free Market'

1. Friedrich Hayek, *The Road to Serfdom* (Routledge and Chicago University Press, 1944).
2. Robert Nozick, *Anarchy, State, and Utopia* (Basic Books, 1974).
3. Ayn Rand, *Atlas Shrugged* (Random House, 1957).
4. Adam Smith, *The Wealth of Nations* (W. Strahan and T. Cadell, 1776).

2 Globalisation

1. American Friends Service Committee Working Party on Global Economics, *Putting Dignity & Rights at the Heart of the Global Economy* (AFSC, 2005), http://www.afsc.org/resources/pdf/putting-dignity-rights.pdf.
2. Joseph Stiglitz, *Globalization and its Discontents* (Norton, 2002).
3. 'Tide Barriers', *The Economist*, 6 October 2012, http://www.economist.com/node/21564193.
4. *World Development Indicators* (2000), www-wds.worldbank.org.
5. United Nations Conference on Trade and Development (UNCTAD), *Development and Globalization: Facts and Figures* (UNCTAD, 2012).
6. UNCTAD, *Development and Globalization*.
7. UNCTAD, *Development and Globalization*.
8. Barry C. Lynn and Phillip Longman, 'Who broke America's jobs machine? Why creeping consolidation is crushing American livelihoods', *Washington Monthly*, March/April 2010.

3 Stepping Stones to a 'Free-Market' Global Economy

1. Stiglitz, *Globalization and its Discontents*.
2. See, for example, 'Preface' by Bryan Gould in Philip Wyman, Mark Bainbridge and Brian Burkitt (eds), *Implications of the Euro* (Routledge, 2006).
3. John Maynard Keynes, *The Economic Consequences of the Peace* (Macmillan, 1919).
4. The Center for Economic and Policy Research, 'Macroeconomic policy advice and the Article IV consultations: A European Union case study (CEPR, January 2013), http://www.cepr.net/index.php/publications/reports/macroeconomic-policy-advice-and-the-article-iv-consultations.
5. Giancarlo Corsetti, André Meier and Gernot J. Müller, 'What determines government spending multipliers?', *IMF Working Paper* (IMF, June 2012), http://www.imf.org/external/pubs/ft/wp/2012/wp12150.pdf.
6. European Commission, http://ec.europa.eu/economy_finance/eu/forecasts/2013_winter_forecast_en.htm.
7. Ha-Joon Chang, 'The root of Europe's riots', *The Guardian*, 28 September 2012. http://www.guardian.co.uk/commentisfree/2012/sep/28/europe-riots-root-imf-austerity.

8. Gillian Tett, 'EU's FISH economies unsettle US investors', *Financial Times*, 14 February 2013, http://www.ft.com/intl/cms/s/0/851277b2-76a2-11e2-ac91-00144feabdc0.html#axzz2 QyLO5n5U.

4 The Political Response

1. Tony Blair, reported in *The Guardian*, 31 July 2006, http://www.guardian.co.uk/politics/2006/jul/31/mediabusiness.usa.

5 Democracy Surrendered

1. For more on this subject, see H. W. Arthurs, 'The hollowing out of corporate Canada', in J. Jenson and B. Santos (eds), *Globalizing Institutions: Case Studies in Social Regulation and Innovation* (Ashgate, 2000).
2. John Maynard Keynes, 'National self-sufficiency', *The Yale Review*, vol. 22, no. 4 (June 1933), 755–69.
3. S. Wilks-Heeg, A. Blick and S. Crone, *How Democratic is the UK? The 2012 Audit* (Democratic Audit, 2012), http://www.democracy-uk-2012.democraticaudit.com/how-democratic-is-the-uk-the-2012-audit.
4. Elaine Byrne, *Political Corruption in Ireland 1922–2010: A Crooked Harp?* (Manchester University Press, 2012).

6 The Shift in the Balance of Power

1. John Gray, *False Dawn: the Delusions of Global Capitalism* (The New Press, 1998).
2. For the full text, see John Maynard Keynes, *Essays in Persuasion* (W.W. Norton & Co., 1963), 358–73.
3. Tim Jackson, *Prosperity without Growth: Economics for a Finite Planet* (Earthscan and Routledge, 2009).
4. Richard Freeman, 'The great doubling: America in the new global economy', Usery Lecture in Labor Policy (Georgia State University, 2005).

7 Everything Has a Price: Or Businessmen Know Best

1. John Kay, 'The brashness and bravado in big deals', *Financial Times*, 16 October 2012, http://www.ft.com/intl/cms/s/0/5a37d888-16e0-11e2-8989-00144feabdc0.html.
2. Naomi Klein, *The Shock Doctrine* (Knopf Canada, 2007).
3. HM Treasury, http://www.hm-treasury.gov.uk/ppp_pfi_stats.htm.
4. Michael J. Sandel, *What Money Can't Buy: The Moral Limits of Markets* (Palgrave Macmillan, 2012).
5. Steven Levitt and Stephen Dubner, *Freakonomics* (William Morrow, 2005).
6. Joseph Stiglitz, *The Price of Inequality* (Norton, 2012).
7. Corey Robin, reported in *The Guardian*, 26 October 2012, http://www.guardian.co.uk/commentisfree/2012/oct/26/can-company-fire-you-for-way-you-vote.
8. Steve Connor, 'Billionaires secretly fund attacks on climate science', *The Independent*, 24 January 2013, http://www.independent.co.uk/environment/climate-change/exclusive-billionaires-secretly-fund-attacks-on-climate-science-8466312.html.
9. Peter Diamond and Emmanuel Saez, 'The case for a progressive tax: from basic research to policy recommendations', *Journal of Economic Perspectives*, vol. 25, no. 4 (2011), 165–90.

8 Mismanaging Our Economies: The Rise of Monetarism

1. See Bryan Gould, John Mills and Shaun Stewart, *Monetarism or Prosperity* (Macmillan, 1981).
2. For more on this important element, see the work of George T. Edwards, for example, *The Role of Banks in Economic Development*, *The Economics of Industrial Resurgence* (foreword

by Harold Lever) (Macmillan, 1987); and of Professor Richard Werner of Southampton University see list of titles at http://www.southampton.ac.uk/management/about/staff/werner.page#publications.

9   Mismanaging Our Economies: The International Dimension

1. Jagdish Bhagwati, 'America's threat to trans-Pacific trade', *Project Syndicate* (Project Syndicate, 30 December 2012), http://www.project-syndicate.org/commentary/america-s-threat-to-trans-pacific-trade.
2. Mike Moore, on NZTV's TVOne, 19 August 2012.
3. Brent Sheather, 'SOE sales – tell me why again?', *New Zealand Herald*, 29 August 2012, http://www.nzherald.co.nz/business/news/article.cfm?c_id=3&objectid=10829989.
4. Massimo Florio, *The Great Divestiture: Evaluating the Welfare Impact of the British Privatizations 1979–1997* (The MIT Press, 2004).
5. James Meek, 'How we happened to sell off our electricity', *London Review of Books*, vol. 34, no. 17 (13 September 2012), 3–12, http://www.lrb.co.uk/v34/n17/james-meek/how-we-happened-to-sell-off-our-electricity.

10   The Rise of Powerful Rivals and Other Models

1. Mike Rogers and C.A. 'Dutch' Ruppersberger of the Permanent Select Committee on Intelligence, *Investigative Report on the US National Security Issues Posed by Chinese Telecommunications Companies Huawei and ZTE* (USA House of Representatives, 8 October 2012), http://intelligence.house.gov/sites/intelligence.house.gov/files/documents/Huawei-ZTE%20Investigative%20Report%20%28FINAL%29.pdf.

11   Mismanaging Our Economies: Ignoring the Evidence

1. See Dean Baker, 'National income accounting for the *Washington Post* and Robert Samuelson', *Beat the Press* blog (CEPR, 25 August 2011), http://www.cepr.net/index.php/blogs/beat-the-press/national-income-accounting-for-the-washington-post-and-robert-samuelson.
2. John Mills, *Exchange Rate Alignments* (Palgrave Macmillan, 2012).

12   Hubris and Nemesis: The Global Financial Crisis

1. Lawrence Summers, 'America's deficits: The problem is more than fiscal', *Washington Post*, 21 January 2013, at http://articles.washingtonpost.com/2013-01-21/opinions/36473197_1_budget-deficits-price-controls-economic-forecasts.
2. *Growth in a Time of Debt*, http://www.nber.org/papers/w15639.
3. See *Austerity After Reinhart and Rogoff* by Robert Pollin and Michael Ash in the *Financial Times*, 17 April 2013, http://www.ft.com/intl/cms/s/9e5107f8-a75c-11e2-9fbe-00144feabdc0,Authorised=false.html?_i_location=http%3A%2F%2Fwww.ft.com%2F2Fcms%2Fs%2F0%2F9e5107f8-a75c-11e2-9fbe-00144feabdc0.html&_i_referer=#ixzz2Ql.
4. Thomas Frank, *Pity The Billionaire* (Harvill Secker, 2012).
5. Denis Campbell, 'Financial austerity is being used to dismantle the state', *The Guardian*, 3 July 2012, http://www.guardian.co.uk/society/2012/jul/03/financial-austerity-dismantle-state-gabriel-scally.
6. Robert Francis, QC, *Report of the Mid Staffordshire NHS Foundation Trust Public Inquiry* (The Stationery Office, February 2013), http://www.midstaffspublicinquiry.com/report.

13   Our Leaders Are Ignorant of How Our Economy Works

1. Ben Dyson, Tony Greenham, Josh Ryan-Collins and Richard A. Werner, Towards a Twenty-First Century Banking and Monetary System: Submission to the Independent Commission On Banking (Centre for Banking, Finance and Sustainable Development

(University of Southampton, School of Management), the New Economics Foundation and Positive Money, 2011), http://www.positivemoney.org/wp-content/uploads/2010/11/NEF-Southampton-Positive-Money-ICB-Submission.pdf.

2. But see the reservations expressed about the emphasis on 'fractional reserve banking' by Ann Pettifor at http://www.primeeconomics.org/wp-content/uploads/2013/01/Ingham-Review-Essay-FINAL-1st-January-2013js3.pdf. She correctly makes the point that adherence to the concept of fractional reserve banking implies (a) that lending is constrained or disciplined by deposits, and (b) that banks have made sufficient, if limited provision for liabilities and losses by linking loans to deposits or reserves, neither of which propositions is accurate.

3. Ben Dyson, *Banking Vs Democracy: How Power Has Shifted from Parliament to the Banking Sector* (Positive Money, 28 June 2012). See http://www.positivemoney.org/2012/06/banking-vs-democracy-how-power-has-shifted-from-parliament-to-the-banking-sector/.

4. 'The case for truly bold monetary policy', *Financial Times*, 28 June 2012, http://www.ft.com/cms/s/0/024b7a7a-bfa7-11e1-bb88-00144feabdc0.html#axzz2Q9hNG14m.

5. 'Duncan Dough Notes' *The Economist*, 7 July 2012, http://www.economist.com/node/21558311.

6. Jaromir Benes and Michael Kumhof, 'The Chicago Plan Revisited', *IMF Working Paper* (IMF, August 2012), http://www.imf.org/external/pubs/ft/wp/2012/wp12202.pdf.

7. But see again Ann Pettifor at http://www.primeeconomics.org/wp-content/uploads/2013/01/Ingham-Review-Essay-FINAL-1st-January-2013js3.pdf. The argument is not that credit creation should be tightly controlled by some automatic measure (as in the case of the Gold Standard) but that an appropriate level of credit creation should be decided by democratic process.

8. High-level Expert Group on reforming the structure of the EU banking sector, Final Report (October 2012), http://ec.europa.eu/internal_market/bank/docs/high-level_expert_group/report_en.pdf.

9. Independent Commission on Banking, *Final Report: Recommendations* (ICB, 12 September 2011), http://www.ecgi.org/documents/icb_final_report_12sep2011.pdf.

10. John Kay, *The Kay Review of UK Equity Markets and Long-Term Decision Making* (23 July 2012), https://www.gov.uk/government/uploads/system/uploads/attachment_data/file/31685/12-631-kay-review-of-equity-markets-interim-report.pdf.

11. Charles Ferguson, 'Bare-faced bankers should be treated as criminals: prosecuted and imprisoned', *The Guardian*, 20 July 2012, http://www.guardian.co.uk/commentisfree/2012/jul/20/bare-faced-bankers-criminals-prosecuted.

12. Will Hutton, 'Let's end this rotten culture that only rewards rogues', *The Observer*, 30 June 2012, http://www.guardian.co.uk/commentisfree/2012/jun/30/will-hutton-barclays-banking-reform.

13. 'Law that explains bank regulation folly', *Financial Times*, 11 September 2012, http://www.ft.com/intl/cms/s/0/e5436a62-fb49-11e1-87ae-00144feabdc0.html#axzz2QyLO5n5U.

14. Ibid.

15. Prem Sikka, 'Bankers must be made to bear the cost of their reckless risk-taking', *The Guardian*, 4 November 2012, http://www.guardian.co.uk/commentisfree/2012/nov/04/bankers-bear-cost-risk-taking.

14   The Role of the Media

1. Martin Linton, *Was It The Sun Wot Won It?* (Oxford University Press, 1996).

2. Serge Halimi, *When Market Journalism Invades the World*, a paper given to a conference organised in Paris by *Le Monde*, January 1999.

3. See http://www.levesoninquiry.org.uk/about/the-report/.

15   Widening Inequality and Social Problems

1. Stiglitz, *The Price of Inequality*.

2. See Samira Shackle, 'Labour MP slams *Sunday Times* Rich List', 1 May 2012, http://www.newstatesman.com/blogs/staggers/2012/05/labour-mp-slams-sunday-times-rich-list.

3. *GMI Ratings' 2012 Preliminary CEO Pay Survey*, at http://info.gmiratings.com/free-report-gmi-ratings-2012-preliminary-ceo-pay-survey.
4. Zanny Minton Beddoes, 'For richer, for poorer', *The Economist*, 13 October 2012, http://www.economist.com/node/21564414.
5. 'It's all downhill for US equality', *Financial Times*, 21 April 2012, http://www.ft.com/intl/cms/s/2/9a571df2-89b4-11e1-85af-00144feab49a.html#axzz2QyLO5n5U.
6. James K. Galbraith, *Inequality and Instability* (Oxford University Press, 2012).
7. Office for Budget Responsibility, *Economic and Fiscal Outlook* (December 2012), http://cdn.budgetresponsibility.independent.gov.uk/December-2012-Economic-and-fiscal-outlook23423423.pdf.
8. Ministry of Social Development, *Household Incomes in New Zealand: Trends in Indicators of Inequality and Hardship 1982 to 2011* (2012), http://www.msd.govt.nz/about-msd-and-our-work/publications-resources/monitoring/household-incomes/index.html.
9. James Henry, *The Price of Offshore Revisited* (Tax Justice Network, 2012).
10. Frank, *Pity the Billionaire*.
11. Institute for Policy Studies, *Executive Excess 2012: The CEO Hands in Uncle Sam's Pocket: How Our Tax Dollars Subsidize Exorbitant Executive Pay* (2012), http://www.ips-dc.org/reports/executive_excess_2012.
12. George Monbiot, 'I agree with Churchill: Let's get stuck into the real shirkers', *The Guardian*, 21 January 2013, http://www.guardian.co.uk/commentisfree/2013/jan/21/i-agree-with-churchill-shirkers-tax.
13. Winston Churchill, in a speech to the House of Commons, 4 May 1909.
14. Polly Toynbee, 'Accountancy's Big Four' are laughing all the way to the tax office', *The Guardian*, 1 February 2013, http://www.guardian.co.uk/commentisfree/2013/feb/01/accountancy-big-four-laugh-tax-office.
15. Stiglitz, *The Price of Inequality*.
16. Garance Franke-Ruta, 'Robert Putnam: Class now trumps race as the great divide in America', *The Atlantic*, 30 June 2012, http://www.theatlantic.com/politics/archive/2012/06/robert-putnam-class-now-trumps-race-as-the-great-divide-in-america/259256/.
17. Gray, *False Dawn*.
18. Richard G. Wilkinson and Kate Pickett, *The Spirit Level: Why More Equal Societies Almost Always Do Better* (Allen Lane, 2009).

17 The Anglo-American Model

1. John Maynard Keynes, 'National Self-Sufficiency', *The Yale Review*, vol. 22, no. 4 (June 1933), 755–69, see http://www.mtholyoke.edu/acad/intrel/interwar/keynes.htm.
2. *Financial Times*, 20 August 2012, https://www.google.co.nz/search?q=Financial+Times%2C++on+20+August+2012.+Steingrimur+Sigfusson&ie=utf-8&oe=utf-8&aq=t&rls=org.mozilla:en-GB:official&client=firefox-a.
3. Eduardo Porter, 'GOP shift moves center far to right', *New York Times*, 5 September 2012, http://www.nytimes.com/2012/09/05/business/the-gops-journey-from-the-liberal-days-of-nixon.html?_r=0.
4. Lynn Stout, *The Shareholder Value Myth* (Berrett-Koehler, 2012).
5. Stout, *The Shareholder Value Myth*.
6. Nancy Folbre, 'It's the accounting, stupid', *New York Times*, 13 August 2012, http://economix.blogs.nytimes.com/2012/08/13/its-the-accounting-stupid/.
7. Nicholas Muller, Robert Mendelsohn and William Nordhaus, 'Environmental accounting for pollution in the United States economy', *American Economic Review*, vol. 101, no. 5 (August 2011), 1649–75, http://www.aeaweb.org/articles.php?doi=10.1257/aer.101.5.1649.
8. Paul Krugman, 'The conscience of a Liberal', *New York Times*, 30 September 2011, http://krugman.blogs.nytimes.com/2011/09/30/markets-can-be-very-very-wrong/.
9. John Key, on TVNZ TVOne's Breakfast Programme, 13 February 2012.

Index